COUNTING SPECIES

COUNTING SPECIES

Biodiversity in
Global Environmental Politics

Rafi Youatt

University of Minnesota Press

Minneapolis

London

A different version of chapter 2 was published as "Counting Species: Biopower and the Global Biodiversity Census," *Environmental Values* 17, no. 3 (2008): 393–417.

Published by the University of Minnesota Press
111 Third Avenue South, Suite 290
Minneapolis, MN 55401–2520
http://www.upress.umn.edu

Library of Congress Cataloging-in-Publication Data

Youatt, Rafi.
    Counting species : biodiversity in global environmental politics / Rafi Youatt.
    Includes bibliographical references and index.
    ISBN 978-0-8166-9411-2 (hc : alk. paper)
    ISBN 978-0-8166-9414-3 (pb : alk. paper)
    1. Biodiversity. 2. Biodiversity—Political aspects. 3. Nature—Effect of human beings on.
4. Environmental degradation. 5. Urban ecology (Biology)—New York (State)—
New York. I. Title. II. Title: Biodiversity in global environmental politics.
    QH541.15.B56Y68
    2015 577—dc23

                                                    2014019931

Printed in the United States of America on acid-free paper

The University of Minnesota is an equal-opportunity educator and employer.

21 20 19 18 17 16 15   10 9 8 7 6 5 4 3 2 1

For Anna and Owen

Contents

Acknowledgments

This book was born out of a number of years in what used to be called "nature," surrounded by other species, and a number of years in universities and libraries, surrounded by books. In each setting, I was fortunate also to have a great many people who shaped my thinking and supported me in many ways.

In graduate school, I was enormously lucky to have Alexander Wendt as a dissertation advisor. He encouraged me to read across disciplines as an integral part of studying international politics, dispensed reading from his famous bank of file cabinets holding articles on every conceivable topic, and still kept me focused on what mattered. This book is almost certainly less a work of international relations than he hoped for when I started it and more a product of my own meandering interests, but I remain enormously indebted to his guidance, openness, and intellectual curiosity. Patchen Markell and Lisa Wedeen lent themselves to help a wayward IR student form a committee that crossed subdisciplines in political science. This work does not take up nearly as many of their suggestions as it should have, but they each inspired important developments in this book, and were also extraordinarily generous and gracious in other ways that kept me afloat.

While finishing my dissertation, I lived for two years in the mountains in California, writing in the mornings and working as a cook in the evenings. Since then, this book has moved around with me to a number of urban academic settings, from Columbus, Ohio, to Portland, Oregon, to New York City, and this has influenced the manuscript, which includes more about concrete jungles than I ever thought likely. I would particularly like to thank my colleagues at the New School for Social Research for their support and engagement, as well as my former colleagues at Reed College and Ohio State University, where portions of this manuscript were first heard. The Environmental Political Theory section at the Western Political Science Association has been a wonderful forum in which to air many of these ideas. Finally, a number of my students in my graduate seminars read and responded to parts of the book manuscript, for which I am grateful. Chris Crews and Samuel Mueller both provided valuable research assistance, and Nancy Shealy was a great source of support in many ways.

I would particularly like to thank Pieter Martin (my editor) and the University of Minnesota Press, who supported this manuscript from early on and helped me wrestle it into shape. This book improved tremendously during the period that it was with them, and I am grateful for all the effort that they put into it. Thanks are also due to the reviewers, whose critiques of the manuscript served to sharpen it in a number of important ways.

I would also like to thank Murat Arsel, Tarak Barkawi, Chris Buck, Chris Darnton, Andrew Dilts, Charlotte Epstein, Teena Gabrielson, Vicky Hattam, Andrea Haupt, Breena Holland, Patrick Thaddeus Jackson, Aaron Johnson, Kimi Johnson, Sina Kramer, Timon McPhearson, Tamara Metz, Jennifer Mitzen, Alex Montgomery, Michael Nordquist, Tim Pachirat, Darius Rejali, Kimberly Smith, Ted Steck, and Deva Woodly.

Finally, this book would not have been possible without Richard and Alice Youatt, Ani Youatt, and Angele Khachadour.

Introduction   Biodiversity, Agency, and Environmental Politics

"BIODIVERSITY" IS DIFFICULT TO DEFINE PRECISELY. As an ecological concept, it refers to the diversity of species that make up life on earth. But as it circulates in the world, biodiversity is at once a natural fact, a species-extinction event, a scientific field of inquiry, a political referent, a moral discourse, an abstract pattern, and a tool of governance. It embroils humans and nonhumans, spans institutions, and attaches to many sorts of political projects. In spite of all these valences, biodiversity is still a traceable cluster of things that has affected political and environmental outcomes in important and identifiable ways in the three decades since the term's inception. Recognizing the shifting constellations of global biodiversity is thus a way to understand the disturbing linkages between a growing global environmental crisis, on the one hand, and a political response to that crisis that has become increasingly technical, antipolitical, and market oriented, on the other. Such linkages bear on human and nonhuman life alike, but in a diverse set of ways.

This book has two major points of departure. The first is a set of issues pertaining to the troubled state of both the global environment and its politics. On the environmental side, nonhuman nature is under increasing pressure around the world, both from increased material production and from rising consumption. This is true in resource terms, with ocean depletion, deforestation, the overuse of carbon-based fuels, and the desertification that infringes on agricultural lands. Climate change, in particular, has become a major force, with everyone from the American military, to the insurance industry, to the residents of small Pacific islands, to consumers, dealing with the impacts that are already here, and calculating the future risks and investments needed. This pressure on nature is equally apparent if we focus more explicitly on the living, or biological, parts of nature. Seen in biological terms, one species—*Homo sapiens*—is having a lopsided impact on the fate of nearly every other species, ranging from habitat transformation to extinction, in

1

ways that affect human well-being as well. Seen in political terms, the fates of nonhuman species have been tied to a group of people in global centers of power constituted by the twin legacies of colonialism and capitalism. Meanwhile, the impacts of biodiversity loss affect a much broader group of human beings, including those who depend more directly on nature for a living. This impact constitutes what has been called a "global biodiversity crisis," involving the permanent loss of many species and the crippling of local and global ecosystems alike.

In the face of this crisis, one of the most pressing questions is what kinds of political action are possible. For some, greater environmental governance is needed at a global scale, involving both significant cooperation between national governments as well as major international institutional changes so that global environmental issues come to be seen as important as global trade issues. Whereas global trade has the WTO, the global environment might require a World Environmental Organization, or at least a significantly strengthened global network of environmental governance.[1] This line of political questioning tries to understand what appropriate institutional forms and policy levers might be, envisioning a politics in which problems and solutions are relatively clear, but political capacity is lacking at the right scale.

For others, it is precisely an extension of this kind of top-down politics that ought to be avoided. Global environmental problems are understood as being caused by an overreaching of political and economic power, both stripping local communities of material resources in the name of continued economic growth and expansion, and transforming the cultural meanings and political means through which they relate to nature. Environmental problems have become increasingly tied to a global neoliberalization of nature—provocatively called Nature™Inc—and an accompanying form of antipolitics.[2] On these accounts, the new layers of global environmental policy using market mechanisms, the language of ecosystem services, and economic forms of the valuation of nature often seem to accelerate the integration of nature into the economy, without necessarily resulting in significant environmental improvements. Building on dynamics identified earlier in international development regimes, the global environment functions as a new site of international antipolitics. By providing ostensibly apolitical forms of infrastructure, assistance, and ideas for market-oriented solutions to environmental ills, these processes hide their own highly political restructuring of states and societies. Biodiversity in particular has increasingly become a site for this kind of antipolitics, with initiatives ranging from The Economics of Ecosystems and Biodiversity

(TEEB), emphasizing the "economic benefits of biodiversity," to the creation of new forms of environmental surveillance of tropical rainforests linked to international financial assistance.[3]

Another related way to understand the political stakes here is to consider global biodiversity as a site of biopolitics. Following Michel Foucault, biopolitics is a historically specific mode of political power that organizes and administers the domain of the living, working on human bodies and subjectivity.[4] While largely accepting the characterization of environmental politics as Nature™Inc, a biopolitical approach to considering biodiversity emphasizes a way of thinking about how power works not only on humans, but also through them, affecting the way they understand and make meanings in the world as subjects formed by environmental regimes. Increasingly, I argue, biopolitics has come to work on and through nonhuman life as well, and biodiversity has been one important site through which it has been extended. By considering the politics of biodiversity as a form of biopolitics, this book considers the tricky implications of seeing nonhuman life as coming more explicitly into the networks of this new mode of political power. In particular, this book questions whether this extension provides new resources through which to think about resistance and agency by foregrounding the ways that nonhuman life lives. As the human sciences like demography were central to the emergence of biopower as it works on humans, the role of the ecological sciences in biodiversity is also central to the politics of life itself, reaching across the human–nonhuman divide, framing many of the political contours of environmental problems in significant ways, and turning our attention to sites surrounding the environmental sciences as political sites where power and agency are at work.

Finally, following the travels, and travails, of global biodiversity across time and space also leads to questions about how systems of governance absorb crisis-led modes of activism, and regularize them. A political modality of particular concern in recent decades has been the emergence of governance by perpetual crisis, involving ongoing managerial responses to complex emergencies, often in security terms or through outright violence.[5] Biodiversity has contributed to that development in a number of ways, particularly through the green global governance initiatives around conservation of species and in the linking of ecological resilience with security. Its more recent connection to climate-change politics sometimes aims to institute an ongoing state of emergency and monitoring to ensure compliance with green outcomes— for example, initiatives to conserve rainforests in Indonesia and Brazil, which are important both for functioning as carbon sinks and for harboring vast "reserves" of biodiversity, take place via satellite monitoring and through forms of internationalized financial transparency. The creation of seed banks, sunk deep into the permafrost in order to conserve plant diversity, looks to future doomsday scenarios in which biodiversity will have to be engineered anew. Tracing the transformations of global biodiversity across time as a political framing and set of practices does not provide an answer to these difficult political questions with any finality. It does, nonetheless, speak to how global environmental problems that affect nearly everyone and everything on the planet have to come to be understood dominantly as technical problems, lacking only political will and appropriate scale.

This book addresses the political engagement with environmental crises by exploring some of the lost potentials of biodiversity to act as a more fundamental and radical political critique of contemporary relations between humans and nature. As I explore throughout this book, biodiversity's evolution as a global political issue is partially a story of self-inflicted co-optation in an effort to bring about serious reform; yet it has the potential to animate a more political kind of environmentalism that rebalances the relationship between technical management and wildness, both human and nonhuman.

Biodiversity loss—framed as the ongoing extinction of species due to human causes—has, on the whole, been less successful as a political discourse of the environment than its closest cousin, global climate change. The comparison is instructive in considering whether there is something unique about biodiversity in global environmental politics. Both were inaugurated as political issues on the international scene at the same time, in 1992 at the Rio Earth Summit, and they have run partially parallel courses since then, sharing in discourses of crisis and technical management, turning to market-based solutions to solve market-based problems, and failing to alter the course of the problems that they have been most clearly directed at solving. Also, many of their most important effects have occurred outside of environmental politics, narrowly construed. Instead, they have shaped the way people think of themselves as citizens, created new pathways of intervention in developing countries, and, paradoxically, opened new market opportunities for "green" consumption. Without devaluing the sincerely motivated efforts of environmentalists who work in policy and activism, it is nonetheless possible to say that the radical, *political* edge of environmentalism has in many ways been blunted over time through these developments.

But, as this book explores, global biodiversity as a political problem is also different from climate change in a number of ways, marking it as a distinct pole in global environmental politics. It has its own set of discourses, which have drawn on different political ideas than climate change and a scientific lineage that owes much more to biological concepts of species and evolution, and ecological ideas of ecosystems. It has a somewhat forgotten basis in a politics of intrinsic value, which involves recalibrating the foundation of our relations with other living creatures based on a universal conception of rights. And unlike climate change, whose causes and solutions are arguably contained within the material problems of political economy, biodiversity loss stretches further into murkier questions about interspecies relations and the politics of life itself.

Anthropocentrism, Agency, and the Political

There is a second major point of departure for this book, involving a more abstract set of questions surrounding anthropocentrism, nonhuman agency, and the political. Though they are abstract, they nonetheless relate directly to the political issues surrounding biodiversity. Anthropocentrism can be understood to have both an empirical and a moral dimension. Empirically, it means looking at events significantly involving human and nonhuman entities, but mostly foregrounding the human dimension, thereby missing much of the important action, while also overemphasizing the power and scope of human agency. Morally, it is the idea that humans ought to be the sole, or at least the most important, center of value at all times and places. This claim is often rooted in assumptions about human and nonhuman agency. Taking cues from posthumanist scholarship in political theory and science studies, this book opens up questions of whether and how the boundaries of political life stop and start with the human. It asks what politics with a somewhat decentered human subject might look like, and whether an empirically less anthropocentric scholarship can contribute to that endeavor. This book also interrogates the "anthro" in "anthropocentrism" more explicitly—for "human" is too often used unflinchingly as an unmarked, universal referent in global environmental politics, hiding its own political power to mark class, race, and economic development in international arenas. Biodiversity's own use of "human" impacts on the global environment are a paradigmatic case, allowing us to think about nonhuman species extinctions as caused by the human species, rather than highlighting the vastly different kinds of impacts that humans have had at different locations and in political history.

Thinking about these dimensions of anthropocentrism together means changing the focus of analysis in environmental politics and opening up the idea of the political. It means that the actors of environmental politics include human and nonhuman side by side, whether scientists, microscopes, rocks, or insects. In particular, this conception of politics has resulted in approaching environmental problems as involving a kind of politics of assemblages—that is, networks composed of a wide range of human and nonhuman actors who together work to create both disruptive and productive political effects.[6] This does not require seeing politics beyond its existing formal institutional sense that includes elections, government, and treaty negotiations. Instead, it means an expansion and respecification of the political as the field through which contestation, public knowledge, and temporary association take place in order to sort out questions affecting common goods and the common good. In taking a view of the political where the human subject is neither central nor in exclusive possession of agency, it is therefore necessary to consider environmental politics as more than the decision making taking place in dusty hallways and fluorescent-lit conference rooms. This book thus foregrounds both how nonhuman species escape efforts to construct knowledge about them and the potential of a more hands-off rewilding strategy. It aims to highlight the circulation of politics across diverse sites and through human and nonhuman actors.

This book does not endeavor to resolve many of the difficult issues surrounding the theoretical relationship between agency and politics, nor does it ultimately do full justice to the empirical study of nonhuman life from a social science perspective. But because biodiversity involves nonhuman life forms as one of its central protagonists, it invariably calls up questions surrounding the relative weight of human and nonhuman agency, and how accurate it is, ultimately, to think about politics as an exclusively human activity when considering ecological politics. As the so-called "end of nature" closes in on biodiversity, referencing the fact that there are few places on earth humans don't affect, a closer consideration of human–nonhuman relations in the production of environmental political problems provides useful ways for starting to think differently about ecological relations themselves.

The Global Biodiversity Crisis

In environmental circles, global biodiversity loss is sometimes said to be a forgotten crisis. While climate change commands widespread attention, though not necessarily swift action, the slow but irrevocable extinction of species has receded from international political view as a matter of deep concern. The number of species disappearing every year now far exceeds the rate of extinction that occurs naturally through evolutionary processes.[7] Moreover, the global distribution of species is also becoming more homogenous. While globalization has stoked fears about the homogenization of global culture, it has equally been part of the reason that biological diversity has been getting standardized at a brisk clip, with the increased spread of new invasive species through global travel and shipping, the increased monoculture in world agriculture, and the diminishment of local biodiversity.

This is not the first time species diversity has dropped off so precipitously. Five previous times in the known history of the planet massive die-offs have occurred, nearly wiping out life on earth in some cases. Up to 75 percent of species disappeared in these events, and each time a new burst of life restored biodiversity. While this might seem like a comfortable story about nature restoring itself, it is misleading in the time frames that matter for human beings. Each of these previous buildups took millions of years, which for a species that seems to have trouble planning even fifty years ahead is nearly unfathomable.[8] If another species-extinction event is under way, it means a long period of interaction with an ecologically impoverished and fundamentally different kind of nature than we have ever known.

The present day appears to be the threshold of a sixth extinction event, and is the only extinction event that would be caused almost entirely by one species. This time through, species loss is widely acknowledged to be the direct consequence of a somewhat misleading category, "human actions"—accurate, in terms of species, but imprecise when it doesn't specify which actions are responsible. In the general terms of the Millennium Ecosystem Assessment, the human actions undermining biodiversity are taken "largely to meet rapidly growing demands for food, fresh water, timber, fiber, and fuel" (Millennium Ecosystem Assessment 2005a, 1). As others see it, these actions are long-term activities of resource extraction and production, through which some nations have become wealthy, materially secure, and ecologically careless. In short, we may have now ended the Holocene, which started twelve thousand years ago, and entered the Anthropocene—a geological epoch, and increasingly a political era, marked for the first time by the activities of a single species (*Homo sapiens*), at the expense of the extinction of millions of other species, effectively wiping out thousands of years of evolution in the process.[9]

This book works within a much shorter time frame. It analyzes the making of global biodiversity loss as a political problem, starting with the invention of the term "biodiversity" in the mid-1980s, and culminating in its absorption into environmental governance by the end of the 2000s. While there are important structural causes for biodiversity loss that are tied to global political economy and the limits of international treaty making, this book focuses instead on the ways that the logics surrounding global biodiversity themselves have been politically productive. By looking at a series of sites where the idea of global biodiversity is made, this book shows how biodiversity conservation has construed itself as a project of identifying, administering, and governing the living machinery of nature, even as global species loss continues to proceed nearly unabated. It traces some of the paradoxes of global biodiversity as a category of political practice, showing how the conditions of its success in policy discourse and conservation politics are also the source of its inability to articulate and sustain a strong critique of contemporary forms of political-ecological practice.

In the 1980s and early 1990s, global biodiversity loss was indeed beginning to be recognized as an ecological and political crisis. In the wake of the 1992 Earth Summit in Rio, a major international treaty aimed at addressing biodiversity loss was signed, the Convention on Biological Diversity (CBD), and the decade saw a global mobilization of conservation efforts. But the CBD didn't have much teeth.[10] Its strongest obligations are to require "identification, monitoring, and assessment" by its member states and the development of national biodiversity plans to address the problem.[11] Indeed, its clearest effect has been to re-enshrine the idea of nature as property, by pushing forward agreements based on the idea that biodiversity is a resource of the sovereign nation-states where it is located.[12] By the 2000s, biodiversity receded as a global issue of importance, and by the 2010s, you might be hardpressed to find Americans who know that the United Nations declared it the Decade of Biodiversity or who think that biodiversity loss is a major political issue.

The international failure to stem biodiversity loss, and the recession of the sense of crisis, has not meant that there has been a failure in terms of expanding political power and governance in its name, however. Rather, it has meant that biodiversity governance has done things other than stop global biodiversity loss, ranging from the efforts to catalogue and name every species on earth through a global biodiversity census to framing new ways of approaching the politics of heritage. Biodiversity as a form of governance is alive and well, shaping political subjectivities, creating conditions for political intervention and action, and producing forms of anxiety about species loss, and global biodiversity forms a key point of departure for the apparatus that surrounds it.

One of the key tasks this book undertakes is to trace the historically specific clusters of ideas—ecological and political—within which biodiversity came to be meaningful since its inception in the 1980s. Rather than treating biodiversity loss as an ecological fact and analyzing the international politics that surround it, in other words, the book treats biodiversity itself as a political idea with a history, one that has involved three basic dynamics. First, the meanings of biodiversity are partly made by the way it has congealed with other discourses and ideas, especially political ones. In a second dynamic, the political power of other discourses have been legitimated and transformed by their association with biodiversity. Finally, brand-new categories of political action have been brought into being through these associations, often hybridizing biodiversity with other terms. This book traces changes in these three dynamics over the course of biodiversity's three decades of existence, and considers what effects these changes have had politically. It shows some of the ways that the intrinsic value of species and the intrinsic value of biodiversity, proposed by conservationists in the 1980s, were constituted by the political ideas of intrinsic human rights, with an effort to bootstrap those ideas about intrinsicness into the status of positive law. In the 1990s, as "biodiversity" became a term of global policy and was increasingly tied to sustainable development, it clustered with important political ideas, including liberal multiculturalism, and also created new categories of conservation centered around biocultural diversity. By the early 2000s, building both on its earlier affiliation with sustainable development and with the idea of difference as a generative social force, biodiversity became understood primarily as an indirect provider of goods. Biodiversity in this decade became valued as a provider of ecosystem services, with efforts made to value it explicitly in monetary terms in order to write it in as a useful part of the postindustrial service economy. By bringing conservationists on board who hoped to make a pragmatic case for species preservation in the language of economics, it became devalued for its own sake. By the 2010s, a securitized version of global biodiversity had emerged, casting its conservation in terms of creating resilient communities against external threats, ecological (climate change in particular) and otherwise. Through these clusters, this book traces the historical transformation and evolution of biodiversity from the mid-1980s to the present.

Global biodiversity has also been important as a positive articulation of nature, one that renders it in particular ways. On one hand, it contains important parameters that direct political possibilities. Most important, biodiversity puts species at the forefront of environmental politics, privileging the general form over individuals, advancing Linnaean classification as a tool of conservation, and advancing "human actions" as a category of political action. It also generally locates the dynamic, generative power of nature in patterns, such as species richness, rather than in the actions or presence of individual entities. Finally, it emphasizes the constitutive power of difference over homogeneity as a force for systemic resilience and adaptability, and in the process draws some of its political clout from discourses of political and cultural diversity. On the other hand, global biodiversity also has a high degree of conceptual mobility that has made it particularly prone to absorption into governance structures. Biodiversity is a scalable concept, as applicable to a single handful of dirt as to the distribution of species or genetic material on the planet as a whole. This quality has sometimes been to its benefit, but at other times it has facilitated a shift in spatial scale that has led to a misleading redirection of political energies.

Although this book looks at a variety of scales, it keeps *global* biodiversity at the forefront, as an idea that has had important constitutive effects on most of the smaller sites in question. Global conservation politics surrounding biodiversity has brought a variety of non-state actors to the fore that claim to speak on its behalf, ranging from an increasingly internationalized cast of conservation biologists and ecologists, to environmental NGOs, to institutions of global governance such as UNEP and UNESCO. In the context of biodiversity, many of these actors continue to articulate and use global biodiversity as a framing concept and to treat it as a given material reality. So even as the species that make up biodiversity are subject to the political jurisdiction of sovereign states, global biodiversity invokes a political and scientific claim that species diversity is, in effect, commonly shared, or ought to be. It is the patterning of species that is part of the global commons, in other words, while the species themselves and the individuals that make up species are much more irregularly distributed across different sovereign states. How this tension between global biodiversity, as a pattern allowing particular groups to advance political claims, and species and territories, as localized sites claimed by sovereign states and other local political actors, is negotiated forms an important point of inquiry.

Much like "nation" or "community," "global" is always an abstraction that requires active imagining and political making. Global biodiversity does have a referential power, an ability to reference patterns that have a discernible, if usually contestable, basis in material realities across different territorial spaces. But globality can never be directly experienced or encountered as such. Rather, emanating from science, politics, media, and elsewhere, globality is a lens that we learn to see through, and in this act of social abstraction, important political work takes place. At the same time, the ideas necessary to generate global optics also touch back down to the ground in particular locations through the pathways of conservation politics.

In the processes that make up global environmental governance, the meaning of biodiversity is often taken for granted. It is taken as a stable, self-evident referent, to which cultural or political value is only subsequently ascribed. The UN Millennium Ecosystem Report, for example, advances a familiar kind of claim, that "people from all walks of life value biodiversity for spiritual, aesthetic, recreational, and other cultural reasons" (Millennium Ecosystem Assessment 2005a, 6). We all know what biodiversity is and that it exists, we all just value it differently. In part, this framing is simply the result of translating science into politics, the movement of largely objective referents into the realm of value, contestation, and wrangling.

But this kind of assumption about biodiversity understates its ontological instability. Because it is an idea of the natural sciences, we tend to treat its referent as a given, and ascribe national or cultural differences to a matter of interpreting "it" differently. Yet biodiversity does not reference one thing, or one nature, but comes into being as a concept across a wide range of social, political, and natural contexts and actors. Biodiversity in India has not been the same thing as biodiversity in Indonesia, politically or scientifically.[13] Though there are points of overlap across these scales and contexts, it has no single center of gravity, and it is more accurate to speak of "biodiversities."

Studying the Politics of Global Biodiversity: Toward Material-Semiotics

Rather than seeing it as a fact "out there" in nature, I approach global biodiversity as an idea, or as a productive sign, that has had multiple meanings over time and space. I explore the ways in which its multiple iterations cluster, form constellations, and congeal with political ideas to create particular kinds of environmental politics. One example is multiculturalism in the 1990s era of globalization, with which global biodiversity clustered in a politics of cosmopolitan tolerance that did not always recognize its own intolerant outsides. But while these shifts and changes in the idea of biodiversity are, in one very important sense, about human activities and human language, they cannot be understood solely as human descriptions of neutral material realities. Unlike a number of accounts of environmental ideas and discourses, I take seriously the various ways that the meanings of biodiversity are contingent on and shaped by nonhuman actors, or what Bruno Latour (2004, 75) calls "actants." An actant is, simply put, an entity that modifies another actor through a series of actions. In one sense, it is not particularly controversial to say that nonhuman things like trees, rocks, laptops, or DNA are actants, in that they clearly modify the properties of other actants in the context of a relation—a smartphone modifies the way a tourist acts, a wolf modifies the actions of an elk, and cornstarch modifies the way that water acts. Ideas, too, can be actants, though they always have a specific material location that is important to trace. But while it seems self-evident in an everyday sense, we often do not do a very good job accounting for this actancy in academic work. Global biodiversity may be a human idea—a scientific and political imagining that is generated through the prisms of different cultures and contexts—but many of its meanings are forged through the interactions of human and nonhuman actants in ways that cannot be reduced to a function of human agency or the power of discourse to interpret a neutral nature.

Despite extensive critiques of thinking about nature and culture in a binary way, many accounts of global environmental politics nonetheless largely fail to grapple with the hybrid quality of environmental problems—that is, with the way that multiple kinds of actancy across the nature–culture divide intersect in a common plane to produce the problem of species extinction. Indeed, to the extent that environmental problems such as biodiversity loss are themselves a product of thinking about nature and culture in opposed ways, most analyses end up replicating the problem by assuming those very categories, treating biodiversity largely as a natural object to be consumed or preserved, and as a technical issue of management or governance. The role that nonhuman life plays in biodiversity politics is constantly punted back and forth between nature and culture, appearing here as a natural resource, there as an environmental value, and then again as an informational pattern divorced from a material basis. It shuttles back and forth between natural science and international policy and politics, each time causing effects in one realm due to its formation in the other, but it manages never to be present on the inside of these accounts.

In liberal-rationalist approaches, biodiversity tends to appear either as a strictly material concern for self-interested states or as an underspecified, publicly held value for conservation that informs the preferences of states and NGOs.[14] In turn, these concerns drive the "real action" of international treaty making and global environmental governance. Although these inquiries are important for showing the limits and possibilities of international cooperation, they often end up treating environmental problems such as biodiversity loss as an issue area that is not fundamentally dissimilar from, say, arms control, trade, or any other issue of international deliberation. Most of what matters is the issue structure (such as whether a problem is an issue of the commons or a private good) and how states deal with the various incentives and disincentives around that issue. The only actors in most of these causal stories are humans, which is odd given the centrality of nonhuman life processes in environmental politics. When nonhuman life appears, most of the work of fixing its meaning has been done already.

While I endorse the emphasis that these accounts place on the materiality of biodiversity, I don't assume that materiality means "naturalness," in the sense that material things are supposed to have fixed objective meanings that are either waiting to be discovered or are transparently obvious. Rather, drawing on the recent literature on agency and materialism, I think that material entities are also part of cultural, social, and political action—in a very literal sense—and that paying closer attention to what these nonhuman entities do, and how their effects often exceed our expectations, is imperative in understanding how biodiversity is produced.[15] I therefore emphasize materiality in a different way here. I highlight how the materiality of nonhuman species has transformative effects on the motivations of conservation biologists. I show how the materiality of Uluru Rock matters for creating the meanings of world heritage. And I suggest that the material qualities of other species form a place of escape or resistance from the managerialism of global environmental governance.

If liberal-rationalist approaches tend to operate on the culture side of the divide by assuming nature as an objective fact, other scholars take a discursive approach that explicitly calls into question the facticity of "biodiversity" and other environmentalisms.[16] By working with the assumption that, as Timothy Luke (1995, 58) puts it, "nature is arguably meaningless until humans assign meanings to it by interpreting some of its many signs as meaningful," it is possible to explore how nature comes to have multiple meanings for different actors or to show the play of power in construing some versions of nature as more valid than others. Discursive approaches do not take the environment for granted as a space of facts, but rather question how its meaning is produced—and their central concern with the production of meaning is shared by this book.

Yet, like liberal-rationalist accounts, discursive approaches often seem to treat biodiversity as a kind of secondary vehicle through which the "real" questions of inequality, justice, meaning, and power among humans are played out. More important, both the materiality and the active aspects of nonhuman entities seem to drop out of their biodiversity stories entirely. Even when gesturing to the fact that discourse involves concrete practices and language together, many discourse approaches to environmental politics nonetheless tend to put human language at the center of the story, examining the way that meanings are internally constructed.[17] In order to grasp what is happening in the political and scientific action surrounding the term biodiversity, I am interested in more than how human language constructs nature through differences. Rather, I also want to ask how the meaning of biodiversity is made through human–nonhuman interactions: Who contributes to the making of this term, and how? When shifts in its meaning occur, what are its sources? If "biodiversity" (and associated terms like "species") can have multiple but not an infinite number of meanings, what is it about nonhuman actants that compels such a limitation? After some formation within human discourses—when biodiversity is released back into the nonhuman world, so to speak—how can we think about the collision between the idea and nonhuman life? And, if biodiversity is a way of figuring human and nonhuman life together, or of putting humans inside nature, what does environmental politics now mean and how can we write about it in a way that provides adequate textual representation of the messiness of human–nonhuman interaction?

In trying to answer these kinds of questions, I shift from language to the broader terrain of *signs*, or semiotics. Signs in environmental discourses include things like Greenpeace banners and cuddly images of penguins, but they also include the ways that nonhuman actions stand in for something beyond themselves to humans, as when scientists study the actions of ant colonies in tropical rainforests. These interactions between human and nonhuman arguably create some sort of meanings for at least some of the living nonhumans as well, but those are outside the scope of this book. Instead, I focus here on the ways that human signs like biodiversity, species, hotspots, and heritage are made by both humans and nonhumans. Through an analysis of key discursive sites where global biodiversity is made, and through occasionally risky language, I try to bring the materiality and semiotic power of nonhuman agents into the frame by treating them as coauthors of scientific and political ideas. What is claimed as human (biodiversity as an idea) or as natural (biodiversity as a fact) is better understood as a joint articulation that is neither of these.

Political scientists, in short, have largely not generated appropriate methodologies for understanding the sources of meaning production in those parts of environmental politics that are populated by nonhuman life, nor have they adequately reformulated a number of key concepts for an adequate ecological analysis.[18] Part of the hybrid approach I use here also means taking a different view of the natural sciences. Environmental sciences are ground zero for environmental truth claims and politics. The roles of these various life sciences—spanning biology, biochemistry, ecology, and others—is to act as the hinge point between human and nonhuman. How scientists conceive of what they study, and the kinds of epistemological assumptions they hold, are central in producing our map of the natural world—its boundaries, contours, and categories. These maps are also unstable, however, and sometimes involve paradoxical assumptions that, for example, bring us closer to nature as one species among many but also distance us from nature as supposedly providing objective knowledge. In these points of instability, we can find the grounds for thinking about environmentalism in a post-nature/culture way.

Breaking Agency Up: A Three-Part Optics

One aim of this book is to think about biodiversity through a different conception of agency than what is found in most accounts of environmental politics. Agency in political science is traditionally synonymous with human agency, organized around a cluster of capacities like autonomy, free will, and intentional action. These capacity-based versions of agency are one important arena where the strict division between humans and nature is constructed and reinforced—and the ascription of agency to some entities, whether human or nonhuman, has consequences for the boundaries of moral consideration and political inclusion. Yet, as a growing number of scholars have suggested, agency may be more profitably thought of as a distributed phenomenon, existing in the relations of networks rather than held by an individual entity.[19] Agency, as Jane Bennett (2001, 163) puts it, is an alliance or an exchange, and involves the "ability to make a difference in the world without knowing exactly what you are doing," and it is "distributed, to varying degrees, to atoms that move, plants that engage their environment, and animals that communicate, as well as humans that write onto-stories, protest war, engage in hate speech, and so forth." Importantly for these accounts, agency is not something that is determined up front, as a capacity held by a given entity, nor can it ultimately be schematized into types. Instead, a generalized definition of agency walks hand in hand with a case-by-case analysis of the networks or assemblages in a particular moment, in order to see which entities have agentic effects and through which relations.

For example, consider John Law's account of himself as a sociologist. He is a sociologist (and a human agent) only in virtue of the nonhuman agents that contribute to his endeavor:

> People are who they are because they are a patterned network of heterogeneous materials. If you took away my computer, my colleagues, my office, my books, my desk, my telephone, I wouldn't be a sociologist writing papers, delivering lectures, and producing "knowledge." I'd be something quite other—and the same is true for all of us. . . . So the analytical question is this: is an agent an

agent primarily because he or she inhabits a body that carries knowledge, skills, values, and all the rest? Or is an agent an agent because he or she inhabits a set of elements (including, of course, a body) that stretches out into the network of materials, somatic and otherwise, that surrounds each body?[20]

In a similar way, biodiversity scientists and political actors concerned with biodiversity are agents in part because of the networks that help to produce them as such. What those networks are, and where they stretch to, is an important question for biodiversity politics. For example, for E. O. Wilson (1984), and for many conservation biologists, we have an innate biophilia, or love of other life forms, that is hardwired into us genetically. Motivating political action, on this account, simply involves getting people to recognize their innate love for other species. But this version misstates the way that "biodiversity subjects," including conservation biologists themselves, are *made* through a material and semiotic network of experience. It cannot address why people engage with biodiversity in such myriad ways, including feeling no "philia" for it at all. Nor can it address the ways that producing biodiversity subjects is tied to other political moods, such as anxiety over species loss, or to the kinds of human agency it enables or disables, such as decisions over land use. Instead, the agency involved in producing biodiversity subjects—including scientific knowledge about biodiversity—needs to be made a question that is asked, as Timothy Mitchell (2002, 29) puts it, not something that is assumed in advance.

Although the emphasis on deep particularism of context and the material-semiotic qualities that all entities share are both important correctives, one significant problem with this version of agency as actancy is the way it seems to be everywhere and therefore nowhere. As Lee and Brown (1994, 778) put it, Latour's actor-network theory (ANT) "secures the universal applicability of its political metaphorics, and stretches the notion of relational power . . . to cover everything."[21] Moreover, in treating all things as capable essentially only of modifying other entities, we lose sight of some of the unique qualities that some actors have. One way that ANT has dealt with this problem has been to emphasize that complex entities—like a political scientist or an ecosystem—are effects of agency, rather than agents as such. What seems like a human capacity to discover scientific facts about the Amazonian rainforest through a unique faculty of reason, for example, is instead retold as a distributed network of materials, including laboratory equipment, spreadsheets, soil samples, earthworms, and the scientist, all affecting one another through chains of modification and translation.[22] But over time, it nonetheless becomes possible to distinguish different modalities of agency in the scientist, the earthworm, and the spreadsheet. To treat them all only in their capacity as actants might mean missing other interesting qualities of agency, such as resistance, autonomy, reinterpretation, incorporation, or solidity. The analysis here therefore takes a different tack. So long as we are careful about not confusing these qualities of agency with foundational arguments about political worth, and so long as we are clear that such schemas are ways to classify at a secondary level, rather than as a primary ontological one, we should not shy away from using second-tier categories of agency to think through human–nonhuman relations. Here, I introduce three midlevel variants of material-semiotic nonhuman agency: *biotic, techno-informational,* and *abiotic.* These midlevel types guide me between the universal claim of material-semiotic agency (or actancy), on the one hand, and the deep particularism of each and every entity and context (from which no generalization is possible), on the other. Each of these variants functions for me as a spotlight on a particular nexus of human–nonhuman relations in biodiversity, rather than as a definitive ontological ordering based on importance.

I take biotic agency to mean *making a difference in a semiotic world by transforming meanings of others while also interpreting the world in ways that constitute the agent.* Biotic entities, including animals, plants, trees, and bacteria, move in a world of signs in ways not radically different from humans. Even though biotic nonhumans do not have some of the unique capabilities of humans, such as abstract thought, or the capacity to use signs to refer to signs themselves, they are agentic in the sense of being regularly capable of both interpreting and transforming signs in ways that matter for humans and for other agents. In Paul Robbins's (2007) study of lawns in suburban America, for example, he shows the ways that the lawn is not just a product of human action, aesthetics, and economics, but is also an environmental actor that "makes demands," forces behaviors, adaptations, and adjustments, and connects to human desires (38, 133). For Robbins, the story of the American lawn, with its range of chemical fertilizers, monoculture, and pesticides, is importantly about the ways that turf grass responds and reacts to humans, water, insects, and inputs. The creation of anxious "lawn people" who prize perfectly green grass and spend significant resources to achieve it has to be understood as part of a formation of biotic agency that includes the lawn itself as an interpretive agent alongside humans, deer, and raccoons.

Such a conception of biotic agency levels different living things into a common plane of semiotic agency. There are of course important differences in the kinds of semiotic agency that emerge in relations among different kinds of living things. But they are not sufficient to lift human agency entirely outside of this wider semiotic pool within which biotic agency occurs, in part because those differences are context dependent, and in part because such differences are not as clear-cut as they seem in sustaining the case for human agency as an always-existing unique capacity.

Consider one of the most frequently offered defenses of agency as an exclusively human capacity, which has to do with the uniqueness of human language use. The key difference between humans and nonhumans is said to rest on the human ability to engage in abstract thought, symbolic culture that can escape its material basis, and moral reasoning. Because nonhumans do not have such capacities, they remain mired in worlds of instinct (animals), simple reactions to external stimuli, mechanical being, or brute physical forces.

In political terms, this language objection also has the dual function of defining explicitly what politics is, and defining who and what is human.[23] What makes political community possible at all is the special capacity for reasoned speech and public deliberation about the nature of the good life, as substitutes for violence, relations of force, and instinctive behavior. Lacking such capacities, nonhuman things of all kinds are usually outside of political community.

But the language objection is both internally inconsistent and conflates human agency with agency as such. In his final published lectures on anthropocentrism, animality, and sovereignty, Jacques Derrida explored some of the ways that the language objection fundamentally mischaracterizes the way that language works. Some species are able to do much more than just react, for example, but have complex forms of communication and language that amounts to a form of culture. More important for Derrida and for my purposes here, language and signification processes (or traces) have a kind of power and agency of their own, working partially behind our backs in ways that both escape us and make us.[24] The way that signification works, on Derrida's account, means that humans cannot actually claim full ownership of their language as radically independent from the world. To the extent that the uniqueness of human agency is based on a series of shifting claims about the uniqueness and radical world-independence of human language, it is unstable, and perhaps unsustainable.

This suggests that differences in signifying practices exist, but they need not define agency up front. As Cary Wolfe (2003, 79) puts it with respect to humans and other animals:

> The difference in *kind* between human and animal that humanism constitutes on the site of language may instead be thought as difference in *degree* on a continuum of signifying processes disseminated in the field of materiality, technicity,

and contingency, of which "human" "language" is but a specific, albeit highly refined instance.[25]

Moreover, arguments for moral or political considerability based on the capacity of reasoned speech are internally inconsistent because they do not even include all humans, such as infants or comatose individuals.[26] Yet these humans nonetheless have political and moral standing. What this means is not that it is indefensible to have political categories to reference species, but rather that such arguments do not have a firm grounding in capacities possessed by that species. Such a perspective on the language objection suggests that agency may not require the kind of linguistic capacities we have traditionally required of it. Rather, biotic agency, at least, takes place in relations between things that are able to take part in and experience the world of signs and sign relations.

Abiotic (nonliving) things, by contrast, are agents in a different sense. While they are capable, like all things, of producing effects in particular situations by linking with and changing other agents, their capacity to take part in the semiotic aspects of agency means thinking in terms of *virtual semiosis*, a concept I borrow from semiotician John Deely.[27] Because abiotic things arguably lack a recognizable sense of interior experiences, their agency takes place in a different way. For Deely, abiotic entities are best characterized as being virtual sign carriers, ones that are only actualized in encounter with biotic subjects. As such, this means that they cannot be socially constructed by biotic agents to be or to mean just anything. Rather, they carry multiply realizable signs that affect and steer the content of biotic agency. Because sentient beings are able to engage inorganic matter semiotically at all, and meaning cannot easily arise out of nonmeaning, Deely suggests that inorganic matter carries with it forms of virtual signs that are somehow intrinsic to their being. The agency of abiotica is only virtual, however, until it is realized in interaction with a biotic entity, whether human or nonhuman, and abiotic signs are multiple, but not infinite. As such, it is not possible to distinguish the agentic capacities of a nonliving thing in independent terms, only in relational terms.

Yet in these interactions, there is continually the "slight surprise of action," where abiotic elements sometimes interact in unexpected ways to produce an outcome.[28] In Timothy Mitchell's account of development in modern Egypt, for example, these elements include tanks, mosquitoes, humans, dams, and synthetic nitrates—biotic and abiotic elements—all of which contribute to the production of war, famine, and disease. What is important in order to understand the events of this period, Mitchell (2002, 27–28, 30) suggests, is to study the linkages that are "hydraulic, chemical, military, political, etiological, and mechanical"; yet, "it is as if the elements are somehow incommensurable. They seem to involve very different forces, agents, elements, spatial scales, and temporalities. They shape one another, yet their heterogeneity offers a resistance to explanation. . . . There is little room to examine the ways they emerge together in a variety of combinations, or how so-called human agency draws its force by attempting to divert or attach itself to other kinds of energy and logic." Biodiversity politics exhibits similar forms of heterogeneous combinations, mixing the logics of natural sciences with economic practices and moral discourses, and bound at a number of junctures by interactions between biotic and abiotic elements. In this light, I thus consider the agentic effects of abiotic entities, such as Uluru Rock in Australia and the sandstone spikes of Meteora, Greece, as they intersect the politics of World Heritage Sites and a variety of living beings.

Finally, straddling the biotic–abiotic line, technologies like computer systems, databases, earth observation satellites, radio collars, and smartphones are increasingly part of biodiversity sciences and politics, and increasingly challenge the way that we think about the interpretive aspects of agency. As both tool use by crows and dolphins and farming techniques used by leafcutter ants illustrate, humans are not the only species capable of making or using technology. But current information technologies created by humans are deeply sophisticated in ways that challenge the biotic–abiotic boundary. As Donna Haraway argues, computers, scientific instruments, machines, and other technologies are increasingly constituted as sign-interpreters and material-semiotic actors.[29] Yet because they are on the wrong side of the biotic–abiotic divide, and because of the discourse within which they were invented, these technologies are often thought of as dealing in information and not meaning.[30] While information technologies arguably still lack the interpretive moments that biotic agents have, they do engage in other agentic practices that seem to exceed the virtual semiosis of abiotica like rocks—acting intelligibly in response to the world, transforming the meanings of others, and sometimes generating their own signs in unpredictable ways. The density of their informational flows, their increasing enmeshment within the world of the living, and the deep mixing of human and nonhuman elements in their material and semiotic structures give them a particular propensity for surprising action and transformation, and they therefore form a third variant of agency between the biotic and the abiotic.

Each chapter of this book generally foregrounds a different aspect of agency (biotic, techno-informational, and abiotic) and examines its interaction with human agency in the articulation of biodiversity and the practices of environmental politics. The articulation of species and hotspots involves humans alongside a cast of other living creatures. The biodiversity census continues to think about biotic agency of nonhuman life, alongside the techno-informational agency of censusing and websites such as the Catalogue of Life. The chapter on World Heritage Sites turns to a more sustained consideration of abiotic mountains and rocks as agents, the most challenging of these modalities of agency.

Outline of This Book

This book is structured along a generally linear trajectory, with each chapter pursuing a particular moment in the transformation and evolution of the idea of global biodiversity from the birth of biodiversity in the mid-1980s to the present. This linearity allows a tracing of the ways that biodiversity has changed over time, both in its constitution as a scientific-political idea and in the politics of conservation that it has constituted. The book considers the rise, transformation, and ultimate incorporation of biodiversity as a political discourse in global environmental arenas, but also emphasizes that global biodiversity has differed substantially at each moment, depending in part on the political ideas with which it has clustered. Starting with the birth of biodiversity hotspots in 1988, it shows how biodiversity shaped environmental thinking, in ways that sometimes did endeavor to see humans as part of nature again, on the terrain of species. This book then traces the way this worked in the global biodiversity census, promoted and institutionalized by conservation biologists in the 1990s, as a way of advancing scientific knowledge, conservation, and human use of biodiversity, and the changing contours of biodiversity protection in UNESCO World Heritage Sites during that same period. It finishes by considering the emergence of the Anthropocene in the 2000s as a new paradigm for conservation by looking at urban biodiversity in New York City and the politics of rewilding.

Biodiversity hotspots—the label for places where there are high levels of species diversity that are under threat—crystallize a number of the most important assumptions that drive global biodiversity and bring its key political players in sharp relief. Chapter 1 reflects on a number of key nodes in thinking about biodiversity hotspots: species, diversity, and activist scientists. It identifies keys to this early discourse, including the intrinsic value of species, the power of pattern and systems, and a global mapping of key points of species convergence that put an emphasis on conserving biodiversity in places other than the developed North. This early period also began to emphasize an environmental politics based on efficient resource maximization—saving the most species for the least money—that was amplified in subsequent decades.

In chapter 2, I turn to the initiative of conducting a global biodiversity census, aimed at cataloguing all the species on earth. As a political interaction that involves categorizing, naming, counting, and labeling nonhumans, the census seems largely to be about the exercise of power by humans over nature. However, expanding the "bio" in "biopower" to think across species lines, the chapter suggests that the global biodiversity census is one example of the change in disciplinary power when nonhuman life enters the equation explicitly. Nonhuman species are not without agency in this new regime, as they manage to disrupt biopolitical impulses toward the smooth governing of populations in interesting ways. Rather than assuming that the census is purely an act of information gathering that increases human knowledge about the natural world, it is better understood as a kind of hybrid political phenomenon, involving both humans and nonhumans wrangling over the conditions of collective well-being.

Chapter 3 explores what happens when global institutions attempt in a serious manner to move beyond rigid nature/culture dichotomies by articulating new, hybrid categories of practice. Until recently, World Heritage Sites were selected using natural criteria and cultural criteria. Because of the problematic political implications of these categories as well as the pragmatic difficulties in cleanly identifying natural or cultural sites, UNESCO moved toward articulating selection criteria that are more clearly hybridized, such as associative cultural landscapes. I analyze the evolution of UNESCO's heritage site classification over time. Two case studies, one in Greece (Meteora) and one in Australia (Uluru Rock), provide specific, contextual locations to consider the intersection of global categories and local, national, and international politics of heritage sites. As sites composed primarily of rock, they also offer a significant challenge to the idea of nonhuman agency. While I show some of the ways that their abiotic agency matters in shaping the meanings of heritage, I also suggest that they are limit cases for political agency. Finally, I evaluate UNESCO's use of "biocultural diversity" as a promising hybrid category. Rather than reading UNESCO's categories as an inexorable march toward hybridity, though, the chapter shows how UNESCO ended up re-embedding significant, problematic aspects of nature-culture in new forms (especially in its orientation toward indigenous nature-culture complexes).

Chapter 4 compares the rise of two new initiatives, urban biodiversity and rewilding, in the context of a more explicitly designed global nature made by humans (the Anthropocene). Looking both at global policy initiatives and at New York City as a local case, the chapter considers how urban biodiversity is a comparatively new object of environmental governance, emphasizing new opportunities for promoting biodiversity in cities and around them. Rewilding, by contrast, generally emphasizes areas outside cities, particularly in the United States, where corridors for large species form part of an overall plan to create trophic biodiversity. In some ways, it shares with urban biodiversity an emphasis on biodiversity by design, but in other ways, it opens up new opportunities for thinking about biodiversity as a more political project again. Pointing toward a new politics of wilding, the chapter considers how rewilding as a form of practicing biodiversity might able to be less beholden to the technical, market-driven, and antipolitical processes considered in the preceding chapters. The relationship between this different politics of biodiversity and the modes of agency explored in the book is taken up in the concluding chapter.

Chapter 1   **The Awful Symmetry of**
              Biodiversity Hotspots

ONE OF THE EARLIEST OBJECTS of global biodiversity conservation and science was the hotspot, which explicitly fused the new knowledge and language of biodiversity with a politics of efficiency. Referencing places in the world with particularly high densities of species that are also highly at risk, hotspots involved overlapping imageries of heat. In their first iteration in the 1980s by conservation biologists, they were identified as being predominantly in tropical regions, contrasting with the air-conditioned corridors of Western capitals where global conservation policy was often worked on. Tapping into long-running colonial and postcolonial narratives about tropical fecundity, biodiversity hotspots grew out of and fed on a Western environmental imaginary that had grown to prominence in the 1970s partly through an emphasis on exploding populations in the Global South. Containing thousands of species whose vitality produces furious evolutionary competition, hotspots emphasized not only the heat of natural life processes and the generation of biological diversity but also the fact that the tropical forests in hotspots were being burned down and logged at a furious pace, feeding the material needs of local citizens who, for a variety of political and economic reasons, had turned to the forest for a living.

Hotspots such as the Brazilian Amazon were internationally hot in political terms, as the impassioned target of decades of Western environmental activism and scientific analysis and as key objects at the middle of a long-running debate about the relative obligations of developed and developing countries. Though biodiversity hotspots were not the only way that tropical rainforests were painted in environmental imaginaries, they were a particularly important one for the developments in global biodiversity politics that were to come afterward. As E. O. Wilson (1992, 272) later put it, the conservation problem for biodiversity became framed as an "awful symmetry" in which "the richest nations preside over the smallest and least interesting biotas, while the poorest nations, burdened by exploding populations and little scientific knowledge are stewards of the largest." This awful symmetry, and its assumptions, framed much of the international biodiversity politics of subsequent decades, and contributed to many of the current standoffs in global environmental politics.

Along with hotspots, this chapter also explores the emergence of the idea of biodiversity itself, including the thought that it was something that could be experienced as such, not just scientifically defined. In one story from this early period of biodiversity, as told by David Takacs, American conservation biologist Thomas Lovejoy began taking United States senators and others out to the Amazonian rainforest to show them biodiversity "in action." Flying in from Washington, the senators arrived late in the evening, with almost nothing in the way of introductory lectures or reading. Before rising early the next morning to take a guided tour of the forest, they would spend the night in the rainforest, hearing the cacophony of sounds in the darkness, feeling the heat, and smelling the unfamiliar smells. As Lovejoy describes it: "They [the senators] will have spent the whole night listening to all these voices. That becomes biological diversity in their brains. If they don't spend the night, they don't get the experience."[1] The nighttime in the rainforest, Lovejoy said, is the key experience of conversion for his guests, one to which he gives further shape in the morning tour. By the end of the morning, the senators experience biodiversity as a concrete phenomenon—they see and feel it in ways that Lovejoy says books, lectures, museums, or video documentaries are unable to convey. How does the experience of those senators come to pass as it does? What does it mean to "experience biodiversity," given the broad definition of the term? How does this experience begin to shape thinking about environmental politics? In particular, it is important to ask how people come to care about something as abstract as global biodiversity loss, and on what terms. Tracing the early conceptual development of biodiversity in the late 1980s and early 1990s, and engaging with the emergence of biodiversity hotspots as a particular conservation object, this chapter illuminates the ways that biodiversity works in political terms, and as an experience.

The focus on the global distribution of species in biodiversity hotspots was an abstraction with particular power. Because species are unevenly distributed around the world, and because biodiversity hotspots directed attention at concentrations of species as the target of conservation, biodiversity generated an environmental politics directed mostly at tropical regions, using efficient allocation of money as one of its main rationales. This laid the groundwork for the kind of green governance that came to be dominant by the 2000s. At the same time, this period also witnessed interesting innovations within biodiversity science and politics, including an open embrace of green values in the science of conservation biology and arguments about protecting species for intrinsic value versus instrumental reasons.

Biodiversity and the Centrality of Species

The idea of the diversity of life is not a new one. The concept of biological diversity has scientific forerunners in biology and ecology, ranging from Charles Darwin to Aldo Leopold.[2] But as it emerged in the 1980s, biological diversity—and then "biodiversity"—became a new object of political and environmental policy, knowledge, and passions, with its own particular dynamics.

Most of the working definitions of the concept in policy and politics are broad and inclusive. In an early and widely used definition in the United States, the U.S. Office of Technology Assessment (OTA) (1988, 3) anchored a 1988 report on biodiversity by defining it as "the variety and variability among living organisms and the ecological complexes in which they occur." At the international level, the point of negotiated consensus is found in the text of the Convention on Biological Diversity (CBD), signed in 1992: "'Biological diversity' means the variability among living organisms, from all sources including, *inter alia*, terrestrial, marine and other aquatic ecosystems and the ecological complexes of which they are a part; this includes diversity within species, between species, and of ecosystems."[3] Growing out of a disparate set of international treaties on species protection and conservation, the CBD ultimately enshrined a commitment to biodiversity as an economic resource, but the definition in article 2 of the CBD does little itself to move in this direction. Rather, like the OTA definition, its most important move is to go from the more tangible reference point of endangered species protection—actual species—to naming the variability of life itself—the pattern—as the key point of reference.[4]

These broad, conceptual definitions of biodiversity encompass the entire variety of life. As the United Nations Environmental Programme (UNEP) puts it, biodiversity is "essentially a synonym of 'Life on Earth.'"[5] Yet it is difficult to take something as general as "life on earth" as a useful synonym. Such a generality necessarily calls up some other imagery or other particulars to concretize it. In the case of biodiversity, when this point of reference is made explicit, it usually meant turning to a hierarchically organized taxonomy, breaking biodiversity down as a kind of three-part Russian nesting doll. The highest level (or biggest doll) is ecosystemic diversity, referencing different environments such as deserts, marshes, temperate forests, and rainforests. This level encompasses the lower ones, but it is not widely used as an indicator of biodiversity per se. At the lowest level, but increasingly seen as an important driver, both ecologically and economically, are forms of genetic diversity. The most widely used level, however, is the middle one: species diversity.

The emergence of the term "biodiversity," as a contraction of "biological diversity," is a useful way to start to understand its central political points of reference. The creation of the biodiversity neologism is credited to plant physiologist and National Research Council (NRC) member Walter Rosen, who spearheaded the first national conference on biodiversity in 1986, sponsored by the National Academy of Sciences (NAS).[6] He created the term as part of organizing the conference, to the initial dismay of E. O. Wilson and others who found it "too glitzy."[7] Rosen's notion was that "biodiversity" is less unwieldy than "biological diversity"—it sounds less technical and less scientific, and the ability of the term to appeal to nonscientific communities was important. Asked about the term in an interview, Rosen neatly frames how the word itself transforms the affective power of the concept.

> All you do is take the "logical" out of "biological." . . . To take the logical out of something that's supposed to be science is a bit of a contradiction in terms, right? And yet, of course, maybe that's why I get impatient with the Academy [of Sciences], because they're always so logical that there seems to be no room for emotion in there, no room for spirit.[8]

The semantics of the word are slightly transformed here, with one effect being that the power of the term to affectively connect humans to other living species is enhanced. The subtraction of *logos*, or reasoned discourse, turns out to add the important hint of an experiential connection. Biodiversity, as a term, was thus created in part as a strategic public relations necessity, a simple way of making a scientific term more accessible and appealing, similar to "global warming" for climate change scientists or, more recently, efforts to use "ecological resilience" instead of sustainability in the Transition Towns movement.[9]

For many of the scientists who were asked to operationalize biodiversity, the meaning of biodiversity was nonetheless significantly up for grabs. One review article in the mid-1990s worked through no less than eighty-five different definitions of the term![10] In *The Idea of Biodiversity*, Paul Takacs (1996) interviews twenty mostly American ecologists and conservation biologists who come up with a highly heterogeneous set of definitions. While some echo the multilevel definitions of the OTA and CBD, other responses range from "plain species diversity" to "the total number of genetic lineages on earth" (Thomas Eisner) to "shorthand for all the richness of life" (Reed Noss) to having no definition at all (Paul Ehrlich) or outright laughter (Vickie Funk) (46–50).

Most of those interviewed do nonetheless point to a multilevel system defined by differences, relations, and emergent qualities among parts.

Part of the problem comes from having somewhat incommensurable scales within the concept of biodiversity. The three Russian dolls—ecosystems, species, and genes—do not neatly connect with one another, just as the levels of analysis problem that is familiar to political scientists. Just as individuals, nation-states, and international systems are not all the same "kinds" of things, and so may not be theoretically integrable, so too are genes, species, and ecosystems in an uneasy relationship.[11] Putting these different units of biodiversity together at national, international, or global levels requires careful scientific work in ways that are not always easy to communicate politically in a simple definition. But although there is no easy general agreement among scientists on what biodiversity is (which is perhaps unsurprising), and as of yet, no grand synthesis among these levels of analysis, there was nonetheless significant agreement on species as the most important unit of biodiversity in the 1980s and 1990s.[12] In part, species is an easily communicable category, both among scientists and as an object of policy. Yet in a number of interesting ways, the practice of using species belies its apparent conceptual transparency.

Compared to biodiversity, the concept of species has been field-tested for much longer, with origins, perhaps, in ancient Greece, Egypt, Mesopotamia, and China.[13] Its modern Western variant originated with Swedish botanist Carolus Linnaeus in the mid-1700s, but this iteration has not been any more prone to definitional consensus. The miracle, in a way, is that species works at all, given the wide heterogeneity of definitions, both in the current and the historical species concept debates in biology.[14] Species are a cornerstone of evolutionary theory and of biodiversity science and politics, but the different meanings of the term require ongoing concatenation and lamination, where groups who disagree about the meaning of the term in the broad scheme of things can nonetheless find zones of overlap and contact that allow them to hammer out functionality.[15]

From Linnaeus until the nineteenth century, species were generally defined by the degree of observable (phenotypical) differences that could be categorized into existing taxonomical structures. One distinguished species from one another based on whether they displayed outwardly different characteristics that could then give guidance on taxonomical organization. Yet this phenotypical approach ran into what biologist Ernst Mayr (2001, 165) understatedly calls "practical difficulties." Victorian-era biologists complained at the vast proliferation of taxonomic schemes used to classify species, presaging a later desire for smoothness and consistency in practice.[16] Taxonomists became convinced that species were not essential types, but rather that they were diverse populations of diverse genetically unique individuals. How then could species be defined as a population? Put simply, if there was no essence to a species, what criteria should be used to lump them commonly together?

Since the beginning of the twentieth century, biologists have largely settled on the biological species concept (BSC), which solves the problem by using sexual reproduction as the key basis for establishing species barriers. The BSC defines species as "groups of interbreeding natural populations that are reproductively isolated from other such groups."[17] In its inverse form, "Members are able to interbreed freely under natural conditions."[18] In short, a species is defined as a closed reproductive community, where that which allows or denies reproductive compatibility is what determines species difference.[19] These factors include direct physical compatibility, but they also include behaviors that reproductively isolate similar groups from another, such as mating calls and geographical range, and physical indicators like plumage or scent. In situations where the populations are not geographically proximate, the biologist must infer the potential reproductive compatibility. While lions and tigers have been interbred in captivity to produce tiglons, for example, they have not interbred outside of zoos, and are therefore considered distinct species.

Certain biological populations fall outside the BSC classification system, which remains a nagging problem for the proponents of the concept.[20] In what is otherwise a robust defense of the BSC, Wilson (1992, 45) admits that "from the beginning of its first clear formulation at the turn of the century, [the BSC] has been corroded by exceptions and ambiguities." Most clearly, biological entities that are not sexually reproductive, either because they reproduce asexually or because they are hermaphroditic, are not part of a species concept organized around sexual reproduction. For example, a number of lizards, mites, fungi, and plants all regenerate without sexual reproduction. Yet these organisms are generally able to maintain biological integrity—that is, the genes of these populations remain closely clustered and their anatomy and behavior remain highly similar. This integrity is taken as a viable proxy for reproduction, and thus they are considered to be species.

A second exception to the BSC is temporally based—species that are evolutionary ancestors of another species (chronospecies) might or might not interbreed freely under natural conditions, but the BSC cannot be used to make this judgment. *Homo sapiens* and *Homo erectus* are considered two different species, for example, but not by way of the BSC.[21] Semispecies, which are the result of populations that partially interbreed, but not enough to produce a new, completely closed gene pool, also challenge the BSC. Semispecies are distinct in phenotypical terms and by distinct habitats, but they cross-fertilize with other organisms that are not part of the semispecies. A great number of plants and trees on the Pacific Coast in North America fit this description, and accidental hybridization that results not in sterile offspring but in new species is one way that speciation occurs; yet semispecies do not fit neatly into the BSC definition and exist, as Wilson (1992, 47) puts it, in "a state of ambiguous tension," neither fully a BSC species nor a nonspecies.

These challenges reveal a pattern among the groupings of scientists that neatly mirrors the organizing logic of biodiversity itself. Those scientists most in favor of BSC are taxonomists, typologists, or systematists, who are most interested in classifying and ordering species. For them, as Mayr (2001, 84) puts it, "the type (*eidos*) is real and the variation an illusion." Population biologists, who are interested in studying specific populations and the process by which difference is created, are more skeptical of the BSC, and revel in the challenges that particular biological entities pose to the BSC. Rather like anthropologists compared to political scientists, for populationists "the type (average) is an abstraction and only the variation is real. No two ways of looking at nature could be more different" (ibid.). The logic of biodiversity involves the simultaneous positing of irreducible difference within irreducible commonality; that its organizing collective concept should contain the same tension is therefore fitting.

The co-configuration of abstracts and particulars in biodiversity discourses ultimately bears on what is seen as ethically considerable.[22] This occurs on two levels. On one level, to experience biodiversity is to see the world as fundamentally configured into abstract, common units—*species*—and it is to experience the massive plurality of species that constitutes the category *diversity*. On a lower level, biological species are also united by being internally plural, to borrow from Hannah Arendt's (1958, 8) description of the human condition—this is a "plurality such that we are all the same in that nobody is ever the same as anybody else." No single specimen of a species is exactly like any other, just as, at a "higher" level, no two species are exactly alike. Indeed, species themselves are diverse or at least seem to require a conjunctive definition in order to be held under a common term. Yet this fact of diversity is also the commonality that life forms share as a fact of existence.

While scientists largely settled on the BSC by the early twentieth century, the matter is far from settled.[23] Debates over the species concept in biology continue to include a rowdy variety of positions. The BSC remains the dominant concept (especially for ecologists), but a number of other species concepts are in active use and are vigorously defended. Divisions exist about how to define species—reproductively, phylogenetically (based on descent from a common ancestor), genetically (based on common DNA), or ecologically (based on occupying a common ecological niche)—to name a few. There is also broad disagreement over whether species, in principle, can be unified under a single concept or whether it is inherently a pluralistic idea, where in order to define species, one must say that species are a number of things (more like family resemblances).[24] Are species populations of individuals, or are they statistical patterns? Finally, difficulties of scale rise again. An ecological analysis of biodiversity within a ten-square-kilometer plot can yield thousands of species, while one gram of beech-forest soil yields four to five thousand bacterial species.[25]

As the emergence of biodiversity hotspots in the next section shows, using the number of species in a particular location as an indicator for biodiversity is both readily communicable and has had rhetorical appeal. But the scalability of species diversity—its potential applicability to a large ecosystem or a handful of soil—does not mean it is scalable in ecosystemic terms, since different species matter more than others for ecosystem functioning. Its scalability has had other impacts, however, allowing it to produce a kind of environmental political efficiency that constructs new targets of conservation policy.

The Birth of Biodiversity Hotspots

Species, whatever their definition, are not evenly distributed across the earth. Due in part to the effects of planetary orientation and orbit, which cause different climactic zones, and in part to the uneven histories of global economic development, biodiversity is much more prevalent in some places than in others. Summarized in the broadest terms, a mere 1.5 percent of the earth's land surface holds 45 percent of existing plant species and 35 percent of existing vertebrate species.[26] Tropical forests, concentrated in the equatorial regions and held by developing countries, contain between 50 and 90 percent of all species.[27]

Given both limited conservation resources and political constraints, a number of scientists and Western conservationists mobilized around this uneven distribution of species over the last two decades, arguing that efforts to preserve biodiversity in the face of the current anthropogenic extinction event should prioritize those "hotspots." Even though hotspots, and the strategies of conservation that follow from them, have sometimes been contested on scientific merits as well as political grounds, the logic that they embody helped to inaugurate a period of global conservation policy and governance that was evocative and passionate, and yet also coldly efficient and abstract, rooted in the new idea of biodiversity. Managing nature for maximum sustainable return was not new to either American conservation and resource management, or to global environmental discussions.[28] But the innovation of biodiversity hotspots was in its construction of the general space of the global environment on a new scale of intensity involving the threat of species extinction, and its translation of that imagery into a marriage of efficient spending and efficient conservation. How did such an unusual mode of talking about nature come to be accepted as common currency?

The idea of biodiversity hotspots was first formulated by the ecologist Norman Myers in 1988.[29] His definition, which persists in most hotspot analyses and applications,[30] brings together two features. First, they must have a high count of *endemic species.* An endemic species doesn't necessarily originate at a given location, but it "occurs there and nowhere else."[31] The idea of endemism thus extends traditional measures of biodiversity based only on the species richness of a locale by adding a criterion based on the existence or nonexistence of similar entities elsewhere. As such, it is a twist on the classical botanic distinctions of native and exotic species that drew on notions of authenticity through originary roots in a place. Endemism emphasizes instead the idea of cloistered survival in a world of continual erasure.

Myers's (1988) second criterion for a hotspot is that the biodiversity of the area must be *threatened.* Localities with high levels of endemic species must "face exceptional degrees of threat" to qualify (187). Hotspots must not merely have high concentrations of endemic biodiversity, which might occur independently of extinctions or environmental change; it must also face biological destruction, mostly anthropogenic in nature. By the time Myers's 1988 analyses were adopted by Conservation International (CI) in 1990 and funded by the Macarthur Foundation, and the subsequent CI-sponsored research at the Center for Applied Biodiversity Science into hotspots was published, that threat became a well-quantified threshold—a region must have lost at least 70 percent of its original habitat to qualify as a hotspot.[32] Based on these two criteria, CI identified twenty-five hotspots across the world in 2000, upgrading this list to thirty-four in 2005 (see Figure 1).[33] For CI, the conservation of biodiversity hotspots functions as a "silver bullet" strategy for global conservation efforts, and both scientific work and conservation agencies have taken up the concept as a tool of ecological management.[34]

Both in ecological conceptualization and in political promulgation, these initial conceptualizations of hotspots openly depended on a normative valuation of species conservation in territories thought of as outside of political-economic history, with particular calculations that then followed about how

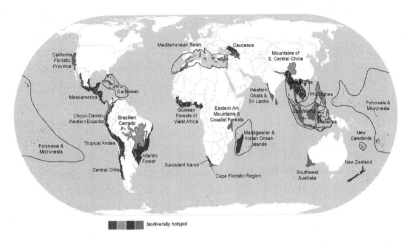

Figure 1. Conservation International's Map of Biodiversity Hotspots, 2000, showing areas with high numbers of endemic species and high percentages of habitat loss. Copyright 2000 Conservation International Foundation. Biodiversity Hotspots.

to achieve conservation objectives. Geography and climate were taken to be sufficient to explain the global distribution of species, rather than the trajectories of the global economy, with the exception of present practices of road building, logging, and slash-and-burn farming. The tangled history of conservation strategies emanating from outside the countries being conserved was also generally ignored.

At the same time, hotspots were not just an idea that conservation groups or other actors took up and acted on. Rather, the conceptual object of biodiversity hotspots exerted pressures and constraints on the actors who used it.[35] How did this quasi-object affect practices and understandings of conservation?

As noted in the introduction, hotspots mix multiple registers of heat imagery. They draw on the fecundity of life and evolution in largely tropical regions. Ecological tropes of heat and fecundity in the tropical zones also mix up humans and nature into a potent reproductive image, using the colder language of demographics to draw on older colonial narratives. For example, one analysis of hotspots mixes demography with ecology to find that "population density in the hotspots was 73 people/km^2, a figure 71% greater than that of the world as a whole."[36] The analysis is intended to highlight the difficulty of conservation under conditions of demographic stresses on the environment. But it also involves a problematic figuring of demographic explosions as part of an overall hotspot reproductive power, without referencing the contextual factors—economic, political, historical—that data come from, and without addressing how changing those factors might be one of the important solutions. As chapter 4 shows, such analyses continue to pervade global biodiversity policy in the 2000s as well.

The merging of species diversity and human demographics into the singular figure of hotspots is complemented by a temporal elision, integrating the long-term evolutionary time frame of species endemism and species richness with the short-term frame of destruction and threat. It melds these temporalities together seamlessly, uniting them under the common heading of "ecological crisis," which has the effect of redirecting attention toward an open-ended future of crisis. It is striking how many works on biodiversity hotspots open their arguments with the observation of crisis. The centrality of threat to hotspots is made visible right away in how Myers frames his argument, which begins by pointing to the mass-extinction episode currently under way, in which millions of species are being eradicated due to largely anthropogenic causes. Such an opening is a common strategy in biodiversity writing. Mittermeier and Myers (1998, 516) open their article by noting the irreversibility of "the accelerating and potentially catastrophic loss of biotic diversity," while Olson and Dinerstein (1998, 502) start by suggesting that "the current extinction crisis requires dramatic action to save the variety of life on Earth." E. O. Wilson (1992, 259), using considerably more inflammatory rhetoric, refers to this mass extinction as a "holocaust." As one might expect of a holistic ecological perspective, discourses of bodily death are also common modes of describing the extinction event, using terms like the "hemorrhaging" of biodiversity, and describing the hotspots strategy as "triage."[37]

In spite of its sound scientific basis, the rhetoric of environmental crisis puts forward an open-ended political combat task to which there is no foreseeable end. It constructs a time scale for success that is in the order of decades, if not centuries, and leverages this for calls for action in the present. The current mass extinction episode is thus at once a well-tested scientific fact, an artifact of the geological record, and a rhetorical and political strategy, and it sets out a frame that carves out the discursive space for action on behalf of the environment and biodiversity.[38] Specifically, the trope of extinctions suggests a common struggle for life on earth against annihilation.

Mass extinctions are distinct from background extinction by their speed in geological time. Background extinctions are an ongoing part of evolution, where new species gradually replace old species, whereas mass extinctions are both rare (there have only been four major ones) and outside of the slow changes that occur through evolution. Past mass extinctions have been due to a variety of causes that have been called "random" and "physical"—most famously the massive asteroid impact that provoked massive climate change and the end of the dinosaurs—but there have been three other mass extinctions in which 75–85 percent of living species became extinct.[39] By contrast, the present loss of biodiversity is attributed to human impact, primarily from habitat destruction and pollution. The conservation implication, of course, is that it is neither random nor unstoppable.

Given this context of biodiversity loss, Myers (1988) is convinced that there is a conservation need for "priority-setting." Priority-setting here means justifying the idea of hotspots in highly utilitarian terms: "By concentrating on such areas where needs are greatest and where the pay-off from safeguard measures would also be greatest, conservationists can engage in a more systematized response to the challenge of large scale extinctions impending in tropical forests" (187). As CI later put it, "In which areas would a given dollar contribute the most toward slowing the current rate of extinction?"[40] As much as it seems like a simply pragmatic approach, this taken-for-granted quality of utilitarianism does also hide other factors. The original hotspots that Myers proposed are all tropical forests, which were later expanded by Mittermeier's concept of "major tropical wilderness areas." These findings are correlated with research in ecological science that finds particularly high levels of diversity in tropical climates, which is called the problem of "tropical preeminence."[41] Concentrated in the equatorial zones, tropical rainforests cover roughly 6 percent of the earth's land surface, but hold more than half of the world's species of organisms.[42] But because these species are concentrated in the poorest countries, conservationists saw an awful symmetry here between biodiversity and wealth.

The focus on hotspots in tropical areas, which are largely located in developing countries, means that the success of biodiversity as a conservation program has had to navigate social inequality, regimes of development, and postcolonial politics.[43] By emphasizing the efficiency of conservation dollars as a decisive factor, biodiversity hotspots also end up reinforcing some of the logics of global inequality that underpin the loss of species in the first place. Environmental capital must be spent where it can get the highest return, in hotspot calculations, and conservation in developed countries is ultimately inefficient by comparison. By mixing the apparent natural accident of the global distribution of species (with the greatest biodiversity at the equatorial regions and the least biodiversity at the poles) with the naturalized imperative of efficient allocation of conservation dollars, hotspots sidestep the tricky questions of why Wilson's "awful symmetry" is in place. CI's hotspot list includes a number of hotspots in the developed world as well. The California

Floristic province, Japan, and the Mediterranean Basin all qualify under the rubric. Yet when biodiversity hotspots in the developed world are considered as targets for conservation efforts, the question of efficiency can quickly become a cleaver once more—the costs of acquiring land or undertaking other conservation measures is comparatively more expensive in these regions.[44]

Additionally, the discourse of efficient allocation of resources is, to a certain extent, also a constitutive factor of the very ecological destruction that hotspots are aimed at halting. That there may be a global biodiversity crisis, in the sense of species going extinct at an abnormally high rate, need not mean that it be strategized in these utility-maximizing terms, or that wealthy Western conservation groups should necessarily lead the way in halting it. In many ways, bringing a management perspective to bear on global ecological problems is itself part of a modern apparatus of logic that is manufacturing the ecological degradation itself. Here, the greatest social good is achieved through the maximally efficient use of scarce resources, which is coordinated from above where possible through global governing agencies and international coordination.

Perhaps most important, it is not clear that saving the most species for the least cost really achieves ecological goals in a broader sense. To the extent that the conservation of biodiversity is not just an objective preservation goal but also a normative project of transforming the ways in which people and the environment relate, addressing the loss of biodiversity may need to be more openly values based and explicitly political, rather than utilitarian, if it wants to achieve its broader aims.[45]

The Double Life of Biodiversity Scientists

As the previous section suggests, we cannot easily understand biodiversity simply by looking at it as a series of scientific facts that warrant clear political action. While I have been highlighting some of the ways that biodiversity is an unsettled idea within both the sciences and conservation, and suggesting some of the political ramifications of its early commitments, I do not want to draw the implication that conservation biologists were themselves creating the idea of global biodiversity from scratch, as sovereign agents. Having held conservation scientists steady, so to speak, in the previous section in order to relate something about the agentic qualities of the biodiversity and hotspots concepts, I now examine how conservation biology itself worked to acknowledge some of these difficulties and to navigate them. While the previous section cast a politically critical eye at some of the discourses that biodiversity tapped into, this section casts a more sympathetic net over some of the politically unusual ways that biodiversity was articulated, as both an objective science and a normative project. Looking ahead to the chapters that follow, which trace biodiversity's later political formations, this section also suggests the resources that might be drawn on for biodiversity to be rearticulated in politically more critical ways.

Scientific achievements depend on social mobilizations outside of the laboratory as well as inside it.[46] For example, Latour's (1999, chapters 4 and 5) account of Louis Pasteur's research into spontaneous generation shows how Pasteur did not just "discover" yeast as a cause of lactic acid fermentation and then propagate that knowledge into society. He also had to mobilize the French Academy of Sciences, lobby government officials, move within theological disputes between Protestantism and Catholicism, overcome resistance to the acceptance of local scientific experiment as a social mode of demonstrating fact, reject an incorrect replication of his experiment by his competitor Félix Pouchet, obtain financing for his research, and so on. From this perspective, even though science and society are often thought of as separate domains with distinct operating logics, they are much more intertwined in practice, a fact that might be embraced rather than hidden away. But this intertwining remains hidden because of the way that scientific expertise is rooted in its procedural requirements to banish personal bias and social norms from social life.

The key point of Latour's argument is that the apparent descent into relativism of truth claims that is implied from this perspective—that is, that any scientific truth claim can be valid if it mobilizes sufficient social support—only exists if we forget that the network of relevant agents is limited to (human) social actors. By triangulating scientists, society, and the array of nonhuman "things" such as laboratory equipment and natural phenomena, the stability (or instability) of any given truth claim over time can be better explained, and without recourse to either objective truth or relativism. Thus, the laboratory equipment, Pasteur's testimony in front of the Academy of Sciences, and the newspapers publicizing the results are all part of the same effect—that which is labeled "yeast." Indeed, they build on one another, translate one another, and connect to one another in ways that involve an interplay of agency between yeast and scientist.

There is little need to go all the way, as Latour does, and say that undiscovered species literally did not exist until they came into contact with a conservation biologist.[47] Rather, the utility of his perspective here comes in examining how a particular concept—like species or biodiversity—emerges and through what assemblages. What matters analytically is to follow the *ongoing production* of an effect, and how it crisscrosses social and natural lines.

Biodiversity, in other words, is always social and natural at once, constantly moving like a shark who cannot stop without suffocating, but not moving necessarily in a straightforward linear fashion either.

What is unusual and laudable about many conservation biologists involved in biodiversity is their open ambivalence about the usual terms of thinking about science. In some contexts, they reject the strong distinctions between science and society, and facts and values, and yet they also rely on such distinctions for parts of their authority. Whereas Pasteur and other scientists whose work is traced by science studies scholars had to alternately play each side of the science–society divide in order to create a viable scientific fact, conservation biologists produce facts by alternately jumping on and off the fence separating those two realms. By openly embracing the value-laden nature of their work, rather than hiding it, and by making it the center of their discipline, they straddle the fence; but by writing in the objective language of science, and insisting that something of their expert knowledge is outside of social bias (and not reducible to a localized form of knowledge), they jump back to the classic terms of the divide. From this somewhat awkward "double life," biodiversity scientists are moving closer to an articulation of science as a social activity undertaken by both human and nonhuman agents involved in the production of knowledge.

An often-repeated self-description of conservation biology is that it is a "mission-oriented discipline," the mission being "not merely to document the deterioration of Earth's diversity but to develop and promote the tools that would reverse that deterioration."[48] It is a science of discovery (of ecological functioning and biological rules) and social action (conservation advocacy), rooted in the sense of ecological crisis. The discipline generally wears its values on its sleeve. In an article introducing the discipline of conservation biology in 1985, Michel Soulé (1985, 731) writes that the discipline's "fundamental" starting point is that "biotic diversity has intrinsic value." The discipline's flagship journal, *Conservation Biology (CB)*, openly declares the desirability of the dual role of scientist and advocate.[49] The strict divide in which science takes place separately from subjective or social values does not seem to hold sway. Normative commitment, ethical orientation, and advocacy politics are as much a part of the scientific endeavor as data collection, fieldwork, and objective analysis.

But these commitments are not rooted directly in the observations, cataloguing, and calculating parts of scientific practice. Many conservation biologists rather candidly admit that it comes instead from a leap of faith in valuing what they study. David Takacs (1996, 229–47) catalogues the testimony of ecologists who speak in nearly religious overtones about the personal moments of transformation they have undergone to spur them to research biodiversity. The Ehrlichs, for example, suggest that the conservation premise of conservation biology is outside science: "This is fundamentally a religious argument. There is no scientific way to 'prove' that nonhuman organisms (or for that matter, human organisms) have a right to exist"(248). David Ehrenfeld likewise points out that "for biological diversity, value just *is*. Nothing more and nothing less"; when asked to explain, he says, "Well, I couldn't prove it, I guess. I just believe it"(249). The transformational moments for conservation biologists come in participatory interactions: "When surrounded by biodiversity, the very dualism that suggests a phrase like 'surrounded by biodiversity' vanishes, and one identifies with the natural world; one is inextricably part of it" (230).

Wilson (1984), in fact, pushes the plausibility of this transformative connection into his controversial "biophilia hypothesis," in which he suggests that humans are neurally hardwired through evolution to be receptive to life. Yet by making this relationality a largely hardwired fact of evolution, Wilson misses an opportunity to consider why some people (and, in particular, some scientists) are moved in this way and not others, a question that is better suited to the language of sociality than that of hardwiring. On their own terms, ecological scientists seem to simultaneously understand that they have undergone experiences of transformation in a common world with nonhumans and that there is an irreducible gap in explaining, translating, or rationalizing it.

There is also pragmatic public reasoning about what to do with this paradox. Myers says, "However much I may agree that every species has its own right to continued existence on our shared planet, I do not believe that the world yet works that way." [50] Therefore, in spite of their personal beliefs to the contrary, conservation biologists and ecologists, and their allies in environmental ethics and political ecology, also develop a broad range of carefully worded justifications and defenses of biodiversity. It is particularly interesting to see how the defenses are framed, and how they intersect with the experiences scientists say they have with biodiversity. The reasons offered, moreover, are often transposed yet again into other contexts of action where they are often objectionable. The point here is not to demand consistency between personal beliefs and public arguments, but instead to ask how the paradoxes of the "double life" might help us think differently about biodiversity and the relation of science and politics.

One regular defense of biodiversity is that it, or its generative power, is instrumentally useful for humans in largely economic terms. We should defend biodiversity because it creates goods that are directly valuable for humans. Biodiversity produces various sources of food that can be harvested. Bioprospecting in tropical forests by the pharmaceutical industry consistently discovers new plants and herbs for modern medical uses. New crops, forms of timber, and industrial materials are generated through biodiversity. Ecotourism in biodiversity reserves generates revenue. Were biodiversity to decline, those economic goods would not be available for improving the quality of human life. Similarly, biodiversity helps produce indirectly valuable goods. These "ecosystem services" are taken-for-granted goods like clean air (recycled through trees) and productive soil, which is regenerated through the activities of unsung species like dung beetles and earthworms.[51]

A second justification is that biodiversity is a necessary condition for human life, and protecting biodiversity therefore strengthens the long-term survival of human populations. Even granting that modern economical and technological advances have mitigated direct reliance on naturally produced goods, the ecological-technological complexes in which most groups of human populations live still indirectly depend on functioning ecosystems. Ecosystems have higher survival possibilities when biodiversity is high; therefore biodiversity should be preserved. The generally established scientific relationship is that greater diversity leads to greater stability.[52] But the relationship is not exact. The loss of a few species will not necessarily cause an ecosystem to collapse. The loss of an important keystone species, however, may cause a snowballing of species loss and ecosystemic collapse.[53]

Third, biodiversity is often said to be intrinsically valuable—biodiversity is good in its own right and should be protected as such. The structure of asserting intrinsic value as a public defense for biodiversity makes the paradox clear, where "value" is (arguably) formed through social relations and experienced subjectively, while "intrinsicness" is an extrahuman quality, located in the thing itself. Entomologist Terry Erwin, grappling with the idea of intrinsic value, says, "We're trying to say something else, but we can't say something else. It's impossible." Intrinsic value, says Takacs (1996, 253), is "a feeling many biologists and others have about the world, a feeling disconnected from English vocabulary. When I read eco-philosophical treatises, I often find them tortured: their authors are struggling to express the ineffable." The notion of intrinsic value was central to much of the deep ecology literature of this period as well. Its aim is to escape the perceived anthropocentrism in instrumental justifications for protecting nature and to locate a source of value that is outside human use.[54] Yet it is deeply problematic in the way it purports to find value outside of relational values. However satisfying it may seem to remove nature from social discussions of value, positing it as intrinsically valuable, or good "as such," "without regard to other entities, without regard to effects on other entities,"[55] it runs counter to the very ecological perspective it purports to promote, in the sense that it denies the embedded web of relationality. It plays the human/nature dualism in reverse, putting biodiversity's value outside social discussion into a realm of natural objectivity, where it cannot be engaged by humans, but then importing it back in again in order to justify forms of positive law.

This defense of biodiversity, enshrined internationally in the preamble to the CBD, also drew on the idea of intrinsic rights from the human rights context that was gathering increased political salience in the 1990s as grounds for humanitarian military intervention, and as part of the so-called Asian values debate, pitting cosmopolitan and communitarian perspectives against one another.[56] Human rights, framed as rights that we enjoy simply in virtue of being human, are seen as powerful, as Chris Brown (1997, 45) notes, precisely because they refer to a general morality that is not dependent on context. Yet even if such intrinsic rights can be deduced or agreed on, in order to bring human rights into the political sphere they need to take on the form of positive law and be applied within contexts that themselves have diverse sensibilities about the value of species. For biodiversity advocates, intrinsic value of species as a political tool seemed to offer a way to transcend the failure of positive law when it came to addressing species loss. Yet they encountered the same paradox when it came time to translate such intrinsic values into positive forms of legal and political protection.

Moreover, are all species really intrinsically valuable, and are some species more intrinsically valuable than others? Dobson and May (1986, 345) point out: "No conservation group mourned the passing of the wild smallpox virus, and no organization speaks for the conservation of the gut nematode species." Intrinsic value of species appears to have pragmatic limits, at least. One way around this is to displace intrinsic value from one level to another, from individual to community (as in collecting ant specimens so long as the ant colony survives) or to ecosystem (as some environmental ethicists have argued) or biodiversity as such, or from individual to species. By identifying one level as intrinsically valuable but not others, it always becomes possible to make a kind of end run to find instrumental reasons to "lose" at least some individuals.

Consider entomologist Terry Erwin's (1983) research on the diversity of beetles in the canopy of the rainforests of Central and South America. The predominant, if antiquated, image of the entomologist is one crawling around on the ground with a magnifying glass, examining anthills and beetles. Yet in the rainforests, there are twice as many species in the canopy as on the ground. As a way of bringing these species in, Erwin developed a method of fumigating treetops using a bug bomb. The process, as described by E. O. Wilson (1992, 137), produces a visceral reaction:

> Walking into the rainforest in the evening, they select a tree for sampling and lay out a grid of 1-meter-wide funnels beneath it. The funnels feed into bottles partly filled with 70% alcohol, the specimen preservative of choice. . . . The crew forces the insecticide upward into the canopy from a motor-driven 'cannon.' They continue the treatment for several minutes. Then they stand by for five hours while the dead and dying arthropods rain down in the thousands, many falling into the funnels. Finally, the collected specimens are then sorted, roughly classified to major taxonomic group (such as ants, leaf beetles, or jumping spider), and sent to specialists for further study.

From the violent shakedown of this tree, Erwin estimates that there are over eighteen thousand species in one hectare of Panamanian rainforest.[57] Though neither Erwin nor Wilson argues for the intrinsic value of individual creatures, Wilson in particular advocates for the intrinsic value of species and biodiversity.[58] Even though it is perfectly consistent internally to value the whole without giving equal consideration to the parts, the image of the fumigation process is nonetheless startling, looking more like bug extermination than a defense or exploration of intrinsically valuable life. The use of "intrinsic" or "religious" language by ecologists can be read as an acknowledgment that the individual motivation to study beetles and to find them valuable comes somewhat from outside the scientists, involving the capture of individual desire. In political terms, it has a different role, functioning as a way of removing nature from political discussion, and then leveraging it back in. This moment, where a scientist feels compelled to kill what he studies, displaced by a commitment to the abstract form of species or biodiversity, shows the powerful kinds of multilevel gear-shifting required for the functioning of biodiversity politics and science. In the end, the roundabout fashion by which biodiversity, as a political sign, is made and reproduced speaks as much to the limited conditions under which we are prepared to hear the claims of other species and to consider our relations with them as it does to the ethical life of scientists.

Conclusion

The birth of biodiversity hotspots in the late 1980s and early 1990s showed conservation biologists giving two sorts of reasons to preserve biodiversity:

instrumental and intrinsic. Work during this period framed some of the basic terms of global biodiversity for the coming decades, rooted in abstracted patterns of species, which in turn meant a focus on the "awful symmetry" of their global distribution. The work that took place in this abstraction became focused on efficiency and resource maximization, only aimed at conservation ends. The paradoxes of biodiversity as a tool of governance were apparent at the individual-level arguments advanced by conservation biologists as well as in the new discipline of conservation biology.

The argument for sustaining biodiversity is in many ways a "won argument," at least in ethical terms, and perhaps in scientific terms as well. There are almost no serious arguments that defend the destruction of biodiversity, per se, or call for eradicating hundreds of thousands of other species at a time, as such. Although there are arguments about the uneven implications of conservation politics, or arguments for extracting resources for development, the reasons advanced by conservation biologists about biodiversity are largely accepted to be true. Instead, what we need to focus on is what intervenes to prevent the won argument from having greater purchase.

Part of the answer this chapter has explored is that discourses of environmentalism like saving biodiversity hotspots end up importing many of the very logics that prevent a more full-fledged response—efficiency, dollars for species, and the dying energy of "saving" and "crisis" all work to shield us from asking better questions about biodiversity. These questions are a way to start to think about relations—not about what biodiversity can do for us (which, as the newly dominant discourse of ecosystem services exemplifies, never tries to think about relations with other species), but only the goods provided by them. The language of service provision opens the Millennium Ecosystem report, and includes "disease management" and "spiritual fulfillment" as among the services provided by ecosystems. Other species work together as service providers to manage disease and fulfill human desires: this is a kind of anthropomorphism that asks to see bright, shining faces of servants, but ones who we do not even have to see, as they live in the servants' quarters outside the great house and provide services before quietly stepping back into the dark recesses.

One implication is a defetishization of species in some strands of conservation politics, or more precisely, the idea of species. As the story of the entomologist fumigating the tree to collect samples suggests, it is possible to simultaneously believe that species have intrinsic value, while chemically emptying a tree of thousands of actual insects, who have no apparent value as individuals. Part of the effect of biodiversity sciences that have moved to informatics and systemic biology has been to emphasize the preservation of the type, and therefore to dematerialize biodiversity. Biodiversity hotspots, for example, rest on the importance of saving species. Zoos and seed banks also save species by saving a few isolated instances. This chapter raises the question, at least, as to whether a politics, science, and ecology organized around the category of species is ultimately the best way to engage with the world.[59] It might thus be important to begin thinking about ecological politics after Linnaean taxonomy in order to rescue the material aspect of biodiversity and redirect the experience of it. As the next chapter explores, however, such developments remain far off on the horizon, and counting and cataloguing species is in fact a central and complicated part of the global biodiversity project.

Chapter 2   Biopower, the Global Biodiversity Census, and the Escapes of Nonhuman Life

DRIVEN BOTH BY THE GLOBAL LOSS of biodiversity and by the lack of knowledge about the vast majority of species that are being lost, conservation biologists and some of their allies in the environmental movement called for and started a massive global census of biodiversity in the 1990s.[1] Most prominently, E. O. Wilson (1992, 318) proposed a new mobilization of scientific resources to complete a global survey of species. The identification of biodiversity hotspots, considered in the last chapter, was merely the first step in a cascade of biodiversity investigation, Wilson hoped, which will culminate in a full inventory of global biodiversity and of the places where it is being lost. The hope is that with complete information about the global population of biological species we can undertake more refined conservation measures and ultimately move toward greater sustainability.

In this chapter I trace the further evolution of biodiversity in the 1990s, focusing on the political optics of the global biodiversity census, on one hand, and the way that political power and ideas about political community are challenged by how nonhuman species interact with censusing, on the other.

I take the position that the global biodiversity census is as much about power and political life and the boundaries between nature and society as it is about scientific information gathering for conservationist ends. Drawing on Foucault's concept of biopower, I suggest that the biodiversity census provokes us to think about the ways that biological nonhumans are embroiled in and challenge the technologies of power that see life itself as a political object. To the extent that the "action" in the biodiversity census seems to rest largely with the human scientists who do the categorizing, naming, counting, and labeling of nonhuman species, one analytic stance toward this scientific practice is an anthropocentric one. Here, the focus is on considering the field of social power in which scientific efforts take place, and asking questions about the discourses, resources, and networks that make a biodiversity census plausible and possible.

But what if nonhumans are active participants in the field of biopower, just as human subjects who are censused are? Can nonhumans be sites of resistance to biopower, and disrupt its governing impulses? I argue that it is possible, and indeed necessary in the context of biodiversity, to extend the idea of biopower to include nonhumans as participants. Like human subjects, nonhumans are regulated and rationalized in matrices of scientific knowledge, through which they are readied as productive resources for capitalism and mined as repositories of genetic information. Nonhuman participation in an ecological field of biopower also involves being part of an array of authority in environmental discourses, with effects for both humans and nonhumans, and constructing new possibilities for biosocial collectives.

However, because nonhumans generally lack the capacity to be self-regulating subjects but are nonetheless necessary authorities in figuring biodiversity truth discourses, they hold a different kind of place in biopower than the self-regulating human subject does. More specifically, because nonhumans constitutionally, rather than intentionally, refuse to internalize the meanings of human language, they are able to resist becoming self-regulating subjects to a significant extent, relying instead on their own semiotic interpretations of the environment and acting accordingly. For example, through migrating, reproducing, consuming resources, and filling ecological niches in unexpected ways, biotic nonhumans are constantly challenging the normalizing will of biopower. At the same time, because environmental interventions to save species come to be justified on the grounds of global environmental well-being, the health and continued existence of nonhumans becomes an increasing imperative. In spite of the fact that the biodiversity census may extend the reach of an ecologically unfriendly capitalism, I conclude that it will also reap important ecological goods in hybridizing political practice and acknowledging extrahuman locations of power.

The Global Biodiversity Census Proposal

Spurred by the problem of a major extinction event in which we do not even know what or how much is being lost, the global biodiversity census is aimed at counting and describing all the species that currently exist in the world. According to the United Nations Environmental Program's (UNEP) Global Biodiversity Assessment, the best ecological estimates of extant species range from 3.5 million all the way to 111.5 million species, with the most likely figure at around 13.5 million.[2] Yet only 1.75 million, or about 13 percent, of those species are currently identified and described.[3] Each year, only 13,000 new species are formally described, a snail's pace given the magnitude of the task.[4] Even when species have been described, the data often remains limited. Some species may have become extinct since being identified. May, Lawton, and Stork (1995), for example, estimate that about 40 percent of identified beetle species are known from a single examination in a single locality, sometimes an observation made decades ago.

E. O. Wilson's (1992) census proposal includes training and deploying a cadre of thousands of specialists in systematics, taxonomy, and classification. He calculates that, given forty years of productive classification work per scientist, at the pace of ten species identified per year, approximately twenty-five thousand professional lifetimes are needed, a number that "falls well short of the number of enlisted men in the standing armed forces of Mongolia, not to mention the trade and retail personnel of Hinds County, Mississippi" (318). In the perfectly rational system that he hopes for, each expert would be assigned to a specific classificatory activity. While there are currently only three people in the world who are sufficiently expert in classifying termites, for example, Wilson would up their number proportionally to match the fact that termites make up 10 percent of the total biomass of tropical regions.

Wilson also champions investment in new computer technology that can combine scanning electron microscopes with image-recognition software. Its goal would be to process and identify species instantly and to flag new specimens as they are passed through. The data held in the GenBank project, a computer database aimed at collecting information on all known DNA and RNA sequences, could be folded into this process.

Given the massive numbers of species and the difficulty of resource mobilization, other proposals suggest sampling procedures to get representative data on the global biopopulation. For example, Terry Erwin suggests that we aim for "massive but achievable biotic inventories" that give us a relative fix on biodiversity.[5] While it may not achieve Wilson's goal of describing all species, targeting specific taxa and sampling certain species would have the effect of rationalizing what is currently an *ad hoc* process. In the face of an ever larger human population, the United States census now uses representative sampling procedures, which its proponents argue make it more accurate than a large-scale but flawed collection of data about every individual.[6] A global biodiversity census would aim to do the same.

Some of the questions that surround the biodiversity census are scientific ones, such as concerns over the basic species concepts it employs and the problems of scale involved in identifying microspecies like bacteria.[7] Given that the activities of science are not self-contained but always embedded in social relations, additional kinds of questions need to be asked, however. Yet little scholarly attention has been paid to what this biodiversity censusing effort means in political or social terms.

Political ecologists have usefully inquired into the general effects of biodiversity discourses and the ways in which they are intertwined with regimes of power and governmentality,[8] but they have not asked whether there is anything specific about the language and practice of censusing nonhuman bioentities that is politically important. Environmental ethicists seem to have ignored the ethical dimensions of the topic altogether. Anthropologists and ethnobotanists have looked increasingly at the relationship between biological and cultural diversity, finding strong geographical and evolutionary correlations between the two and suggesting that a broader biocultural value linking nature and humans might be found in diversity complexes.[9] However, they have not inquired into the importance of censusing as a technique by which the differences in biocultures might be constituted. Political scientists have written extensively and insightfully about the practice and effects of censusing human populations,[10] but they have not taken up how censusing nonhumans relates to political questions about power. The rest of this chapter aims to fill some of these gaps, particularly with respect to questions of how power functions in contemporary environmental science and politics.

The Biodiversity Census and the Social Power of Scientists

Taken as a socially embedded activity, the production of successful scientific knowledge necessarily requires mobilization of economic resources, expansion of institutional power, and discursive legitimation.[11] Successful science, in other words, must be socially forged. This point does not suggest that the status of scientific truth claims is fully dependent on social interests; rather, the point is that thinking about a scientific activity like the biodiversity census requires attending not only to activities of classification and arguments over species concepts but also to how those activities are made possible in the first place. In short, what kind of social power does the biodiversity census draw on, depend on, and reproduce? What makes the use of a biodiversity census seem intuitively obvious as the right tool to address biodiversity loss?

Here I consider two forms of social power, both crucial to the census project. First, I address what financial and institutional resources are necessary to allow agenda-setting power and the capacity to steer future resources in advantageous ways.[12] Second, I suggest that the allure of the census rests partly on the way that biodiversity scientists are able to tap into discursive power, particularly the seductive power of discourses like panopticism and discovery.[13] I consider these forms of power in turn.

The institutional push for a global biodiversity census is centered in the United States, where it has harnessed major sources of funding from major institutions such as the National Science Foundation (a $14 million fund for "planetary biodiversity inventories"), the Packard Foundation, and Harvard University. It has created a network of scientific-political organizations mainly based in the United States and Europe dedicated to censusing different parts of the natural world and promoting the "completion of the Linnaean enterprise"[14] into a "Catalogue of Life"—the Census of Marine Life, NatureServe, the Global Taxonomy Initiative of the Convention on Biodiversity, Species2000, and the All-Species Foundation. There has been increased funding for the academic fields of taxonomy and bioinformatics.[15] New professional lives have opened up around these resources—"each species merits careers of scientific study and celebration by historians and poets," as Wilson (2003, 78) puts it. The biodiversity census makes these possible first through the act of species identification and then through the subsequent study of species behavior, ecological roles, and potential uses for humanity.

The key institutions of the global biodiversity census are organized around information and communication technologies, which worm their way right into the names and missions of the organizations involved. The Global Biodiversity Information Facility (GBIF) and the Integrated Taxonomic Information System (ITIS), in partnership with U.S. federal agencies including the Environmental Protection Agency (EPA) and the United States Department of Agriculture (USDA), are two of the global clearinghouses for establishing quality species-level data, aiming to be "open portals" of biodiversity data.[16] GBIF's mission is to "develop methods for sustainably using biodiversity . . . [by] rapidly, openly, and freely delivering primary data about biodiversity to everyone in the global community, using digital technologies."[17] The political intent is universal access, while its method of delivery is technological. The universally wired nature of "the" global community is taken for granted, even as a global digital divide and the barriers of expertise suggest that no such community exists.

One critical role that information technology plays in organizing the global biodiversity census is in its ability to suggest a panoptic biological future.[18] "Imagine an electronic page for each species of organism on Earth," Wilson (2003, 77) asks us, "available everywhere by single access on command." Genealogically related to projects like Diderot's *Encyclopédie*, the modern

"Encyclopedia of Life" is the endpoint and ultimate goal of the censusing project, organized in a technology that claims to outrun space and time.

The rhetoric of "achieving" a global biodiversity census also taps into complex Western narratives of discovery and the conquest of nature (ironically, since the conservation agenda of the census is aimed in part at preserving the wildness of nature). This rhetoric also draws on the position of social power held by the modern sciences to reveal the unknown to human publics. Wilson (2003, 79) exhorts supporters of the census to have "faith in the sprint to the finish of the global census," promising that "unknown microorganisms . . . will be revealed" and that "never again, with fuller knowledge of such extent, need we overlook so many golden opportunities in the living world around us." Similarly, the All-Species Foundation tells us that the global biodiversity census "offers an unsurpassable adventure: the exploration of a little-known planet."[19]

Finally, the discursive power of the census is connected to economic life in the way that it renders nonhuman agents ready for postmodern capitalism as semiotic constructions (as in genetic codes for bioprospectors or images in nature videos).[20] As Arturo Escobar (1995, 195–208) argues, whereas "nature" marked modern capitalism's attitude toward the nonhuman, "biodiversity" is a term of postmodern capitalism, in the way that it readies nonhuman nature for semiotic rather than material use. Indeed, postmodern capitalism may protect nature materially even as it commodifies it semiotically, as in the case of protecting the Amazon rainforest for its pharmaceutical potentials.[21] Yet, as Escobar (1995, 57) argues, "once the semiotic conquest of nature is completed, the sustainable and rational use of the environment becomes imperative." That is, once biodiversity discourses help conserve an area as a biodiversity reserve which is made valuable in terms of commodity codes, it also becomes part of a political system of global environmental governance that continues to manage it for capitalism.

Thus, conservation biologists have mobilized an expanding pool of financial and institutional resources, drawing in part on the seductive qualities of the dream of panopticism and the historical glory of exploration. To the extent that the agenda of global environmental governance is steered by their expertise, consensus, and public statements,[22] they have also garnered increased authority in speaking about matters of conservation, ecotourism, and economic development. While these forms of social power (institutional, financial, technological, and discursive) explain some of what is at stake in the biodiversity census, the power of a global biodiversity census also rests in its hybridizing force. It reintroduces nonhumans into the discursive heart of an otherwise anthropocentric politics, economy, and knowledge that has generally denied that nonhumans have formed an active part of these projects.[23] It creates a framework through which humans interact with, pattern, and position the diversity of natural nonhumans, in material as well as semiotic terms. Understanding the importance of the biodiversity census therefore extends questions of power past its traditional human context into an ecological context.

The important questions here are in many ways similar to those political scientists ask about human politics: For whom does this extended politics and power work?[24] What happens to anthropocentric understandings of power if we recognize an active participation of nonhumans in the process? And what does the reintroduction of nonhumans tell us about the "whereabouts of power," to use John Allen's (2004) phrase? To answer these questions, I turn to the idea of Foucaultian biopower, which considers how power works at the microlevels of individual life in relation to the more traditional forms of power considered thus far.

Biopower and the Census

Because biopower is concerned with the ways that techniques like censusing operate on the terrain of "life itself," it is particularly suited to thinking about the biodiversity census, which similarly involves a strategy for administering and rationalizing life in ways that reaches into nonhuman biological life as such.[25] The consideration of censusing nonhuman life through the lens of biopower involves a basic trade-off. On one hand, the extension of biopower into nonhuman realms raises the specter of a more subtle, but nonetheless corrosive, form of human power over the natural world. On the other hand, because power and resistance are always coexistent, nonhumans may disrupt the functioning of environmental governance in new and distinct ways. Specifically, biopower faces difficulty in creating self-regulating nonhuman subjects who internalize conditions of subjection.

Self-Regulating Subjects and the Justification of Power

In contrast to the absolute power commanded by the Hobbesian sovereign to "take life or to let live," Michel Foucault (1978, 140) argues that the modern form of biopower that replaced it in the nineteenth century was a regulatory and disciplinary form of power that involved "the administration of bodies and the calculated management of life." Biopower organized and administered life through a variety of techniques or methods of power that dragged human life itself into the grid of power-knowledge. Institutions such as universities, public health agencies, and the army; and regulatory forms of knowledge, such as demography and modern medicine; not only analyzed life processes but permeated them as well.

Yet it was not just the use of these techniques or the presence of these institutions that characterized nineteenth-century biopower. Two parallel political shifts made biopower distinct from sovereign power. The first shift was that the right of the sovereign to have power over life and death was no longer justified based on protecting the sovereign from external threat (as in conscription in cases of war) or internal threat (as in the death penalty). Rather, the power over life and death was now justified in terms of the population itself, in modern democratic language. When war was waged, it was not to protect the sovereign, but in the name of the people and their continued existence.

The justification for biopower's interventions into the lives of people—their reproductive health, the ways they die, their vaccinations—was similarly made in the name of the population. One effect of this shift, Foucault (1978, 138) notes, is that the death penalty became more difficult to sustain logically: "How could power exercise its highest prerogatives by putting people to death, when its main role was to ensure, sustain, and multiply life, to put this life in order?" In other words, the justifications for power's activities have social effects that exceed the justifications themselves. What effect, then, will extending "protecting life" to "protecting biodiversity" have if we consider the biodiversity census as an extended example of the logic of biopower?

Part of the answer is that direct resource exploitation becomes more difficult, since power over the life and death of animals, plants, insects, or trees can no longer be justified by needs of the human population (or sovereign) to fight natural necessity with all its might.[26] Ecological biopower thus involves both broader social trends like the rise of modern ecological consciousness and the emergence of conservationist ethics as part of it structural logic. At the same time, what becomes easier is both the management and regulation of nonhuman biological life by humans and the direct intervention in, and mutation of, biological and ecological life processes, all in the name of bio- or ecosystemic "health." Here, biopower can be understood as a logic of eco-governance that simultaneously subverts the resource-driven agenda of modern capital by trying to conserve material nature *and* enables and rationalizes an entirely new form of intervention in life itself. The ecological sciences, on this reading, are crucial institutions through which interventions into life occur, and the biodiversity census is one of their primary power-knowledge techniques.

Thinking about biopower as involving nonhumans also has the consequence of changing the population in whose name power's exercise is justified. If the idea of biopower adequately describes the intrusion of scientific,
economic, and regulatory techniques into the lives of nonhumans, then
administering nonhuman life must be justified in the name of an expanded
population as well—in this case, in the name of a global ecological population
of species (and their genes), guided by an ethic of preserving and fostering
biodiversity. In sum, in the name of planetary health (a metaphorical extension of modern biopower's concern with human public health to a planetary
scale), a new population is configured into which biopower intervenes, one
explicitly composed of human and nonhuman members participating in ecosystemic communities.

The second, parallel shift that Foucault (1978) notes was involved in the
move from sovereign to regulatory power: it had an unsettling effect on
the practice of governing. Unlike sovereign power, regulatory biopower had
the imperative to promote life, to "optimize forces, aptitudes, and life in general," and its "highest function was perhaps no longer to kill, but to invest life
through and through" (139). Yet, crucially, it had to do so in ways that did
not make the population more difficult to govern.[27] In other words, however life
was politically managed, it had to be done in ways that ensured governability.
This aspect of biopower was aimed at producing self-regulating subjects who
internalized the qualities that promoted life but did not fundamentally disrupt social functioning. Self-regulating subjects were both efficient for power
(since subjects did power's work for it) and governable.

Yet in this respect, the movement of nonhuman entities into the population in whose name biopower acts represents a potential location of freedom,
or at least resistance, precisely because many nonhumans are constitutionally incapable of being self-regulating subjects who can internalize the conditions of subjection in biopower's own terms. Nonhumans do not "know"
that they are a species or a member of a specific phylum, in those terms, or
that they have a particular gene sequence; rather, they have their own frameworks of understanding the moments of interaction with scientists and modes
of environmental experience that guide their actions. In this respect, biotic
nonhumans differ from the human subjects of biopower, who, as Foucault's
analysis suggests, become self-regulating subjects partly in virtue of the way
that their consciousness is structured by biopower—by its language, its categories, and the techniques of self-making.

When one looks at the minority of bioentities that could be made partially self-regulating—genetically modified crops, pet clones, lab-grown tissue

replacement—they form a small fraction of the biopopulation. Even in those cases, moreover, there are significant doubts over whether they can be made into self-regulating subjects in the same sense as humans. Their ability to accede to and internalize the normalizing effects of power is limited by their biological constitution. Though they have varying kinds of subjective experience, they cannot be said to have the self-reflexive kind of subjectivity that humans do. Whereas human subjectivity is marked by being a distinct self in contrast to the environment and the ability to have the reflexive thought that "I am a self," nonhumans are generally limited to the former possibility.

If biopower cannot make most nonhumans into self-regulating subjects, then their governability rests solely on whether they can be controlled indirectly through the patterned grids of scientific prediction. Yet as groups and individuals, biological nonhumans routinely confound predictability, within their own kinds of subjectivities. They respond to ecological change by unexpectedly shifting migration patterns and locations. They expand into unexpected ecological niches that humans open directly (e.g., suburbs as feeding grounds for raccoons, rabbits introduced in Australia for hunting which subsequently overran the countryside, garbage dumps as sources of food for omnivorous bears) and indirectly (e.g., red-tailed deer population explosions in New England upon the overhunting of deer predators, causing substantial economic damage and fatal car accidents). Some species mutate at evolutionary speeds that far exceed those of humans (e.g., pesticide-resistant strains of bugs or penicillin-resistant viruses). They sometimes form new relations with other species to the detriment of humans (e.g., birds as carriers of Asian bird flu). They remake ecosystems into new stabilities and undermine others.

In short, while the lack of subjectivity and reflexivity in nonhuman populations is usually read as a source of acquiescence to human interrogation, it seems to also have the opposite effect by enabling resistance and disruption to the desires of biopower to establish governable populations. Foucault (1978, 143) says of biopower: "It is not that life has been totally integrated into techniques that govern and administer it; it constantly escapes them." Nonhuman agents effect some of the very same escapes simply by living. Life itself escapes biopower.

Array of Authorities

A second component of biopower is "one or more truth discourses about the 'vital' character of living human beings, and an array of authorities competent to speak that truth."[28] In the context of the nineteenth-century societies that Foucault was analyzing, these truth discourses about living beings included fields like demography and medicine. In the context of twenty-first-century biopower, Paul Rabinow and Nikolas Rose suggest that they might be extended to include fields like genomics, cloning, and reproduction. What is critical to the truth discourses surrounding these fields is that there can be an array of authorities like the human sciences, public health agencies, or social theorists that both problematize a certain issue and endeavor to intervene in the field raised by that problematization. These authorities both render the issue socially visible and strive to rationalize solutions.

Just as scientists play a central role as authorities in the truth discourses of human sciences, so too are they central to the truth discourses of biodiversity loss. The project of the biodiversity census involves conservation biologists as a critical part of the authorities competent to create a truth discourse around species loss and conservation, through the rationalization of species into an ordered catalogue of nonhuman life. But the involvement of nonhumans in this truth discourse exceeds a simple presence as scientific objects and raises questions about whether we can think of biopower as authoritative about nonhumans without any account of how nonhumans might themselves testify to those truth claims, resist them, or actively participate to some degree in the making of scientific knowledge.

An alternative account of scientific practice that moves toward such a distributed model of authority comes from Bruno Latour and others involved in theorizing an actor-network approach, in which human and nonhuman agents are seen as collaboratively involved in the construction of scientific truth claims. On this account, scientific authority depends in part on the (non-linguistic) "testimony" of nonhumans who are marshaled by scientists to establish the veracity of scientific accounts.[29] While it is still human scientists who problematize the field of biodiversity loss, then, the array of authorities competent to speak the truth discourses surrounding that field is distributed among both humans and nonhumans.

This line of argument about authority has three consequences. First, it speaks to the question of the "whereabouts of power." One of the criticisms of Foucault's analytic of power is that once it is taken past a specific institutional site into the broader practices of governing it seems to be everywhere and nowhere.[30] In a broader sense, space and place themselves seem to disappear from power. In the case of biodiversity sciences, at least, extending the participants in the biopower formation to nonhumans gives power concrete locations—in the places where data is collected, in the laboratories where representative samples are brought under the microscope, and in the bodies of species who experience different life possibilities and pathways because of the process of classification. What makes biodiversity discourses potent at all, in other words, is the marshaling of human and nonhuman authorities to its truth claims in particular places and particular biological bodies.

Second, the intrusion of nonhuman life into authority-generating processes like the biodiversity census disrupts the human subject as the center of modern biopower by forcing a new set of constituents into the political field who cannot quite be captured by it in the same way. Because the biopower depends on the relative flourishing of life, it cannot speak and act authoritatively on behalf of the health of global biopopulations *and* simultaneously extinguish them. The necessity of nonhuman life for biopower both enables its extension and increases the living things that disrupt its desire for smooth governing. To return to Foucault's analysis of the death penalty, if biopower (in contrast with sovereign power) challenged the right of the state to kill its own citizens, then so too should ecological biopower be seen to challenge the domination of nonhumans (in modern relations with nature), including the ongoing anthropogenic species extinction event.

Finally, if the Latourian understanding of authority as distributed between both scientists and scientific objects is correct, this critique should also apply to humans, in the human sciences that Foucault was considering. The authority of scientific claims depends not only on scientists, academics, and public servants, but on the very human subjects that make authoritative claims possible. Not only is resistance coexistent with power within human subjectivity, as Foucault claims,[31] but a more distributed kind of authority also resides in the practices of biopower—among the subjects who take part in its data collections, experiments, and interventions.

Biosocial Collectivities

In Foucault's historical analysis, the formation of biopower occurs within the context of the rise of the modern nation-state. Yet the biodiversity crisis, which I have been thinking of here in terms of an extension of human biopower into biodiversity power, presents a political situation in which there is a veritable state of emergency (species loss), and yet there is no political state in which to declare it. This observation is true in two senses. It is true, first, in a spatial sense, in that the biodiversity crisis is global, yet there is no global state in which such a crisis could effectively be addressed.[32] While a layer of global environmental governance may be growing (and even while using environmental problems as a way through which its expansion is made plausible),[33] it does not yet have the logical or practical means to resolve the wider problems of social justice and development involved in the biodiversity crisis.

In a second sense, there is also no political formation that accepts the *participation* of nonhumans within its confines. The nation-state is a modern, secular, and thoroughly human mode of organization, one that is based on a community of humans who in turn decide what is right or good for themselves and the environment. As considered in chapter 1, its reasoning is often decidedly and openly anthropocentric, as ecologists who advance biodiversity's cause almost all accept as a necessary part of communicating the biodiversity crisis to human publics. Similarly, the discourses of global governance draw on a thin kind of global political community, but they do not grasp nonhumans as participants in their ideological vision.[34] Global governance is hardly democratic with respect to humans, much less politically inclusive of nonhumans.[35] Understood in this way, when global governance discourses address biodiversity loss, they do so either as the next logical step in the postcolonial mission (moving from "civilization, progress, rationality, poverty alleviation and now, environmental sustainability")[36] or as simply another problem area for governance to address.[37]

In the context of biopower that I have been considering, what, then, is the effect of a global biodiversity census without a global state? If the modern census was part of a power-knowledge formation that was both organized by and constitutive of the nation-state as part of biopower, then a global biodiversity census should have some transformative effects in constituting political forms. The hypothesis I want to suggest is that a biodiversity census helps construct new ideas of a multilayered and multispecies global community.

As a way into this hypothesis, consider the effect of the modern human population census on ideas of community. Benedict Anderson, for example, argues that the modern census was integrally related to the creation of the categories necessary for the creation of postcolonial nation-states. Anderson (1983, 165) maintains that the "(confusedly) classifying mind of the colonial state" created identities through the census that might not have been recognized as such by those who were censused and classified. The census involved a "totalizing classificatory grid, which could be applied with endless flexibility to anything under the state's real or contemplated control" (184). Yet by undertaking this project, the conditions of postcolonial nationalism were shaped and forms of intelligibility were constructed (and imposed) that were not otherwise there. For present-day aspirants to statehood, a census remains an important marker of a consolidated national citizenry, as in the push for a Palestinian census as a way toward achieving a de facto Palestinian state.[38] Similarly, then, a global biodiversity census might be understood as part of constructing a global biocitizenry and in forming a global ecopolitical community.

Rabinow and Rose (2003, 2–3) suggest that biopower must include "strategies for intervention in the name of life or health, initially addressed to populations that may or may not be territorialized upon the nation, society, or pre-given communities, but may also be specified in terms of emergent bio-social collectivities." Like Foucault, Rabinow and Rose are concerned with human populations, but their use of "bio-social collectivities" that are not necessarily dependent on a territorial population suggests the possibility of forms of community that are not tied to the nation-state. If the nation-state is not necessarily the right analogy for biosocial collectivities of humans and nonhumans, then Michael Hardt and Antonio Negri's (2000) expansion of biopower past Foucault's state-bound apparatuses of governing points toward how a deterritorialized collectivity might be theorized. If Foucault's use of biopower was used in the concrete historical analysis of the transition in nineteenth-century Europe from the sovereign state of absolute power over life and death to one "in the name of the people" of disciplinary and regulatory power, Hardt and Negri push the historical analysis forward another step by drawing from Gilles Deleuze the idea of a transition from a Foucaultian disciplinary society to a society of control.

Disciplinary society exists in relation to individual subjects, setting the parameters of what is normal and deviant, prescribing the rules of social behavior, and constructing the boundaries of the social space in which its citizens rattle around. Power in disciplinary society is concentrated in institutions. By contrast, a society of control moves into the very interior of its subjects. It regulates not from the outside but through its distribution and internalization into "brains and bodies."[39] It is a form of power that exists in networked interiorities (i.e., the linked, self-regulating consciousness of subjects), not in external impositions, limits, sanctions, or structurings. Power in a society of control is also unique in the way that it is able to make biopower its exclusive terrain of reference. For Hardt and Negri (2000, 24), it is also a more totalizing form of power than disciplinary power—it "extends throughout the depths of the consciousness and bodies of the population—and at the same time across the entirety of social relations." It is such an organizing power that Hardt and Negri see as globally operative in the social production of subjects.

But Hardt and Negri are critical of the way in which the global society of control has been considered in a disembodied way. They argue that the abstractions of language, communication, and intellectual ideas have been given productive precedence over the material and corporeal.[40] In their neo-Marxist reading, the potential of a biopolitical analysis rests with its study at the level of labor, production, and bodies. If Marxist analyses of modern capitalism understood communication as external or secondary to the material relations of production, Hardt and Negri want to read it as internal and immanent to production in postmodern capitalism. The semiotic reconfiguration of postmodern capital that Escobar suggests is thus the very productive activity in Hardt and Negri's framework, and biopower is a Foucaultian/Marxist hybrid.[41] In such a framework, biodiversity is something produced, and the "things" of biodiversity—the individuals, the species, the communicative fabric of science around which knowledge of them is built, the development projects of which biodiversity is a component—are implicated in a global society of control.

Like Foucault's conceptualization of power, Hardt and Negri's vision of biopower as a field or fabric of social and capitalist production is an image that makes us see a total matrix of power. Yet their relative exclusion of nonhumans is curious, since there is a slew of nonhuman agents outside of that productive field. There is a multitude of nonhumans, which includes the "bacterial proletariat," in E. O. Wilson's colorful metaphor,[42] and the nomadic animal populations that routinely ignore national borders.

Moreover, if biotic nonhumans have a kind of interiority, in the sense that they are experiencing entities capable of semiosis and embodied knowledge, then the amorphous and diffuse nature of biopower moves through those interiorities as well. This movement takes biopower beyond a Cartesian focus on the human body, mind, and social relations, and into an ecological view. Whereas biopower tends to take nonhumans as a kind of cinematic "bluescreen" against which human dramas unfold, an ecological view of biopower gives nonhuman actors active roles.

Nonhumans, in short, participate in the relations of biopower with humans. They are constituted by those relations, and they also are sites of resistance against them, by the very fact that they do not live like human subjects. The "society of control" that operates through networked interiorities is a hybrid society, one with material embodiment in sprawling networks of human and nonhuman agents. Biopower moves into the subjective lives of biological species, and their actions and transmutations in turn transform biopower.

For different reasons than mine, Rabinow and Rose (2003) argue that Hardt and Negri's conception of biopower is much too broad. Their critique is that it operates at a level of generality that is not useful for analysis. It is able to "describe everything but analyze nothing" (4). What they commend about Hardt and Negri's concept is the attempt to "extend the scope of traditional analyses of economic exploitation and geopolitics to encompass their relation to the living character of the human species, and *perhaps to all living beings*" (ibid., emphasis added). Although I disagree that "living beings" is necessarily the place at which a line of political regard should ultimately be drawn, I do agree that extending the analysis of biosocial collectivities past the human species is important in order to understand the work that phenomena like the global biodiversity census are doing.

What kinds of biosocial collectivities might be formed or reinforced through the global biodiversity census? First, the global biodiversity census could reinforce but also subtly transform existing forms of political identity. The centrality of the species concept to the biodiversity census reinforces the biological basis of "humanity" in human rights discourses or global cosmopolitan identity—that is, "humans" are not just related through politically constructed discourses, but through material-semiotic networks of meaning that include similarities in bodies and biological capacities.[43] Yet the very category of "human" owes a large part of its meaning to the existence of the plethora of nonhumans who are its Other. However, pushing the species basis of "human" also offers a way of remaking that Otherness, by foregrounding the category within which difference is made (species) and a new context in which they relate (ecosystems), rather than taking the difference itself as self-evident or made exclusively through human discourse. If ecosystems (global, regional, local) function by virtue of a multitude of species of which humans are one, then the terms of radical human/nonhuman difference are altered from one comparing differences in capacities between species to one of difference in ecological function.

This move certainly carries political risks, as some of the dubious deep ecological claims to making the global ecosystem the primary unit of allegiance highlight.[44] But the global biodiversity census also offers the potential for a consideration of interspecies difference within new biosocial collectivities that are not only global but also regional and local. Contra the deep ecological claim, there is no inherent primacy to a global or regional ecosystem over a local one.[45] As such, the use of the species concept to frame "humanity" need not only mean a global ecopolitics that erases local difference; it can also be a progressive way to build local identities that are linked ecologically to one another and to an emergent global ecosystem. In short, the global biodiversity census offers a way of reterritorializing the category of "human," grounding it relative to other species and to the wide variety of local ecosystems that make up the global ecosystem.

Second, then, in those local and regional ecosystems, the identification of species could contribute to building political units that are bioregional in nature. In one way, it can reinforce existing political units like the nation-state that coincide with ecosystemic boundaries. The island ecosystems of New Zealand or Madagascar are bioregional but also national. Without resorting to the tired warhorses of "biologically determined" communities, bioregional identities can involve a human openness to building political community around the perceived meanings and boundaries of watersheds, mountain ranges, and ecosystems. Arguably, at least, these bioregional identities can involve a more responsible treatment of local environments, since they involve a greater sensitivity to the places in which humans live and to the nonhumans on which we depend.

In some cases, the global biodiversity census assists in building bioregional identities that are internationalist in nature—for example, the ecosystemic complex of the North Americas, with its migrating human and nonhuman multitudes and interlinked ecosystems, makes a mockery of the aluminum-siding fence separating Canada, the United States, and Mexico.[46] In this particular instance, the overlap of a North American bioregional identity with free-trade agreements like NAFTA can offer a critique of the ecological effects of free trade. For example, understanding the movement of transgenic corn from the United States to Mexico or determining water use in the international watershed of the Rio Grande may be better served by embedding free trade into ecological thinking rather than by relying on the rather more narrow principles of Ricardian trade theory. Identifying the species that make up the Rio Grande ecosystem and understanding the ecological relations between them offers a source of moral consideration that goes beyond economic thinking.

Third, species identification is a biological peg for local social movements. For example, the identification of heirloom tomatoes and the particular qualities that those strains offer to humans is a source of political leverage to the organic food movement in the United States. Similarly, the Chipko peasant movement in India to assert local eco-rights and indigenous rights is based on the relation of a local human community to its local ecosystem and the particular tree species on which it depends for livelihood.[47] Local social identities need not always be progressive or ecologically sound, of course. The Corn Belt in the United States, composed almost entirely of the relationship between one species of corn and a chain of agricultural production, is a biosocial collectivity at the heart of the industrial food chain.[48] Nothing about species identification is inherently conservative or progressive, which is perhaps what makes it so worrisome to modern notions of ideology, identity, and politics. But those species undeniably shape the life conditions of the biosocial collectivities in which we live, and progressive movements must both take heed of them and endeavor to ally with them where possible if they do not want to cede their power to others.

In sum, the global biodiversity census constitutes in human minds the category of species with which we necessarily have relations and, arguably, to which we have responsibilities given their sentience and conativity.[49] It highlights our embeddedness in the ecosystems in which we always participate and have effects. And it creates a sense that the diversity of life forms is both an ethical good and a prerequisite for the long-term sustainability of human and other planetary life.

Conclusion

As I have tried to extend the concept, biopower is no longer something that exists purely in human populations and communities. Rather, biopower can be thought of as a form of ecologically distributed power that involves interventions in human and nonhuman lives and is enacted by human and nonhuman subjects. Nonhuman entities are both active and complicit in these practices of power. The self-regulation of human subjects is even partly made by nonhumans, as in the nonhuman battle between vaccinations and viruses on which social medical practices are built. Nonhumans are required to testify to the truth claims of biodiversity science and constitute part of its authority. They constitute and transform the biosocial collectivities on which ecological interventions take place. They have their own strategies for intervention in those collectivities (adaptability, migration, reproduction), and they shape the kinds of human strategies for intervention that are possible and desirable. In analyses of power, authority, and community in environmental politics, the "bio" in biopower should be taken seriously as involving all of life.

were rewritten into new combinations, their power to separate and order did not disappear entirely in these new modes of what I call *hybrid heritage*. Hybridizing nature and culture in heritage categories such as "associative cultural landscapes" did not, in and of itself, ensure politically or environmentally just outcomes, though this was indeed part of the reason that it was done. Hybridity opened up new possibilities, but it often carried traces of the past forward in equally powerful ways, transforming and reinscribing nature and culture in world heritage.

This chapter traces the way that natural and cultural sites were assumed to be different, examines the criticisms of a dualistic nature-culture heritage framework, and shows how UNESCO tried to respond to these problems. In between sites that were either natural or cultural, and sites that were later preserved under the new hybridized rubrics, there is a small subset of sites that exemplified *hyphenated heritage*—sites that were nominated for exemplifying both natural value and cultural value, but separately, called "mixed sites." Preserved under the old rubrics of nature and culture, but also hyphenated together, mixed sites are a kind of intermediary step in the history of world heritage preservation. I examine the clues that this hyphenated heritage offers for thinking more clearly about the possibilities and limits of hybrid heritage.

Of the political dynamics that drive all the hyphenated heritage sites, I identify national sacred heritage and postcolonial heritage preservation as two of the most prominent, and I use the case studies of Meteora in Greece and Uluru Rock in Australia as ways to explore these two dynamics, respectively. The relationship between politics, on the one hand, and secularism and the sacred, on the other, reaches into many significant aspects of contemporary international politics, ranging from the conditions of possibility for U.S. foreign policy to the boundaries of European identity. One significant question is how secularism constructs itself as an unmarked category, relative to religion and the sacred, and how this construction itself involves and enables the exercise of political dominance. Put in slightly different terms, are religious and secular political formations commensurable, or is there ultimately an unbridgeable chasm between them?[1] The secular act of preserving sacred world heritage is a complicated political act, raising similar questions of commensurability and dominance. In contexts where the preservation is aimed at ecologically important sites, a cognate set of questions arises about the relationship between environmental preservation and religious or sacred grammar, particularly given the proclivity of major parts of Western environmental movements to use sacred language in defense of nature. Both Meteora and Uluru Rock raise these issues. They differ, however, not only in national culture and geographical setting, but also in the important political differences between claiming a Christian site as part of a secular national heritage (Meteora) and negotiating a postcolonial politics between white Australians and Aboriginal Australians, and this chapter explores the unique dynamics at these two sites as well.

The hyphenated heritage sites I discuss are also unique because of the central importance of large rock formations to both their cultural and natural value. In Greece, the sandstone spikes of Meteora rise up on the edge of the Plain of Thessaly, where Orthodox Christian monasteries have been perched for almost one thousand years. In Australia, Uluru Rock is the sole high point for miles around, with a mini-ecosystem thriving around its base; it is culturally important because of its centrality to Aboriginal natureculture.[2] This chapter considers the agency of these abiotic rock formations, foregrounding the ways in which their virtual semiosis has worked to transform human meanings, and to be transformed by human action. Unlike other modes of nonhuman agency, the agency of abiotica is not characterized by an interior sense of self on the part of the agents—in the case of these rock formations, or the other mountainous sites, it would be difficult to do any more than "think like a mountain," in Aldo Leopold's famous phrase, as a kind of helpful anthropomorphism that might allow us to better understand ecological processes or our entanglement with them.[3] They are therefore limit cases for me in thinking about political agency. But as virtually semiotic agents, the rock formations in these stories do have a kind of power to shape meanings in ways that are not quite reducible to a brute version of materiality, and this chapter explores what this variant of agency looks like.

What frames the politics of nature, culture, and biodiversity in this chapter, then, is the idea and practice of heritage at a global scale. Sharing in some of the environmental conservation language of "saving biodiversity" in material terms before repackaging it as a material and semiotic commodity for tourist consumption, world heritage also has distinct logics that redirect the way that biodiversity is understood. To understand these dynamics, this chapter examines the intersection of global heritage categorization and local heritage sites.

Making Heritage, Making History

One useful way of thinking about the practice of heritage is together with history. Although heritage and history are sometimes understood to be opposed in their aims and commitments, they are more often linked enterprises that share some common orientations and modes of justification. They both tap into, and are tapped by, networks of material objects laden with a variety of cultural meanings and political values, in the service of narrating an ultimately inaccessible past. Each also practices a good deal of what the other preaches. Heritage does not float freely of historical record, even if it does bend it in fairly deep ways. History does more than engage in an objective analysis of past, working to create experiences of the present in new ways, much like heritage. Moreover, what they have in common comes into sharper relief when we look at the ways that nonhuman agents are embroiled in the practices of heritage and history, rather than only at the intellectual justifications used to distinguish those two endeavors.

Historians might see heritage as a distortion of history involving a selective use and even invention of historical material to fit or create a set of identity needs. Consider the site of Plymouth, Massachusetts, where the *Mayflower* is supposed to have first landed and where the town administers the site of Plymouth Rock. Yet there is little concrete historical evidence to suggest that the Mayflower Pilgrims, led by William Bradford, first landed on a rock, or even that they first landed at Plymouth.[4] The rock, which now sits in the hallowed site, complete with Ionic columns, was only identified over a century after the initial landing. It was subsequently split into pieces (it is now 5 percent of its estimated original size), and moved to its current location. It is even questionable whether the rock has any historical merit as the actual Plymouth Rock. Yet tourists now regularly visit Plymouth Rock where the Pilgrims landed, complete with the date "1620" carved into it. Historians cringe at the rewriting of history into heritage and at the deviation from what "actually" happened.

But David Lowenthal (1998) persuasively suggests that heritage is not bad history; rather, it has both different social aims and different modes of persuasion. Historians aim, however imperfectly, to narrate the past in the service of making it less opaque. History's mode of persuasion is rational proof, subject to the critical analysis of others and to contradictory evidence. Heritage makers, by contrast, aim at something entirely different—their aim is to "clarify pasts so as to infuse them with present purposes" engaging in both a "creative art" and an "act of faith" (xv, xvii).

On Lowenthal's (1998) account, heritage persuades by creating the possibility of experiential interactions with things in ways that create desired meanings. But unlike history, whose power rests on its claim to a more accurate story of the past, heritage "exaggerates and omits, candidly invents and frankly forgets, and thrives on ignorance and error" (121). One approaches Jefferson's Monticello and the slave quarters there rather differently than one reads a critical history of Jefferson's activities. The point of heritage is "not that the public should learn something, but that they should *become* something" (23). Therefore, "heritage is immune to criticism because it is not erudition but catechism—not checkable fact but credulous allegiance" (1995, 7–8). For Lowenthal, this dynamic exonerates heritage practitioners from charges of historical inaccuracy.

Lowenthal (1998, 88–104) does acknowledge that heritage sometimes has negative political consequences, such as aggravating national chauvinism, erasing historical memory, and bonding too closely with commercial tourism.[5] But because his starting point is that heritage, in all its historical fuzziness and self-creating splendor, is an irreducible component of collective identities that are themselves unavoidable and even desirable, he ends up arguing that heritage *as an activity* is worthy of defense against charges of historical inaccuracy. This imaginary involves a strong dichotomization of history and heritage as involving separate logics with separate goals and separate sets of effects.

But heritage and history are not quite so distinct in practice.[6] Heritage regularly draws from the past as framed by historians in order to create a given idea of the past. The heritage industry at Plymouth Rock did not access the actual past of 1620 before installing their rock; rather, they drew from the historical and cultural narratives surrounding the Mayflower that told them that there was an "actual" first landing at Plymouth Rock and that it was significant.

The material of historians, similarly, is sometimes that of man-made heritage. Historical research into the Great Pyramid in Egypt, for example, involves researching the cultural fields that surrounded the pyramid at the time of construction and on into the present, and not just a historical object. Cultural histories of the French Revolution involve not only a retelling of the events, but also a telling of how the Bastille came to have cultural significance. Historians also do battle against heritage "myths," working in synergistic tandem with the heritage makers that construct them. It is not always clear where heritage stops and where history starts.

Moreover, if an actual past exists but is ultimately inaccessible, then heritage and history are even more closely intertwined, since they are drawing not from an actual past but rather from one another. In one sense, both heritage and history shore up the idea of an actual past—a past in which all presumed events and experiences, everywhere and at once, are imagined to have taken place. For Lowenthal, the idea of an actual past allows him to frame heritage and history as distinct endeavors, as they each take a different orientation to and select different elements from that omniscient abstraction. His acquittal of heritage as a distortion of history necessary for collective identity is really also a way of reinstalling the fiction that history is the actual past. Heritage likewise relies on the idea of an actual past in order to realize its power— tourists to a heritage site encounter not a mythologized history, but a presumed actual past, one that is carefully maintained and presented. The site of Plymouth Rock is encountered as the real Plymouth Rock.

But rather than asking only about the relationship of heritage to an actual past, which would involve a posture of scholarship aimed at debunking myth, it is equally important to look at how the experience of the actual past is produced, an endeavor involving the organizing categories of heritage and history, and varying networks of human and nonhuman agents. Assuming that such a past exists but is ultimately inaccessible does not entail forgoing efforts to clarify what really did happen; rather, it means asking what happens in efforts to bring to life a replicable experience of the past, and inquiring into the ways that heritage and history are linked in this endeavor through networks of objects. To borrow from the sociological language about boundary objects, then, heritage materialities must be "both plastic enough to adapt local needs and the constraints of the several parties adopting them, yet robust enough to maintain common identity across sites."[7] Plymouth Rock as a boundary object brings a kind of solidity and an air of irrefutability to the site, and its naturalness is part of its cultural power, but it also requires inscription with a date to prove its cultural bona fides, and there must be an ongoing elision of "actual Plymouth Rock" with "the Rock that has traditionally been identified as Plymouth Rock." Heritage, like history, is neither self-evident nor fabricated out of whole cloth. Rather, it requires selective entwinement with material elements. It must use organizing categories to make these squirrely things meaningful, but it also must navigate the challenge that these elements manage to pose to the coherence of the narrative and address the varying properties that these materialities offer.

Transforming UNESCO Heritage Rubrics: Nature-Culture and Its Critics

UNESCO adopted the Convention Concerning the Protection of the World Cultural and Natural Heritage (hereafter "the Convention") in 1972.[8] The Convention is steeped in the assumption that cultural and natural heritage are two substantively different kinds of heritage that require different mechanisms of selection and different criteria defining their universal value. Article 1 defines cultural heritage, which is split into three types: monuments, groups of buildings, and sites. Monuments, which dominated the early cultural heritage sites, included "architectural works, works of monumental sculpture and painting, elements or structures of an archaeological nature, inscriptions, and cave dwellings." Groups of buildings are similar to monuments, valuable because of their architecture. Sites involve the "works of man or the combined works of nature and man."

Natural heritage, defined in article 2, is also broken into three types: natural features, habitats of threatened species, and natural sites. The first group is simply any "physical or biological formation" that is deemed to be valuable. The second kind of heritage, habitats, is defined by threat—any area that is the habitat of an endangered species, as long as the species is also of "outstanding universal value." Finally, natural sites are a generic type.

Both articles explicitly include the "point of view" from which the sites are deemed to be universally valuable. The value of cultural sites is determined by the fields of history, art, architecture, anthropology, and ethnology. The value of natural sites comes from ecological and biological sciences, conservation needs, and the aesthetic perspectives of judges who remain unspecified. These initial nature/culture criteria thus allow that neither realm's value was self-evident. In acknowledging the "point of view" of science and conservation, the language of these articles tacitly acknowledges that natural sites are necessarily engaged with cultural (human) processes that make them intelligible as sites of value. Similarly, in the cultural sites, the acknowledgment that some cultural sites might be the "combined works of man and nature" allow that culture might sometimes be built by nonhuman as well as human forces.

As of 2006, there were 812 World Heritage Sites, out of which the vast majority (628) were exclusively cultural properties and a significant minority (160) were exclusively natural properties. From an environmental perspective, this straight numerical imbalance itself is a problem, underestimating the long work that nature has put into creating material that is as valuable as cultural heritage, and even sustains it. But at least up until the mid-1990s, when UNESCO undertook a revaluation of this conceptual schema, the *content* of the categories themselves was equally an issue. Because monuments were mostly what counted as cultural heritage and wilderness was what counted as natural heritage, these categories enforced a variety of exclusions, including indigenous nature–culture relations and nonhuman nature that was not pristine wilderness, and it passed over many of the appropriations of nature in culture and culture in nature.

But if the categories of nature and culture require an ongoing border operation and a policing of boundaries in order to mask the crosscutting agency of nature in culture and culture in nature, then we should see evidence of human agency in the natural sites and nonhuman agency in the cultural sites. Consider some of the exclusively cultural sites, in which the cultural significance of the property is at least in part due to its natural location or properties. The tropical rainforest is central to the site of Angkor Wat, which even includes one temple (Ta Prohm) left to interact with the rainforest, as evidence of the power of the surrounding jungle to the site.[9] Similarly, even though they are preserved as cultural sites, the Royal Botanic Kew Gardens in England and the Orto Botanico in Italy are forms of cultural nature. The Mining Area of the Great Copper Mountain in Sweden may be preserved for its cultural importance, but the importance of the natural copper and the mountain itself to that culture are equally central.

In the reverse direction, the purely natural sites are constituted in all kinds of ways by culture.[10] The wilderness designation of Yellowstone National Park is in part a cultural construct that erases previous human habitation and sets up a strict boundary where wild nature begins and ends. Moreover, its importance as a heritage site consists not only in the population of grizzly bears and buffalos or its thermal vents, but also in the way that it was exported beyond the United States as a model of organizing national park systems.[11] The Galápagos Islands are surely of critical natural importance, but are deeply constituted by the cultural history of Darwin's explorations and theories of evolution.

If Bruno Latour is right that hybrids are proliferating not just underneath the nature-culture radar but because of the very acts of purification, then natural-cultural hybrids should be worming their way into heritage discourse because of the very attempts to keep them out.[12] Latour's argument is that the act of keeping nature and culture radically separate constructs modern sources of power—the power of nature as an objective fact and of society as a political force. Creating these dichotomous poles, however, relies on denying ontological hybridity. Over time, the act of constructing nature and culture as radically separate means that increasing numbers of hybrids are mobilized and then denied. It is not clear in Latour's account what would happen to hybrids if they were recognized rather than denied. Nor is it clear why entities should be recognized as hybrids at one point rather than another. But the broader contours of Latour's speculative onto-story map closely onto the changes over the last forty years of World Heritage Site history, in which UNESCO has increasingly come to recognize the hybrid nature of the dichotomized heritage it once insisted on.

Beginning in 1987, UNESCO undertook a series of studies in which it reevaluated its selection procedures and the patterns and distribution of outcomes that resulted from those patterns. Ultimately, UNESCO recognized that its nature/culture system of classifying sites was no longer sustainable. Its natural sites were shot through with culture. Once expanded beyond Europe, its cultural criteria ignored those cultures that had a living culture of nature. And both natural and cultural criteria were bound up with problematic projections of global power by a European-dominated body.

To its critics, UNESCO was paying too much heed to European academics in this moment of reflexivity. [13] To its supporters, these studies represented a welcome moment of self-criticism that resulted in a more just and equitable version of "world" heritage. The debate is an interesting political moment for the way it reflects the slowing confidence of Euro-American cultural hegemony, acknowledges and constructs the collective voice of a hodgepodge group of peoples called "indigenous," and rethinks the nature–culture relationship as crystallized in heritage.

One basic problem, as outlined by UNESCO's group of experts in June 1994, was that cultural heritage had mostly been taken to mean "monuments," thereby privileging a very narrow view of cultural heritage. A study of heritage site distribution conducted by the International Committee on Monuments and Sites (ICOMOS)—a partner organization of UNESCO—from 1987 to 1993, concluded that "Europe, historic towns and religious monuments, Christianity, historical periods and 'elitist' architecture (in relation to vernacular) were all over-represented on the World Heritage List; whereas, all living cultures, and especially 'traditional cultures', were underrepresented." [14] This last problem, the ICOMOS study suggested, was partly due to the fact that because "traditional" cultures did not build large monuments they were ignored as locations of cultural heritage. More important, it was also due in part to "an over-simplified division between cultural and natural properties which took no account of the fact that in most human societies the landscape, which was created or at all events inhabited by human beings, was representative and an expression of the lives of the people who live in it and so was in this sense equally culturally meaningful." [15] By privileging monuments on the cultural side, and wilderness areas on the natural heritage side, it ignored functioning, living cultural systems and the environment through which they existed.

The ICOMOS study was followed up by a World Heritage Committee initiative for a "Balanced, Representative and Credible World Heritage List," culminating in the adoption of a new Global Strategy in 1994. Its aim was to find ways to "ensure that the List reflects the world's cultural and natural diversity of outstanding universal value." [16] Procedurally, UNESCO revised the language in the natural and cultural criteria in articles 1 and 2 to reduce the emphasis on "dead" cultures over living cultures. It also limited the number of nominations a state could make each year, in the hopes of limiting the flood of European heritage, and it took measures to increase the nominations from geographically underrepresented countries.

In terms of establishing a better balance of natural and cultural sites, the strategy has not yet produced results. From a ratio of about 3:1 cultural to natural sites in 1994 (304 cultural sites and 90 natural), the disparity had increased to almost 4:1 (628 cultural and 160 natural) as of 2006.[17] However, an IUCN (2004) study found that natural sites were much more geographically well balanced at the global level than cultural sites. While cultural sites remained highly clustered in Europe, natural sites "cover almost all regions and habitats of the world with a relatively balanced distribution." From an environmental perspective, the geographical balance of natural sites might be understood to reflect the even distribution of natural beauty and the fact that all cultures necessarily find significance in the natural landscapes that surround them. Yet it also suggests that UNESCO's world heritage program has been far better prepared to acknowledge the global ubiquity of natural sites of significance than to recognize equal standing for global cultural diversity. In this frame, given the way that colonial and postcolonial discourses rendered non-Europeans as part of nature, as a way of seeing them as passive objects ready for the power of the civilizing mission, UNESCO's geographical balance in natural heritage sites alongside a geographical imbalance in cultural sites could be read as a part of a continuing projection of Western cultural power over global spaces figured as "nature."[18]

Conceptually, the Global Strategy recommendations also included the creation of new categories of heritage that moved past the cultural and natural criteria of universal value in the Convention. New categories included trade routes (e.g., the Silk Route), itineraries or religious routes, industrial heritage (e.g., railways and canals), and small-island sites (especially in the Pacific). The most important conceptual innovation here, arguably, was the idea of "cultural landscapes," which openly aimed at overcoming a dualistic conception of nature and culture (or "wilderness" and "monuments").[19]

The Creation of Cultural Landscapes
and Global Indigenous Politics

Most broadly, cultural landscapes build on the language in article 2 that refers to the "combined works of nature and of man." Cultural landscapes are particular constellations of people, social systems, and their natural environment, particularly where the constellation is still functioning. They remain explicitly cultural properties, though they may also be nominated for natural criteria.

Pushed to its conceptual limits, Susan Buggey (1995) and Adrian Phillips (1995) both note that the influence of humans on landscapes over time has been so pervasive that all landscapes are cultural landscapes. There is, according to Phillips, only "a spectrum of human impacts varying from negligible to comprehensive" (385). In this sense, there are no cultural landscapes per se, since this term suggests that there could be noncultural landscapes—there are only landscapes.

The assertion that all landscapes are cultural to varying extents is eminently reasonable in one sense, in that we are talking about human valuations of nature, and it would be impossible for humans to value nature as heritage nonculturally. But if UNESCO categories are going to be reflexive enough to recognize culturally constituted landscapes, then they ought to apply similar reflexivity to objects of culture—natural culture, in other words. By implication, the ubiquity of cultural landscapes is only half the equation. One might equally well reverse Buggey's claim to point out that all culture involves landscapes, that culture always involves a spectrum of natural impacts.

Though important, their criticism ultimately misses a broader point: given the need for organizing constructs, one that stresses the relationality of nature and culture is an advance on one that construes them as radically different. The ubiquity of cultural landscapes is no reason to dismiss the category as a starting point. It remains important, however, to be more specific about what kinds of cultural landscapes count as heritage. Cultural landscapes must refer to a particular density of human impacts on the landscape, say, or to a specific kind of interaction between humans and the landscape.

More specifically, then, UNESCO (2005) identified three different kinds of cultural landscapes, each reflecting a slightly different attempt to frame a post-dualistic heritage: intentionally designed landscapes, organically evolved landscapes, and associative landscapes.[20] First, then, is "the clearly defined landscape designed and created intentionally by man," a category that includes gardens and urban parklands. The emphasis is on the design of the landscape by a human landscape architect, such as Frederick Law Olmsted's Central Park or South Side Chicago parklands. While nature continually exceeds the intentions of its designer, what is being preserved as heritage is the human experience of a designed landscape.[21]

A second type of cultural landscape, the organically evolved landscape, "results from an initial social, economic, administrative, and/or religious imperative and has developed to its present form by association with and in response to its natural environment." For example, terraced rice fields in the Philippines are designed by humans but also reflect the contours of the mountainsides and patterns of flooding and erosion, resulting in an ongoing evolution of the landscape. If the first type involves overwhelming human agency in design, function, and ongoing maintenance of the landscape, the second type allows for initial human agency followed by an ongoing period of co-evolution with natural agents.

The third type is associative cultural landscapes, and it is the strongest challenge to the organizing power of nature and culture in heritage preservation. Associative cultural landscapes are inscribed as heritage on the basis of "the powerful religious, artistic, or cultural associations of the natural element rather than material cultural evidence, which may be insignificant or even absent."[22] In other words, what is being staked out as heritage is a mind/matter relationship, the experiential association itself between a people and a landscape.

Unlike the protection of monuments that are described as objects in the first place, an associative cultural landscape must be described in terms that are alien to that which the heritage status seeks to protect. The removed perspective and language of anthropology must be used to describe the "beliefs and attitudes" of a culture toward a landscape. In so doing, some of the power projections that were problematic in the nature-culture version of heritage are written back in, but in new form. More precisely, the production of "outstanding universal value" through the heritage of associative landscapes is a continuing dualistic intervention in nondualistic cultural schemas.[23] As an example of how this process works, I consider the case of Uluru (Ayers Rock–Mount Olga) National Park in Australia in the next section (as both an associative cultural landscape and a mixed property).

The term "associative cultural landscapes" is widely, though not exclusively, employed by UNESCO to mean *indigenous* associative cultural landscapes. The narrow usage of this category leads to at least two problems. The first issue is that the specificity of associative cultural landscapes to protect indigenous heritage means that there is no longer a broader rethinking of Western relationships between nature and culture. If the point is to rethink the dualistic relation between nature and culture, as UNESCO is aiming to do, then it must rethink that relation not only with respect to indigenous cultures but also with respect to industrialized societies, suburban ecologies, Idaho potato farmers, and global circuits of economic exchange.

A second issue is a conceptual challenge that comes from trying to use the term "associative cultural landscapes" in nonindigenous contexts. Here, a new set of values needs to be articulated to succeed nature/culture, and this cannot be done by simple conceptual extensionism from indigenous associative cultural landscapes. What the Western binary of nature/culture allowed was the gradual building of value systems that gave greater meaning to some cultural or natural heritage sites than others. In the case of nature, wilderness areas and the ideal of the pristine landscape untouched by human hands offered the guiding rationale, later augmented by scientific values of biodiversity conservation. In the cultural case, the emphasis was on monuments and material artifacts that showcased human power. In associative cultural landscapes, these rationales lose some of their power to organize. Natural and cultural rationales cannot always be easily combined, as evidenced by the fact that so few cultural landscapes are also mixed sites (only four out of fifty cultural landscapes are mixed properties—Uluru, Tongariro in New Zealand, St. Kilda in Scotland, and Pyrenees/Mont Perdu). Instead, a new set of values and discursive concepts must be articulated to judge what is worthy of heritage designation.

These two problems frame the inquiry in the rest of the chapter as I look in detail at mixed-criteria sites (selected for both natural and cultural criteria) and the modes of interaction between natural heritage and cultural heritage that they display before turning to a sympathetic critique of the idea of biocultural diversity, organized along sustainability and adaptability, as a workable orientation for hybrid heritage.

The Hyphenated Heritage of Mixed Sites

The process by which a site becomes a World Heritage Site requires the nominating country to select the natural and/or cultural criteria that best describe its outstanding universal value. There is no prohibition on a site being both naturally and culturally nominated (mixed sites).[24] Yet as of 2007, out of 812 World Heritage Sites, there were a mere 24 properties selected as having both outstanding cultural and natural value.[25]

These sites were mostly nominated under joint criteria. Nineteen of the 24 properties were initially proposed as mixed sites, though the national story of each site usually reveals that, over the history of the site, there is a dialectic between natural and cultural justifications for protection. For example, Tassili n'Ajjer in Algeria was initially protected as a national park by the Algerian government in 1972 because of the cultural significance of its cave paintings. The cave paintings depict ancient local flora and fauna, though, already suggesting a connection between nature and culture. When the Algerian delegation nominated Tassili n'Ajjer as a World Heritage Site, however, it was nominated as a mixed property, inscribed in 1982. Ignored in the national context, the natural features of the site were highlighted in its global heritage nomination, including both its geology and its biodiversity.[26] Four years after its inscription as a World Heritage Site, the Algerian government extended natural national park protection to the site in 1986 and expanded its boundaries. This back-and-forth between natural and cultural is common in the mixed properties; part of the task of this section is to show both how this shifting emphasis is deeply political, with varying stakes for different social actors, and how these mixed sites provide clues about the kind of natural-cultural hybridity that this chapter is aimed at uncovering.

The hybridity of heritage in these mixed-criteria sites is limited, in the sense that these are generally hyphenated or concatenated forms of nature-culture heritage, rather than forms of heritage that are preserved under new, hybridized rubrics that fuse nature and culture into something new (associative cultural landscapes are an exception). These sites are important, however, for the signposts they offer for future thinking about the entwinement of nature and culture, human and nonhuman. By starting with places where outstanding natural and cultural heritage coincide but are separately justified, I try to uncover the possibilities for a deeper hybridization and to think about the limits to that kind of project. UNESCO has itself pursued similar kinds of clues, engaging in studies of places where biodiversity and cultural diversity coincide as a way to understand the linkages between nature and culture.[27] What, then, joins nature and culture in these mixed-criteria sites, if anything? What is the quality of the interaction between natural and cultural agency at these sites? And what do they suggest for hybrid heritage?

As a way into thinking about these issues, I identify three modes of interaction between the natural and cultural elements at these mixed sites and code each mixed site according to these modes (see appendix 1): a living, dominant national culture that is bound to nature through *religious* or *sacred* means; *postcolonial* or *postimperial* contexts that endeavor to preserve the association of a nondominant culture with nature; and an extinct or *declining national way of life* rooted in a natural landscape, important for the direct reproduction of a dominant culture's national identity. Except for a few cases where there is not a strong relationship between nature and culture, almost all the mixed sites exhibit one of these three modes of interaction.

One form of natural and cultural heritage interaction in mixed sites involves a declining or past way of life rooted in a natural landscape, often important for the direct reproduction of an existing national identity and/or the national tourism industry. The cultural way of life is largely secular and is rendered as a past object, often as "traditional." This differs from the sites in which sacredness is an important component. Unlike postcolonial sites, the cultural heritage here is directly claimed as "authentically" belonging to the dominant national group's cultural tradition. This form of heritage hews closely to Lowenthal's understanding of heritage as a past artifact in the service of creating present-day collective identities such as national identity. I therefore focus here on the remaining two modes, which have different dynamics.

The Sacred and the Secular in Meteora, Greece

Another mode of interaction between natural and cultural elements at mixed sites involves a living human culture that is built around a natural site, where the bond between the two involves a religious, sacred, or devotional context. Mixed sites directly invoking a religion or a quality of sacredness are mostly in China and Greece. Each country approaches the nature–culture relationship in these sites in specific ways, depending on their forms of religious practice, national histories, and geographies, but these sites are nonetheless linked by a grammar of sacredness that structures the nature–culture relation. My primary focus is on the Greek site of Meteora, which provides an outstanding instance of how this structuring works.

The site of Meteora is structured around Orthodox monasteries built for seclusion. The monasteries are improbably perched on sandstone spikes and pinnacles that jut up and out into space, giving the illusion that they are "floating on air."[28] Until the recent hacking of steps into the mountainsides, reaching a number of the monasteries required climbing wooden ladders

Figure 2. Monasteries atop the rock towers of Meteora, in the World Heritage Site of Meteora, Greece. Source: Creative Commons.

pegged into the rocks or being hauled up in a net by the monks. Like the isolating effect of water at Mont St. Michel, the sites are intended to remove the monks from worldly concerns and create the possibility of an austere devotional practice.[29]

These sandstone spikes provide isolation relative to other people, but they are more than functional ways to enable ascetic practice. The spikes of Meteora are visually arresting and compelling in their effects on the psyche of hermetically oriented people. There is evidence that they induced religious hermits to live on them as far back as AD 1000, before the building of the monasteries. If religious asceticism can be pursued anywhere away from others, this leaves staggeringly large spaces as potential sites. What explains the choice of one site over a multitude of others can be better explained by the virtually semiotic meanings of those areas that draw humans in repeatedly over time.

One meaning these rocks repeatedly co-create is the idea of being closer to divinity, creation, or the cosmos. In the spatial imaginary of Christian cosmology, to be up in the air is to be closer to God. The very idea of a God residing in the heavens rests on a vocabulary of space where heights are divine and depths are fallen—to be an earthly mortal, striving toward a higher state of grace; or to be pulled up into heaven, with hell below. To be lifted up, then, particularly relative to one's surroundings, is more than metaphor—it is an actively embodied experience that requires the physical geography and virtual semiotic presence of mountains and towers of rocks.

The affective power of the rocks also creates an experience of the world that is stark yet contoured, one that exists between grounded earth, solitude, and divine communion. It is insufficient to simply be high up relative to one's surroundings, as in, say, a skyscraper—though as Jane Bennett (2001, 53) notes, even the vertigo experienced in a skyscraper has potential political meaning, in the way it lets us see a world that is not blocked by "actualities." One must also be high up in the "right" place, in a place where the specific meanings of things is apt to transform one's purpose in the right ways.

European visitors, particularly nineteenth-century Romantics, were apt to notice and describe these sensations. Henry Holland, visiting in 1812 in pursuit of manuscripts, describes his approach in typically flowery Romantic language:

> When we approached the spot, the evening was already far advanced, but the setting sun still threw a gleam of light on the summits of these rock pyramids, and showed us the outline of several Greek monasteries in this extraordinary situation, and seemingly as if separated from the reach of the world below. For the moment, the delusion might have been extended to the moral character of

these institutions, and the fancy might have framed to itself a purer form of religion amidst this insulated magnificence of nature, than when contaminated by a worldly intercourse and admixture. How completely this is delusion, it requires but a hasty reference to the present and past history of monastic worship, sufficiently to prove. It is the splendour of nature alone, which is seen in the rocks of Meteora.[30]

As any good Romantic would, Holland finds the sublime to be in nature rather than in culture. Yet he also catches himself eliding the affective power of the rocks with the spiritual grace of the monastery. He is not just reading nature onto culture here, but rather fully forgetting the distinction between them, if only for a moment. Even as Holland catches himself, we find the kind of meaningful experience that the rocks create in relation to humans. Holland's own Romantic religion finds expression in the way that the visual meanings of the rock imprint themselves on his consciousness. The rocks even call out a human hand where none has been laid—Holland again forgets his Romantic bent and says that they seem to be "formed rather by the art of man, than by the more varied workings of nature."[31]

In more recent times, the existence of a sacred or religious relationship between culture and nature at Meteora has also revealed the limits of the nature/culture dualism, in the politics of its heritage inscription. Even though Meteora, like the other sites in this category, is protected under both natural and cultural criteria, nature—as wilderness, empty of human presence or biodiversity "as such"—is not what is being protected. Rather, it is a cultural relationship with nature that seems to matter, where agency is more ambiguous. And although culture seems to be the dominant reason for protecting the monasteries, the winding history of Meteora's inscription shows the difficulties involved in "purifying" this site, to use Latour's term, into a cultural thing alone.

The Greek government initially proposed that Meteora be protected for both cultural criteria and natural criteria in its nomination. However, in initial reviews of the site in 1988, the two advisory bodies to UNESCO that review cultural and natural aspects, respectively, came up with a split decision. ICOMOS recommended that the site be inscribed for four different cultural criteria (i, ii, iv, and v). IUCN concluded that although "the sandstone pillars which form the foundation for the monasteries provide a striking setting which man has used to advantage . . . the natural values on their own are not of universal significance and the site is best evaluated on its cultural attributes."[32]

A few months later, however, UNESCO's World Heritage Committee reconsidered, acknowledging the difficulties involved in evaluating properties that "had an indissociable combination of cultural and natural elements."[33] Part of the problem was inconsistency in the criteria, in which natural heritage could sometimes involve the "combined works of nature and man," but at other times involve only natural heritage without reference to cultural elements. Similarly, UNESCO suggested, while article 1 referred to natural aspects of cultural heritage, the criteria did not provide any place where such natural aspects could be evaluated. They concluded that ICOMOS should reevaluate a number of cultural properties that had a natural setting of importance, including Meteora, and that rather than "artificially split[ting] the evaluation of World Heritage into 'culture' and 'nature,'" ICOMOS could evaluate properties using the cultural criteria and natural criterion iii, which, at the time, referenced the "natural beauty and the exceptional combination of cultural and natural elements." After ICOMOS's reevaluation, Meteora was eventually inscribed as a mixed site and protected as heritage because of the presence of "superlative natural phenomenon or areas of exceptional natural beauty and aesthetic importance," as natural criterion iii (now vii) puts it, alongside cultural criteria.

One lesson from Meteora's inscription process is the difficulty of distinguishing nature from culture in sites where both are outstanding. While the bureaucratic process of inscription ultimately required that some cultural and some natural criteria be used, the process itself showed that it was difficult to capture the power of the site under these dichotomized terms. At each turn, natural things appeared to be cultural, and cultural products had significant natural aspects. But there is also a more specific set of questions to ask about these mixed sites that are characterized by a sacred or religious grammar. The issue is whether secular frameworks for thinking about heritage preservation, such as a secular use of the nature/culture distinction, are capable of sustaining a deeper hybridity between human and nonhuman, particularly when the sites involve a sacred or religious aspect. In Meteora and other sites, for example, the language of sacredness, constituted against secularism, is central to distinguishing cultural value. Put more plainly, can nature and culture be dissolved without also dissolving secularism and sacredness?

The fact that environmental and ecological political movements (and the fantastical elements of technological culture, science fiction, and cyborgism) always teeter precipitously on the edge of mysticism and spiritualism might suggest that there is something important about aspects of human–nonhuman relations that lend themselves to challenging secularism. In the context of heritage, the specific question is whether secularism depends too strongly on the distinctively human character of culture to move toward a construction of heritage categories that admit to "indissociable" relations between human and nonhuman agents *without* deploying a language of sacredness.

One route to answering this question would be to consider whether explicitly secular heritage sites in fact contain sacred or religious elements of their own, and to show how such elements have been both denied and understood as part of the nonhuman. On this reading, secularism is in a denied relationship of dependency with sacredness, in much the same way that culture is in a denied relationship of dependency with nature. As long as this relationship remains denied, then heritage preservation would remain mired in the kinds of circularities that characterized the Meteora nomination process, where natural qualities of the site were accepted as important for its cultural importance, and indissociably so. These hybrid qualities ultimately had to be split back into cultural criteria and natural criteria. The way forward, then, might be to continually emphasize the presence of the sacred in the secular, just as we are able to find the secular (heritage) in the sacred-religious sites, and the natural in the cultural. One could point to the strongly mystical or religious aspects of secular practice as a starting point—secularism's faith in rationality, faith in progress, the quasi-divinity of sovereign figures, Rousseauvian civil religion—and extend such an analysis to secular heritage sites. Perhaps the mythmaking aspects of heritage are forms of secular-sacredness, in other words.

But to equate the secular with the human and the cultural and the sacred with the nonhuman or the natural is not quite right. This kind of parallelism assumes that there is one generalized binary language in play, one that lines dominant terms up on one side and subordinate terms on the other side, rather than crosscutting elements among these terms. Even though secular and sacred, nature and culture, and human and nonhuman are joined as binaries in one sense, it is useful to see how different elements from these three pairs interact to structure one another.

Moreover, as Talal Asad (2003) notes, what is needed in thinking about secularism is to understand the kinds of concepts that make "the secular" intelligible and apparently real. Therefore it is insufficient to show the presence of the sacred in the secular, since this leaves those categories intact without inquiring into how they came to have their current meanings. In other words, while the previous approach tried to move forward by finding secular heritage that were "actually" a hybrid of secular and sacred as a way of also being a hybrid of nature and culture, Asad challenges us to ask how the grammar of nature and culture came to be operative as self-evident, and how secular and sacred interact with those elements.

As the Meteora example shows, sacred elements are translated into secular language across both cultural and natural justifications. On the cultural criteria explicated by ICOMOS (1988), Meteora is lauded as "one of the most forceful examples of the architectural transformation of a site into a place of retreat, meditation, and prayer"(1)—human agency in transformation is what drives its importance (rather than divine inspiration or communion, as the monks who built the monasteries might have thought), along with natural agency (the sandstone pillars are important as a backdrop, and as something that needed "transformation" in order to become a place of religious practice). Sacredness, in other words, is secularized through this language, turned into a more mundane architectural activity. The same is true of the secularizing logic that casts Meteora's monasteries as important for, among other things, "symboliz[ing] the fragility of a traditional way of life that is threatened with extinction" (2). The sacred, here, is a *relationship* between human and nonhuman that is translated into secular, human terms. In that process, however, the relational quality of human–nonhuman interaction at Meteora is lost.[34]

What a genealogy of the secular might also include is that secularism has a particular relationship with abiotica—it must take the rocks and mountains in these sites, and abiotica more generally, to be brute but largely meaningless physical facts that language and culture must constitute. In part, this necessity stems from the fact that the grammar of the secular depends on denying and then repositioning those integrative cosmological schemas of religion that might give these abiotica an important role in meaning creation. But all of this is not to imply that bringing abiotica to a fuller presence requires a sacred context or a turn to a new environmental religion—at least if the sacred is still articulated from the perspective of the secular. Rather, it suggests that pursuing the virtually semiotic agency of abiotica as a source of meaning creation requires a kind of devout agnosticism about where that agency falls on a secular-sacred spectrum, and that admitting abiotic agency—even on virtually semiotic terms—is a way of pushing that devout agnosticism a little bit closer to its boundaries.

As the next section examines, heritage practices have tried to account for this problematic relationship with sacred sites in part through the idea of cultural landscapes, where the language involves trying to admit sacredness through a post-nature/culture framing of the relationships people have with particular lands. Yet secularist language remains a potent part of these new heritage formats, with slightly different effects from those at Meteora.

Postcolonial Heritage and Uluru Rock

A different form of interaction between nature and culture in mixed sites is characterized by a postcolonial or postimperial political context, in which the dominant political group proposes as a heritage the natural-cultural complex of a recently colonized group. The difference in the structure of political power between these sites compared to the "national identity" sites creates a radically different dynamic in which the mixed status of the heritage site functions as a proxy for a kind of postmodern rewriting of nature-culture by guilty postcolonials. As a form of hybrid heritage, it provokes a series of questions on guilt, power, and narration. The stories of two heritage sites in Australia show how this rewriting happens and some of the political limits to postcolonial guilt.

Kakadu National Park

Kakadu National Park in Australia was established in its current form in 1979, and was first inscribed as a World Heritage Site in 1981. Its national history stretches back further, however. In the area currently within the park, there were the Woolowonga Aboriginal Reserve (dating from 1964) and the Alligator Rivers Sanctuary (a nature reserve). In 1979, these two areas were incorporated into the combined jurisdiction of Kakadu National Park.

From a conservation perspective, the park's primary value lies in the fact that it contains an exceptionally large monsoonal river system, replete with the flora and fauna characteristic of such a river ecosystem. The area provides a habitat for a wide variety of rare and sometimes endemic species, including the ghost vampire bat, the loggerhead turtle, the estuarine crocodile, and a number of threatened plant species.[35] Culturally, the park is dubbed a "unique archaeological and ethnological reserve" by UNESCO,[36] containing "living cultural heritage"[37] in the form of Aboriginal populations whose continuous presence in the area has been traced back forty thousand years. Aboriginal art, largely cave paintings, stretches back at least eighteen thousand years, and the remaining Aboriginal inhabitants have maintained "sacred" relationships with the land. The land ownership arrangements involve a classic legal double-move, whereby the Kakadu Aboriginal Land Trust and the Jabiluka Aboriginal Land Trust are the official owners of approximately one-third of the land in the park, but have agreed to lease it to the Australian government to be managed as a national park.[38]

A series of uranium mines was established within the borders of the park, the most controversial of which involved an expansion of mining in the late

1990s. Mirrar Aborigines objected to the new mining at the Jabiluka site, citing both the harmful ecological impacts of the existing operations in the Ranger mine and the fact that the area near the new mine contained over two hundred sacred and cultural sites. Scientists and activists also raised a number of environmental concerns with the new mine, including the impact of radioactive leaks into local rivers and the negative effects on threatened species.

The Jabiluka mine ultimately became a target of international activism, drawing in a number of NGOs, along with UNESCO and IUCN. Already a World Heritage Site, UNESCO moved to designate the Kakadu World Heritage Site an endangered site, based on the expansion of mining. The World Heritage Committee held an extraordinary session on the mine in 1999, at which it voiced "deep regret" that the mine project had not been voluntarily suspended, given the possibility of "serious impacts to the living cultural values of Kakadu National Park posed by the proposal to mine and mill uranium at Jabiluka."[39] The committee further chided the Australian government for its lack of "confidence and trust building through dialogue" with the Mirrar Aboriginal People.[40] However, framed against the necessary deference to Australian state sovereignty, enshrined in the 1972 Convention, further action was not taken. After further wrangling, and a drop in uranium prices, the mining company reached a tentative agreement with the aboriginal owners of the land, who asserted the right to veto future uranium mining at the Jabiluka site in the park. Even as the cleanup of the Jabiluka site started in 2003, uranium mining continues at the Ranger mine, and future mining at Jabiluka may still take place.

In certain respects, the changing political contours of the Kakadu National Park project highlight the growing political clout of indigenous groups within Australia in recent decades, and show the ways in which their unique relationship with the land has become a source of political power, even if that power is still very limited. Heritage status also helped to create a category that the Mirrar people could embrace at international and global scales, with their indigenous status providing a way of speaking in global media, acting in and being spoken about in international political institutions, and mobilizing global sympathy. Yet the status of the park as global cultural heritage also showed just how permeable that assertion to "outstanding universal value" is, by the resource needs of Australia's industrial economy, the obfuscations of private property and law, and the final resort to sovereign prerogative against international pressure.

By positioning Aboriginal-land relationships and culture as part of the World Heritage complex, moreover, the Mirrar's political status relative to

Australian society and global societies was rewritten in ways that combine postcolonial themes with the nature-culture themes of heritage preservation. To gain an international political voice, Aboriginal communities also took on, or were given, the label of being "living cultural heritage"—a peculiar position that simultaneously acknowledges the importance of Aboriginal nature-culture to Australia and to the world, but denies its very vitality. The importance of that nature-culture in the present is justified by the needs of non-Aboriginal Australian society to come to terms with its past and by the unsettling memories of settler colonialism that emerged in UNESCO and other parts of the international heritage movement. But the categories invented to address this guilt involved relegating Aboriginal culture to a living museum status in which the main form of agency is to continue to live so that the culture might be maintained as heritage and to act as the living embodiment of righting past colonial wrongs.

Uluru Rock

Uluru Rock (also known as Uluru–Ayers Rock and Ayers Rock) forms the heart of the Uluru–Kata Tjuta National Park.[41] It is a massive sandstone formation that rises out of the otherwise flat Western Desert of central Australia, and therefore acts as a kind of focal point for the surrounding landscape. At its base, there are two semipermanent water sources as well as a number of edible plants, which made it an important camp and sacred space for Aboriginal peoples in the region. Uluru Rock was initially part of the South West Aboriginal Reserve, established in 1920. But in 1958, Uluru was "excised" from the reserve, made into a national park, and became a popular national tourist destination.[42] It was not until 1987 that it became a World Heritage Site, inscribed under natural criteria. Like Kakadu, a convoluted set of land ownership agreements pervades the land. On the same day in 1985, "inalienable freehold title" to the land was granted to the Uluru–Kata Tjuta Land Trust *and* the land was leased to the director of National Parks and Wildlife for a period of ninety-nine years.

The rock holds religious significance for the Anangu Aborigines. It is said to have been created by the ancestral heroes during the *tjukur* (Dreamtime), the time when spiritual beings walked the earth, created its features, set up rules of social interaction, and imbued the land and the individuals in it with spiritual power and meaning.[43] Yet the site was initially inscribed only as a natural World Heritage Site, selected for its geological importance and "exceptional natural beauty." Only later (in 1994), under the construct of "cultural landscapes," was it also admitted as a cultural property.

For over one hundred years, the heritage preservation path of Uluru thus bounced back and forth between natural and cultural. As an Aboriginal reserve in the early 1900s, its natural character was largely ignored in favor of the cultural needs of non-Aboriginal Australian society vis-à-vis its Aboriginal population. Once the rock was discovered as a tourist attraction in the middle of the desert, the natural side was emphasized, a phase that continued through its nomination as a World Heritage Site in 1987 under natural criteria. Subsequently, a surge of Australian scholarship, a rise in Aboriginal political activism, and a worldwide concern with the rights of indigenous peoples spurred a swing back toward its cultural importance.

Uluru Rock is not just an object of heritage, though, in the sense of being a passive thing on which heritage politics is enacted. Rather, its particularities have mattered in shaping the meanings of heritage at the site. We might start with its spatial scale. While philosophers use "rocks" as a catchall term to denote brute, solid materiality at any scale, a mountain like Uluru Rock differs qualitatively from individual rocks, and not just quantitatively. Whereas an individual rock can be handled, polished, put under a microscope, worn as part of a necklace, or put under ionic columns in Plymouth, the relational quality of scale makes mountains more difficult for any individual human, animal, or plant, to grasp. Uluru Rock's physical size, or at least that part of it visible to human eyes, creates an imperative to gaze on it, or at least to deal with its visual and physical presence in some manner. The current location of Uluru Rock, with vast flatlands in every direction, contribute significantly to its quality. Like Meteora at the edge of the Thessaly Plain, Uluru's height and presence above ground also require a change in optics in order to grasp. Human vision can focus on individual features of the mountain, but taking in the entire mountain requires a wide-angle lens. Its distillation into the images that fill tourist brochures can do some of this work of translation, but this again involves a change and displacement of scale, from the wide-open space of the basin to the manageable image on a computer or photographic print.

Unlike relations between humans and other living things like moss, trees, or creosote brush, in which it is easier to share a perception of a common time frame and activity of birth and death, the arrivals and departures of a mountain is rooted in much deeper time, at a distance that is difficult to internalize in its own terms, whether through scientific dating techniques or through its creation by ancestral creator beings in *tjukur*. Like Meteora, Uluru Rock is made mostly of a form of sandstone called arkose, which dates to six hundred million years ago.[44] As a bounded entity, Uluru Rock dates to about four hundred million years ago, when seas receded and the rock slab, still buried underground, was turned 90 degrees and split. Like an iceberg, whose visible tip often represents only a small percentage of its overall mass, Uluru Rock's mass is still largely underground.

Uluru Rock exists in this context largely because of its stubborn capacity, over tens of millions of years, to resist fracturing and weatherization. Even though it has been turned 90 degrees over time by geologic forces and has been buried by both seas and sand, it has had an endurance and resistance to these processes based on its cohesive structure. In turn, this monolithic quality has contributed to its surface character. Unlike the sandstone at Meteora, which has significant fissures and cracks that are visible to the human eye, Uluru Rock has few surface features. What marks its surface are gullies and ridges running in parallel across its dome, scars that are being formed primarily by water erosion. Its surface is pockmarked with dimples and dry pools that cascade down the side of the rock. Minor fissures in the rock do exist, which come from the release pressure that is created when they become warm and then cool. The oxidizing of iron in the rock also gives it a particularly malleable relationship with light, with its color shifting throughout the day and becoming particularly red to human eyes at dawn and dusk.

Where Meteora's material-semiotics involve the smooth yet distinct joining between sandstone spike and the monasteries on top, which creates a

Figure 3. Uluru Rock, in the World Heritage Site of Uluru–Kata Tjuta National Park, Australia. Photograph by Corey Leopold.

three-part image of natural, human, and divine, Uluru Rock remains apparently unbuilt on. That Uluru Rock is "just a rock" was part of the reason that it was initially inscribed only as natural heritage, demonstrating the European bias toward monuments as the dominant form of cultural heritage. But such a view of rocks misses the way that Uluru has exerted a presence across the surrounding flatlands and has constructed cultural meanings without making them materially present in the form of buildings. The spatial imagery guiding this assemblage is not vertical, as it is in Meteora, but horizontal. Partly, such constructions also involve a different relationship to the agency of Uluru Rock—one that, in effect, feels its semiotic projection across space, rather than by being in its space.

To think about the agency of Uluru Rock (or Meteora) thus requires keeping two frames in mind. The first frame involves the host of material-semiotic acts that occur between abiotic elements—the encounters between wind and rock, rain and sandstone, sun and soil. These have a semiotic quality in that they involve a relation that signifies a number of things and leaves a number of semiotic traces of the encounter. Yet since political agency, as I am considering it in this book, must involve a moment of interior experience where meanings are held and experienced before being turned back out and redirected, mountains are not agentic as such. Rather, the material-semiotic relations between abiotic things become agentic when they encounter living things. In the second frame of a biotic-abiotic relationship, then, relationships of agency can emerge. Virtually semiotic things become actually semiotic, involving a nearly infinite set of traces like mineral deposits that plants may strive toward, the visual qualities that present themselves to human eyes, the ability to trap water in small pools, and the iterated interactions that result in human art. Politics does not take place outside of this, but in it and through it, and it is difficult to talk about the politics of world heritage here without giving the full spread of agentic activities their due. What matters here is the *relation* between human and rock, conceived of as material-semiotic on both sides, and resulting in (among other things) the meanings of heritage at the site.[45]

Even more than the Chinese mountainous sites and the Greek monasteries, Uluru Rock's status as a sacred living site is also central to its mixed status. Aboriginal *tjukur* is a conception of the landscape as imbued with meaning, through walking ancestral pathways and following networks of physical-spiritual tracks. The very existence of the land is continually sung into being through a complex network of songs that are held by individuals. Even while treading very carefully here to avoid romanticization, and acknowledging the removed anthropological gaze and language involved, it is still possible to note that there is not a conceptual differentiation between nature and culture in this kind of perceptual and experiential framework. Other kinds of differentiation certainly take its place—a massive network of differentiation based on ancestral lines, tribal affiliations, and the specific natural entities and places to which individuals are tied through their Dreamings—but nature and culture as such are not distinguished.

In fact, because of the postcolonial political status of Aboriginal peoples, the mixed heritage site status of all the Australian parks as natural-cultural complexes has meant that there has been a continued deployment by UNESCO and the Australian government of a reworked nature/culture axis. Rather than the colonial version, which sought to equate indigenous inhabitants with nature and juxtapose them with the civilized logic of colonial culture, the postcolonial version recognizes the integrated cultural component of the indigenous relationship with the land, and it is precisely *that* component that positions Aboriginal peoples as "living heritage." Thus, that which lives on is culture or nature, while that which is condemned to heritage status, even while it is celebrated for it, is integrated nature-culture. This integrated complex is the idealized past of fragmented Euro-American culture, which tends to think of itself as decisively separated from nature by the veil of culture and language.

Pushing biocultural diversity solely into indigenous–natural relationships, in effect, reinscribes the problematic features of nature/culture (projections of political power from a center to a periphery) along a new axis. Now we have people-landscape complexes that are integrated (cultural landscapes) and those that are not (postcolonial Australian culture or nature). Here, nonintegrated nature-culture retains power and, indeed, organizes the cultural landscapes through heritage. What is lacking, still, are non-Aboriginal approaches to Uluru Rock that differentiate in non-nature/culture terms.

Biocultural Diversity and World Heritage Sites

The mixed sites of Uluru Rock and Meteora show some of the modes in which there was overlapping natural and cultural agency in heritage, even as they were initially inscribed as hyphenated heritage. Yet as UNESCO increasingly recognized, concatenating heritage categories did not adequately represent the thing that was being marked as heritage. In moving toward associative cultural landscapes, a promising hybrid form of heritage was articulated, one that specifically aimed to protect a relational quality between a particular nature and particular culture, rather than between nature and culture as such. In practice, however, cultural landscapes have been heavily weighted toward sites involving indigenous people, which has had the unintended effect of reinscribing a modified nature/culture dualism in heritage categories, only bumped up a level. Put simply, indigenous–nature relationships are seen as holistic, while modern Western heritage retains its nature/culture dualism.

One of UNESCO's broader efforts to find language that stretches across these political chasms comes in the idea of *biocultural diversity* (BCD). On the one hand, it is a form of hyphenated heritage, joining biological diversity and cultural diversity. On the other hand, its articulation has sometimes also involved hybrid criteria by which to judge sites as more or less valuable as heritage. Like associative cultural landscapes, it is possible to see BCD moving dialectically over time, moving from a dualistic structure, to a hyphenated structure with internal contradictions, to a partial synthesis in hybridized categories. Yet in the political messiness of heritage, conservation, and international relations, each moment did not cleanly supersede the next—rather, each of these moments continues to exist side by side, sometimes uneasily. The institutional life of categories is long-lived, while innovative alternatives do not inexorably succeed their predecessors. To unpack BCD, it makes more sense, then, to look at its different usages and meanings. There are three layers to BCD, each progressively thickening the concept.

In the first and thinnest layer, one form of diversity is taken for granted in order to point out how it promotes the other diversity. For example, UNESCO (2007) makes the claim that protecting diverse cultural attitudes toward the land leads to a higher level of biodiversity. Here, "protection of cultural landscapes can contribute to modern techniques of sustainable land-use and can maintain or enhance natural values in the landscape. The continued existence of traditional forms of land-use supports biological diversity in many regions of the world. The protection of traditional cultural landscapes is therefore helpful in maintaining biological diversity." The protection of traditional forms of land use like rice paddies or the French countryside are justified on the grounds of maintaining biodiversity (ibid.). Assuming that cultural diversity is a political good, the argument is that it also leads to biodiversity protection.

From the other side, UNESCO suggests that a biodiverse natural site leads to protecting cultural diversity, and thus should be protected as heritage. For example, the justification for protecting the Amazonian rainforest as a national park has changed from the protection of biodiversity per se to the promotion of global cultural heterogeneity and linguistic diversity. Thus, Western conservation groups like the World Wildlife Fund, which have traditionally been concerned with biodiversity, have picked up on this theme as a way of arguing for the benefits of nature conservancy.[46]

The second layer is a more specific argument about the nature of the relations between diversities: cultural diversity and biological diversity are directly co-constitutive and interdependent. The content of one form of diversity necessarily flows from the other. "The infinite variety of the natural world provides material for cultural inspiration, meaning, and practice. Words, expressions, stories, legends, etc., encode human relationships with the environment. And since eons, human ingenuity has participated directly in enriching biodiversity—from the level of genes, to species, ecosystems and landscapes."[47] At a deeper level, systems that respect differences in one realm automatically constitute differences in the other realm, because they are part of one complex. As UNESCO (2004) puts it: "Biological and cultural diversities are mutually reinforcing and interdependent. Natural systems cannot be understood, conserved and managed, without recognizing the human cultures that shape them. Together, cultural diversity and biological diversity hold the key to ensuring resilience in both social and ecological systems." In short, diversity cannot be separated into cultural and biological components. Rather, cultural diversity and biodiversity are co-constitutive and co-evolutionary phenomena and their dynamics must therefore be considered together. Put in the language of this book, BCD is at root a material-semiotic diversity that cuts across the human–nonhuman and nature–culture lines.

Partly supported by UNESCO, a growing academic and activist literature pursues a neo-Wharfian hypothesis that links language, cultural knowledge, and the environment in a concept of BCD.[48] The analyses find strong correlative relationships between endangered languages and endangered species, and suggest that areas of strong cultural diversity are correlated with areas of strong biodiversity as well.[49] At a more abstract level, the literature has sought to establish how language relates to environmental management in the long term, and to argue that protecting linguistic diversity is an important way of protecting BCD.

On this account, language (and linguistic diversity) is central to the relationship between biodiversity and cultural diversity because it is, very literally, a joint product of human culture and local environment. Peter Mühlhäuser (1996) argues that the ecologically situated view of language presumed in BCD means that language does not describe an environment, mediate reality into human consciousness, or in itself construct the field of differences and meanings through which humans interact with the world. Rather, language is constructed by the interaction of culture and environment. Linguistic diversity is therefore a reliable gauge of BCD in part because it is one of its most important products. It is in this sense that the loss of BCD, as gauged by the global loss of languages, is not the material loss of species or the ideational loss of language, but the "extinction of experience."[50] The experience lost is not (just) human experience, but one jointly made up of human and nonhuman entities in common biocultural complexes.

Language also has functional importance here, in the way that it encodes cultural knowledge of a given environment, which in turn further steers human activities. This relationship creates a series of feedback loops. In negative spirals, to destroy a given local environment is also to destroy the local cultural knowledge that goes with it and to render the local language dysfunctional. In positive spirals, local languages that are specifically tailored to a local environment enable a more nuanced and meaning-rich interaction with that environment. These positive kinds of local relationships take long periods of time to co-evolve, and require a relatively high degree of autonomous ecocultural development.

What is BCD ultimately a diversity "of," and what kind of work can this concept actually do? BCD suggests that "biocultures" are the unit out of which biocultural difference is created and subsequently respected, and that biocultures are forms of "life" in general terms. As Maffi (2005, 602) puts it, "Biocultural diversity comprises the diversity of life in all of its manifestations." BCD, as a concept spanning activist, policy, and academic circles, is thickened from this general definition by being set as a largely self-evident good against the homogenizing forces of cultural globalization. Yet the term itself has insufficient conceptual weight to be able to do more than level a fairly general critique of biocultural activities that homogenize, and promote, those that diversify or stand in contrast to a presumably dominant, homogenous bioculture. In other words, it is ultimately difficult to parse "good" biocultural moments from "bad" ones. If a science lab creates fifteen new species of genetically modified tomatoes and evolves a specialized scientific language and culture to describe and manipulate tomato genes, in what sense does this not constitute part of BCD? Is it when those fifteen species spread too far or dominate tomato growing that they stop being part of BCD and start becoming its opposite? Would biocultures that are relatively homogenous in language and sparse in terms of species, but perhaps ecologically friendly, be a part of the mosaic of BCD, or outside it?

As conceptualized, BCD cannot answer these questions on its own. Rather, it ends up smuggling in—or explicitly importing—further political agendas to make its case, which constitute the third layer of BCD. Like cultural landscapes, one way it has done so is by using the indigenous-nature complex as a shortcut to gesture to valid forms of BCD.[51] For example, Klaus Toepfer, head of UNEP, says: "There is an urgent need to help local, indigenous and traditional peoples safeguard their heritage, which in turn can do much to conserve the biological and genetic diversity upon which we all depend."[52] Here, BCD appears as the complex of indigenous people and their heritage, as generative grounds for preserving global biodiversity. As suggested above with respect to cultural landscapes, however, BCD might try to thicken itself in ways that go beyond focusing mostly on indigenous-nature complexes, since this approach tends to end up writing the nature/culture distinction right back in.

Another, more cross-cultural, route has been to suggest that the criteria of difference that parses one bioculture from another should be built along an axis of sustainability and the outcomes of survival and adaptability that such an orientation tries to ensure.[53] It is the ecological sustainability of a biocultural landscape that makes it more worthy of protection than one that is not. Thus, UNESCO gives special weight to cultural landscapes that demonstrate sustainable land use, such as rice paddies in Asia, oasis systems in desert regions, and the patchwork of farmlands in the French and English countrysides. The value of preserving these cultural landscapes as world heritage is framed in terms of promoting sustainability. Similarly, the preservation of indigenous associative cultural landscapes promotes sustainability on the grounds that those intimate cultural relations with the lands lead to a smaller ecological footprint over time.

A related rationale for BCD is adaptability to change. The simple logic is that the greater the diversity, the greater the likelihood that a given system can adapt to exogenous changes and therefore be sustainable. Arguments about the diversity–adaptability relationship are familiar in biological settings like agriculture (e.g., monoculture farming, genetically engineered crops, and single-species tree plantations). Evolutionary adaptations are also generated through genetic diversity. But UNESCO is pushing the linked strength of diversity in cultural and biocultural contexts as well, in creativity, language, and "development." By loose analogy to the ecological case, UNESCO suggests that a culturally diverse world is more likely to adapt successfully to the homogenizing power of the global economy and culture and to resist its debilitating features. Thus, cultural diversity is a matter of a cosmopolitan ethics of respect and developmental necessity.

Biocultural adaptability pushes beyond a species-based object of adaptability, though. BCD is not aimed at preserving the "human species" as its primary goal, as environmental discourses often frame anthropocentric arguments for conservation. Because its diversity is rooted in complexes that exceed the human, it suggests the idea of a global system that is neither a global ecosystem nor a global political structure. As a way of specifically deepening an internally diverse notion of BCD, sustainability also offers a way of drawing the legitimate boundaries of biocultural difference for a heritage program. It is a big enough term to potentially include indigenous cultural landscapes, Western wilderness programs, local agricultural complexes from ancient rice paddies to relatively new organic farming practices, and eco-techno complexes of energy use (consider wind farms as heritage sites).

Rethinking BCD and Heritage

How can we evaluate this turn to BCD and its relationship to world heritage? The concept of BCD is highly promising in many ways, but it is also hampered. I offer two sympathetic criticisms of the BCD concept before turning to a more theoretical set of reflections on some of the effects of the idea and practice of BCD. At the end of the section, I suggest what some of the future possibilities might be for bringing BCD and heritage together.

The first difficulty with BCD is that it promises some kind of parallelism or equivalence between biodiversity and cultural diversity, but "species" (biodiversity) and "human culture/language" (cultural diversity) are plainly very different sorts of units. Merging these two diversities (rather than just tracing correlations between them) has the effect of overloading the importance of human language and undervaluing species. Even though the academic literature surrounding the term is rather more nuanced in its aims, the way that the term is used by UNESCO and UNEP involves a more simplified link between two kinds of ostensibly equal kinds of diversities. This link builds in a significant imbalance by denying that nonhuman species have culture or language in ways that might matter, while tacitly exempting humans from being part of species diversity.

One can imagine resolving this by thinking fully in terms of species, and subordinating human language and cultural diversity to biodiversity. Many environmentalists, biologists, and conservationists do just this in emphasizing the "human species" as an actor, one species among many. The problems with this approach are legion, as many critics have pointed out. It is more difficult to think about BCD as implying a diversity of culture of multiple species as well as intraspecies diversity, but this is nonetheless more plausible. The growing work in ethology and biology on animal culture and language suggests that it is not just species, as biological life forms, that we are considering in biodiversity, but also species-in-contexts, with learned habits that are transmitted across generations, and modes of communication that are not entirely innate.[54] To take one example, primates have very different cultural habits in captivity than in the wild, to the point that primates raised in captivity cannot be returned easily to the wilds because they lack both the relevant contextual knowledge to survive and the cultural skills to integrate with other primates. The same is sometimes true for other reintroduced species, such as condors, and pets who escape from their owners. In short, we need to pay greater attention to the kinds of semiotic contexts that other species encounter and their potential social relations with humans, in order to make sense of the diversity of cultures within and across species lines. Rather than moving toward biological units (species) or leaving its units incommensurable, BCD could make its units commensurable by utilizing a concept of species-cultures and pursuing the ways in which they interact in particular contexts.

A second problem with the formulation of BCD comes in the assumptions that are made about what that diversity implies in political terms. BCD supporters have used the slogan "sharing a world of difference" as well as other generalized expressions of respect for diversity.[55] But diversity needs political content: *How* do we share a world of difference? Whose differences matter, and when? What happens when, inevitably, others do not want to share in that world of difference? As considered above, one way to understand "respect for differences" is as "respect for indigenous-nature complexes." But while this is a start, it does not tackle some of the most serious issues in biocultural diversity, which lie in the biocultural complexes in the heart of the nonindigenous world, ones that also envelop, affect, and constitute indigenous politics. Another way BCD has been given political content is through the emphasis on sustainability—but given the way that sustainability has arguably been eviscerated of political content, this term needs political revitalization too.

At a more abstract level, BCD also involves a fascinating mixture of meaning-generating assumptions, including one set based on presence and absence, and another based on pattern and randomness.[56] In one sense, the positive meanings of BCD are still located in the presence and absence of languages and species. Species are extinct or exist, while languages are disappearing or present. In this way, BCD is part of an older, modernist tradition that, as N. K. Hayles (1999) puts it, front-loads meaning into a given system, guaranteeing it by originary presences like God, logos, or teleology.

But in emphasizing the power of BCD to generate resilience and adaptability, a different metaphysics is invoked that turns toward systems and information theory. It relies on the rather different pairing of *stability* (i.e., the adaptability or resilience of a system—in short, a pattern) and *diversity*. Here, it is not the presence or absence of particular species that matters per se, nor the particular words, syntax, or grammar of an indigenous or other human language, but the *density* of difference, where those differences can be systematically and without loss captured and compared under a common informational umbrella. Meaning, then, in this metaphysic, "is not guaranteed by a coherent origin; rather, it is made possible (but not inevitable) by the blind force of evolution finding workable solutions within given parameters."[57] Moreover, diversity is not the opposite of systemic stability, but rather, is its very creative grounds. The co-evolution of cultural and biological life suggests that the same dynamic applies to the long-term adaptability of biocultural systems.

What is at stake in this emphasis on pattern/randomness as a generative metaphsyics? On the one hand, it moves away from the kind of subject/object thinking that has traditionally been understood as the problematic Cartesian legacy underlying humanity's relationship with nature, and as such might represent a step toward thinking about human–nonhuman relationships on just the kind of common plane that I have been exploring in this book. On the other hand, by turning toward a more systems-theory metaphysic, BCD brings on board some new, and difficult, commitments. While it emphasizes the study and preservation of local languages, cultures, and ecologies, it translates those into informational form, by abstracting them away into patterns of languages and species. The sciences and policy of biodiversity, as explored in chapter 2, have been central to this dematerialization, emphasizing the ways that patterns of species matter. On the whole, what matters is not the local meaning of a particular species or individual in its relation to others, but rather the patterns of information that generate stabilities in biocultural complexes.

Finally, what of the intersection of BCD and heritage? Using heritage protection to promote BCD has significant limits. Pushed too far, the practice of heritage works against its own political aims. The ideal of preservation is often at odds with the very ecological adaptability and fluid cultural processes that heritage is trying to protect. The challenge that BCD poses to heritage is whether it can be conceptually expanded from the static preservation of things and places to include a designation of fluid processes like biocultural complexes. Can UNESCO remain reflexive enough to change not just what sites it protects but also the reasons why and how it protects them?

While associative cultural landscapes, as applied only to indigenous-nature complexes, appear to represent something from which moderns have fallen, they could be applied directly to transform modern heritage practices in a way that also stakes out a mind–matter relation, rather than a natural or cultural thing itself. In particular, one way UNESCO's heritage concept might transform itself is through rethinking its Western emphasis on authenticity and originality. For example, Alexander Stille (2002) contrasts Chinese and

Japanese ideas about preservation with Western ideas about heritage. Stille suggests that in these traditions of preservation, it is conservation of the form that matters much more than the actual object. Thus, the Terracotta Warriors that are buried in imperial tombs are often replicated and presented as "originals." Chinese art sometimes involves copying a previous master's work as a way of demonstrating skill, not forgery. The Ise Shrine in Japan was excluded from UNESCO protection because it had been rebuilt with new wood and therefore lacked authenticity, yet in Japanese terms, the shrine remained legitimately heritage because the form of the structure had been maintained.

Similarly, digital or virtual heritage is a logical outgrowth of form-based preservation. Such heritage already exists. There are three-dimensional reconstructions of Nefertiti's tomb in Egypt, while virtual reconstructions of German synagogues destroyed during the Nazi era offer a way of recovering a form of heritage that no longer has physical presence.[58] Digitizing ancient Armenian texts not only creates a virtual version of existing heritage but also spreads the possibility of accessing them to widespread diasporas and a global community of scholars. The re-creation of the Lascaux caves in France is not virtual but embodies the same idea of facsimile. In short, a decoupling of heritage from authenticity or originality could animate a very different kind of heritage, one that allows the flow of agency to keep moving on the ground, while using virtuality as a way to translate the meaningful aspects of biocultural existence.

Conclusion

This chapter followed twists and turns of global heritage politics in the 1990s, showing how it grappled with the difficulty of hybridizing nature and culture. In the politics surrounding heritage categories, biodiversity figured prominently as an organizing logic, framing the idea of natural heritage in substantive ways. It also acted as a logical and conceptual bridge between biological figurations of nature and global figurations of cultural diversity, which mutually reinforced claims about the generative power of difference, even on radically different planes. By following the specific politics of two heritage sites, in Greece and Australia, this chapter also pushed further into difficult questions surrounding agency and the ways that political claims to heritage were two-faced—on the one hand, a politics about abiotic objects like mountains and rock formations, and on the other, a politics made in part by those objects, and constituting an important part of the debate about the differences between built memorials and associative cultural landscapes. These sites thus raised important questions about human relationships to land and to meaningful

Chapter 4   Urban Biodiversity in New York City and the New Rewilding

BY THE SECOND HALF OF THE 2000S, biodiversity was increasingly framed through a new conception of nature. Leaving behind the arguments for the intrinsic value of nature and the moral imperatives to stop species extinction that structured biodiversity in the 1980s, and building on its connection with sustainable development in the 1990s, the paradigmatic environmental idea that came to frame biodiversity in the 2000s was the Anthropocene—a nature in which humans are the prime movers, usurping natural processes for better or ill, and the originators of the major decisions about evolutionary trajectories, climate, and basic geophysical processes. While the scientific debates over epoch-naming continue, weighing the appropriate standards for demarcations of geological time, many environmentalists quickly adopted the term, using it as a critical marker to note the degradation of the global environment due to human activity, including biodiversity loss. Fired as a warning shot, the Anthropocene was a way to ask pointed questions about the "end of nature" and to point to the irreversible and epochal quality of the transformations taking place at a planetary level.

Others used the term Anthropocene to try to shift the contours of how American environmentalism thought of its relation to nature, and by extension, how, where, and why it engaged in environmental politics. For Peter Kareiva, chief scientist of the Nature Conservancy, the Anthropocene meant a downshift from "great nature" to "good nature"—that is, moving away from conserving nature in the wild and toward finding ways to "domesticate it more wisely."[1] Others, like Ted Nordhaus and Michael Shellenberger (2004, 2007), were even more explicit, arguing that nature's fate now fundamentally rested on even more human intervention, and of an increasingly intentional kind. For them, the Anthropocene was a moment to leave old environmentalist strategies behind and embrace the construction and support of a new, technologically enhanced nature. Even where the language of the Anthropocene has not been explicitly adopted, its core idea that we live in a fundamentally different kind of global nature now, one that is nowhere untouched by human impacts, has been widely acknowledged, whether as a lament, a spur for a reconciliation with nature, or a new opportunity.

Across these debates, the role of biodiversity in conservation thought and practice has become recast along axes that are now directly more connected to its utility to humans than ever before, in particular through an amplification of the ideas of ecosystem services and natural capital, marrying environmental problems to market solutions of increasing reach and sophistication.[2] Given the marked failure to reach the global targets for halting biodiversity set under the CBD for 2010, a certain amount of this shift can be read as a practical recalibration in conservation circles to accommodate shifting environmental and economic realities. But in this shift, biodiversity itself has become reconfigured and, to borrow a corporate metaphor, downsized. Whereas it earlier emphasized massive hotspots of species, the great diversity of life, and so-called charismatic megafauna, biodiversity in the Anthropocene is just as often the variety that provides adequate water, good-quality soil, and other services. Whereas biodiversity once emphasized species in the wilds pursuing their own life trajectories, it now often emphasizes urban biodiversity and the possibilities of rediscovering nature in places once thought insufficiently wild to harbor nature at all. Both "wild" and "urban" have new meanings in this configuration.

To understand these developments, this chapter examines two comparatively new turns in global biodiversity policy and conservation. The first is the growing emphasis on *urban biodiversity,* both an object of conservation and a proactive tool of environmental governance. The iteration of biodiversity in the 2000s moved further along the trajectory of making it a second-order, generative principle, where it is important to the extent that it underpins ecosystem services, and increasingly, socioecological resilience. A step away from being the primary provider of instrumentally useful goods like medicine, and doubly removed from being intrinsically valued, it is now seen as sustaining the systems that sustain us. Biodiversity is a service to ecosystem services. In many ways, the turn to urban biodiversity is a paradigmatic example of this troubling turn, but urban biodiversity also extends and changes biodiversity in other politically interesting and sometimes promising ways. I examine how it is articulated in new global environmental governance initiatives driven by UN agencies, the CBD, and others, and look at the ways it connects with resilience, focusing particularly on the context of climate change and postdisaster politics in New York City.

New York City is a particularly important site for examining these dynamics. As a paradigmatic "global city" of significant size, it is representative of the new kind of target for urban biodiversity policy. Ecologically speaking, it has a very large footprint, though as urban environmentalists note, carbon footprints per capita are lower in New York than in surrounding suburbs. As a key site of political, financial, and symbolic power in the United States, it is also a critical place to examine the emergence and evolution of disaster politics, both in response to the threat of national security disasters and to the threat of natural disasters. Increasingly, these two are intertwined.

The second initiative the chapter considers is *rewilding*, a conservation strategy with a number of meanings across different contexts. One key version of rewilding, including its American valence, aims to create or restore large swathes of functioning ecosystems, comprising wilderness areas and wildlife corridors, with biodiversity anchored by reintroduced keystone species, including top predators. The Yellowstone-to-Yukon corridor in North America, the corridor along the former Iron Curtain in Europe, and the Gondwana Link in Australia are all prominent examples. A second variant of rewilding involves a more explicit form of creating biodiversity by design, generally in smaller, privately held areas and with a vision of biodiversity rooted much further back in time, as far back as the Pleistocene, and sometimes more explicitly connected with nationalist and racist mythologies.

Though "urban" and "wild" are apparent opposites, and have structured environmental thinking as opposites for many decades, these new iterations show interesting affinities on closer inspection, including a shared sensibility about biodiversity by design, a rethinking of wildness, and sometimes a form of antipolitics. As with other moments examined in this book, these two turns are aimed not just at designing nonhuman life but also at remaking humans, and the chapter explores both the new kinds of biodiversity subjects and the kinds of nature that they help to produce, and might help to produce in the future. Although it raises some cautionary flags, the chapter concludes by asking how rewilding—understood as an ecological strategy as well as a community and personal practice—might help reanimate biodiversity as a political project.

The Rise of the Urban in Global Biodiversity

Thinking about how urban life intersects nature in ways that make cities livable and sustainable is not new. In New York City, for example, it goes back at least to Frederick Law Olmsted and the design of Central Park as a way to alleviate the "miasmas" plaguing public health, alongside a desire to foster a

Romantic engagement with nature. In a somewhat different vein, Victorian-era zoos brought wild nature to the cities.[3] The livable cities movements in the 1960s also emphasized urban spaces that more explicitly included natural elements.[4] But what was new starting in the early 1990s was the explicit linking of biodiversity with urban spaces, in a way that suggested not that cities were fallen from nature, but rather were themselves sites of rich biodiversity. Early proponents of linking biodiversity and urbanization in the 1990s noted that conservation politics and science had largely neglected areas of dense human habitation as sites of study.[5] This disinterest in cities had roots in environmentalism's traditional affinities with wild areas, and scientific roots in the study of nature "out there." Given the rising urbanization of populations across the world, the wilderness-based perspective on biodiversity meant that insufficient empirical attention was being paid to the ecological transformations in the places most affected by the most humans. While environmentalists tended to think about nature in cities as being completely erased, urban ecologists pointed to the interesting and important remnants of nature in city areas, highlighting those species that survived and thrived within city life.

Urbanization also meant that cities were having a greater ecological footprint than before, reaching further out into areas where "natural" biodiversity existed in order to provide resources like water, food, and material goods to city dwellers. Rather than seeing cities, suburbs, and outlying rural and wild areas as separate entities, the new urban ecology increasingly suggested that they be seen as a distinct unit or system in their own right, dominated by the magnetic ability of the city to pull material flows inward, and repel the leftovers back out.[6] Urban biodiversity, in this frame, aimed to link nature in the city with biodiversity in the wild and rural areas that provided ecosystem services and inputs for human health and well-being in the city itself.

At the same time, the urban biodiversity movement suggested that there were new and untapped possibilities in seeing biodiversity and urbanization through a single lens, in focusing more closely on how cities could be made more sustainable and green within their own boundaries,[7] as well as affecting global biodiversity.[8] In a material sense, this meant thinking more explicitly about sustainable design, such as creating green rooftops, promoting parks, greening consumption and its associated by-products, and so on. More broadly, it meant thinking about the material throughputs of cities as a whole—as UNEP notes, "cities occupy 2% of the earth's surface and use 75% of its natural resources."[9]

Finally, at an experiential level, the urban biodiversity movement suggested that ignoring biodiversity in the cities meant that opportunities to emphasize connection with, appreciation of, and education about nature were being lost, precisely when they were needed most. Thus, New York's "Teardrop Park" becomes a paradigmatic site of urban biodiversity: a park covering less than two acres, complete with children's slides and play area, but also containing seventeen thousand mostly native plants and a number of microclimates, such as a miniature marsh.[10] Surrounded on one side by the towering skyscrapers of lower Manhattan, and by the Hudson River on the other, its aim is to integrate nature and culture, and function as an island of biodiversity on the very urban island of Manhattan.

Urban Biodiversity in Global Policy

These early critiques of biodiversity's exclusive focus on wild and rural areas, or on biophysical processes such as water and climate, have increasingly been amplified in global policy arenas such as UNEP, UNESCO, and the CBD in the past half decade. As the global biodiversity targets for 2010 at the Johannesburg Summit (2002) were clearly not going to be met, these bodies turned in part to urban biodiversity as a new way forward. As with previous iterations of global biodiversity, addressing "knowledge gaps" forms a central plank of the urban biodiversity turn. Started by IUCN, the prominent global conservation organization that is also involved with the World Heritage criteria examined in the previous chapter, the Urban Biodiversity and Ecosystem Services (URBES) project is a European-focused initiative aimed explicitly at addressing scientific and knowledge gaps about biodiversity and cities. Other urban biodiversity initiatives emphasize a city-based level of global environmental governance, especially the International Council for Local Environmental Initiatives (ICLEI), which is a group of twelve megacities, one hundred super cities, and a host of smaller cities, who pursue a variety of sustainability projects at the city level. Among these projects, ICLEI runs a Cities Biodiversity Center, which funds projects that develop technical solutions to aspects of urban biodiversity. ICLEI also hosts the Urban Biosphere Initiative (URBIS), a global network of researchers, policy makers, "visionary planners," and environmental practitioners, aimed at creating more "resilient and equitable urban regions."[11]

As with many global policy areas, the organizations involved have expended significant effort to issue a number of reports that describe and construct the global problem in particular ways.[12] One of the most comprehensive global policy documents addressing this relationship is the *Cities and Biodiversity Outlook*, published in 2012 by the CBD, and backed up by the Hyderabad Declaration issued from the CBD biannual conference of parties meeting in October

2012.[13] The report summarizes the relationship of urbanization and biodiversity, starting at a global scale. Whereas many global biodiversity reports start by invoking the crisis of global species loss, this report starts with data on global urbanization, noting that by 2050 the projected urban population will be nearly double what is was in 2010 (7), and that more than 60 percent of the area expected to be part of urban areas has yet to be built. Urbanization is presented as a "challenge" for biodiversity, both in direct habitat intrusion and in terms of indirect resource extraction. From the broad sweep of global statistics, the report moves to regional perspectives, where it elaborates lengthy sections on Africa, which is "urbanizing faster than any other continent" and "near highly sensitive ecological zones with high biodiversity" (12), and Asia, where "minimizing habitat and biodiversity loss . . . will require appropriate urban planning and reformation of the land market system" (16). In a comparatively brief section on Europe, the report notes 70–80 percent urbanization levels on the continent already, with little urban population growth.

The biodiversity-cities nexus is located here less in terms of biodiversity in urban areas, and more in terms of urbanization and population growth in developing countries. The report builds on the global population fears prominent in environmental politics since at least the Club of Rome Reports in the 1970s, though it buries it here under the cover of looking at the relationship between cities and biodiversity. On the whole, existing cities do not appear as undergoing urbanization, turning most of the focus to the "under-researched cities in the global South" (8). The problem is "out there," as are the major opportunities for intervention.

The report then presents an instructive microhistory of urbanization and biodiversity. It explains that "most of the areas occupied by present cities were settled already by people in Neolithic times, when Europe was colonized by agriculturalists (9500 BC)." This "long history" in turn explains "why [Europe's] cities are often characterized by a higher species richness of plants and animals than the surrounding rural areas" and "may also be one factor explaining why European plants and animals *worldwide* tend to successfully establish in areas with dense human populations." Meanwhile, the regional section of the report concludes that "the roots of urban ecology, environmental protection, and sustainable urban development can be found in Europe" (18). But while biological aspects of this brief history may be true, as a long stream of academic work has repeatedly pointed out, environmentalism of the West hardly captures the entirety of environmentalism at global scales.[14] Moreover, such a framing swiftly de-emphasizes the reasons for the success of European plants and animals worldwide rooted in colonial projects, intentional introductions, and global circuits of trade and resource extraction, casting them instead as part of a natural history in which successful organisms adapted to living in cities emerged first in Europe, and then subsequently were successful, entirely on their own terms, on a worldwide scale.

One of the most interesting constructions addresses the unexpected and counterintuitive confluence of urban spaces and "rich biodiversity" (22). The report notes that many cities actually have "high species richness and several are even located within globally recognized 'biodiversity hotspots'" (22). It goes on to note that "while intact natural ecosystems harbor the richest biodiversity, remnants of pristine natural landscape . . . [and] managed and industrial landscapes are increasingly become refugia for biodiversity in cities" (22). One vivid example shows a giraffe outside Nairobi, Kenya, pictured against the skyscrapers, with the caption, "Nairobi National Park, 7 kilometers from the center of Nairobi, is renowned for its wildlife" (23).

Two issues discussed in chapter 1—the reliance of biodiversity on the species construct, and idea of biodiversity hotspots—see further development in the urban context, but with a newfound power of erasure. Whereas the term "species" in early biodiversity politics was used to highlight the "great unknowns" of nature, "species" here functions to privilege the form of the giraffe over both its declining numbers and the ecological/political contexts in which

Figure 4. Urban biodiversity: a giraffe in Nairobi National Park on the outskirts of the city. Copyright Ariadne Van Zandbergen.

it lives. What makes it possible to say that it is now *counter*-intuitive to think of cities and biodiversity as opposed is the species construct: the presence of a giraffe in Nairobi National Park validates the co-constitution of biodiversity and urbanization, while managing to ignore the depletion of giraffe populations in Kenya and the increasing pull of urban areas on the surrounding countryside and forest. Similarly, in the CBO report, biodiversity hotspots, which require that an area have *lost* 70 percent of its habitat in order to be a hotspot, are turned into positive features of cities that are near them.

"Urban biodiversity" does a great deal of flattening at a global level, emphasizing what cities have in common in the way that they interact with biodiversity. "Urban areas all over the planet are currently facing severe challenges" (7). But these reports make clear that this is especially an issue in countries where most future urban expansion will happen—countries with "low economic and human capacity, which . . . constrain the protection of biodiversity and management of ecosystem services."[15] The CBO report sounds the alarms for "Africa, China, and India" (strangely eliding countries and continents), and suggests that "maximizing the biodiversity potential through improved urban governance globally will require more comprehensive local knowledge" (8). This language, and the programs associated with it, are exemplary of what geographers and others have called green governmentality at a global scale, one aimed at expanding the conditions for deeper intervention into and regulation of the lives of people by governments and international agencies through the construction of an environmental problematic.[16] The knowledge gaps (and the activities undertaken to bridge them) that appear quite reasonable from the perspective of building scientific knowledge appear in this political frame as the very technique of governance, gathering up local knowledge in order to maximize life potentials of both human and nonhuman life.

In addition, as urban political ecologists have pointed out, nature in the city is produced through an uneven terrain of political and economic contestation, and is not simply a general, neutral object of governance.[17] In this respect, the neutral appearance of urban biodiversity in these texts as a provider of "ecosystem services" and a general public good obscures the ways that urban environments are themselves highly uneven and mobilized for powerful interests, both in who gets what services and the ways that urban biodiversity can be accessed. Urban nature, moreover, is not just what nature is left after building the city. Rather, as Matthew Gandy (2002) shows in his environmental history of New York City, the urbanization of nature is central to the process of urbanization itself, and produces a distinct "metropolitan nature," both within the city limits and in the surrounding areas. Urban biodiversity, in sum, should not be understood as a ahistorical *remainder* of urbanization, which reads human activities as agentic and nature as passive material. Rather, it is a distinct socionature itself, produced through power arrangements, political contestation, and profit, and involving the sometimes surprising actions of nonhuman nature as well.

Urban biodiversity also allows us to see how the logics and perspective of the Anthropocene affect the way we think about biodiversity. Whereas earlier research into biological diversity often used biophysical categories to organize its knowledge (e.g., the CBD's programs on forest biodiversity, inland water biodiversity, marine and coastal biodiversity, and mountain biodiversity), the perspective of urban biodiversity marks a complete confluence of a species-specific habitat with a biophysical category. It is not just that humans in Beijing, Rio de Janeiro, and New York are a keystone species of that habitat, in other words; rather, their life activities themselves are themselves the habitat. This self-reinforcing logic presents humans as part of the natural world, but loses ecology's power to work with the tension between human-made and natural, between human activities and ecosystems that are always above or outside whatever humans do. It lends a kind of permanence to urban centers, while forgoing the critique of much environmental politics past that cities are built on a fallen nature and urban spaces erase the wild.

Finally, although biodiversity itself references a pattern—the degrees of variety in an ecosystem, for example—and not an obviously material "thing," it is also striking how it comes to take on a kind of coherent, collective presence in these global policy texts that is very thing-like. In addition to biodiversity being a "point of view" (17), the CBO text often suggests that biodiversity itself does things. For example, the text reads that "[t]he contribution of biodiversity to [certain] vital ecosystem services often goes unacknowledged" (11). Likewise, "biodiversity in cities exposes people to nature" (11), where biodiversity is cast much like a television set that exposes people to other cultures. But unlike the kind of actants described by Bennett and Latour, which tend to be things with identifiable, materially discreet boundaries like earthworms or transfats, biodiversity's main material location as a second-order principle is textual. That is, while individual exemplars of species certainly have material existence, "biodiversity" as such is materially semiotic only in textual locations. And in these texts, biodiversity's "actancy" makes specific use of a reader's forgetting its textual location or eliding it with a material location in the world, and thus becomes ideological. Biodiversity, as a thing, now contributes to ecosystem services (itself a textual actant) in a newly organized urban nature, where difference produces services.

Resilience and Urban Biodiversity: Transition Towns Post-Sandy

Increasingly, urban biodiversity is also being linked to a set of ecological and political practices that cluster around the idea of *resilience*. As an ecological concept, resilience is a quality of an ecosystem that can increase or decrease. It refers to "the capacity of a system to absorb disturbance and reorganize while undergoing change, so as to still retain essentially the same function, structure, identity, and feedbacks."[18] Given that disturbances to ecosystems, such as forest fires, the arrival of a new species, or an unexpected change in geophysical cycles, are an everyday part of nature, resilience refers to the ability of a system to respond to that disturbance and right the ship. Resilience and biodiversity are generally argued to be directly related: the ability of an ecosystem to bounce back from a disturbance will be greater where there is greater biodiversity. As a conceptual tool of ecosystem management, resilience emphasizes the ways that human activities have negatively impacted the ability of ecosystems to sustain themselves, through activities like overfishing, logging, or habitat incursion, and to highlight the kinds of conservation actions that can prevent ecosystems from collapsing on themselves. Though it is not usually noted, resilience, in ecological terms, is not always a positive feature, as an ecosystem may be maintaining itself in a way harmful to other species. For example, a eutrophic lake—a lake with an algae bloom caused by an over-abundance of nitrogen—can be resilient to the efforts of fish species and other aquatic species to transform it.

Politically, resilience has been used by environmental movements seeking to transform the negative environmental politics of stopping problems into an active politics of building. The grassroots Transition Town movement, for example, adopted resilience as a key concept for addressing climate change. Started in the mid-2000s in the United Kingdom, Transition Towns aimed to create new ways for smaller communities concerned about peak oil and the overuse of fossil fuels to take concrete action by "being more prepared for a leaner future, more self-reliant, and prioritizing the local over the imported."[19] Frustrated both by the failure of global negotiations on emissions and by the tenor of despair that surrounds much of environmental politics, Transition Towns expressly adopted resilience as a key term because of the way it contrasts with the passivity of "sustainability" and the negativity of "environmental problems." In contrast, Transition Town meetings are "more like a revivalist meeting than a political campaign" and "offer a positive vision."[20] The movement has generated traction internationally, with self-declared Transition Towns in cities around the world.

As with earlier efforts to articulate biodiversity into politics in the 1990s, its expression in Transition Towns nests it within larger, more general formations of diversity. For Rob Hopkins (2008, 38–39), one of the leaders of the Transition Towns movement in England, any given system is diverse to the extent that it has a number of elements—"people, species, businesses, institutions, or sources of food"—but it is resilient to the extent that there are a higher number of connections between those elements. Emphasizing localism and self-reliance in preparation for a future scarcity is in many ways not new as a mode of environmental politics in developed countries. Peak oil augments or replaces fears of global population explosion, while the ecological metaphor of resilience becomes a socioecological principle that organizes the movement. In linking resilience to peak oil and the discourse of scarcity, Transition Towns manage to invoke a politics familiar to us from the security state—one in which a negative and fearful future is used to motivate a patriotic, self-affirming community that works to secure itself and its boundaries against external threats. Resilience and diversity, in the context of climate change and peak oil, is thus linked to security politics and the antipolitics of disaster.

In the New York and New Jersey area, after Hurricane Sandy in 2012, resilience was used in ways that emphasized the securing of cities vulnerable to the effects of climate change. Because cities in the Anthropocene are understood to be equivalent to the local ecosystem as such, the use of the ecological sense of resilience to characterize the political response to hurricanes finds no contradiction. An ecological response and a political response are made to seem equivalent—only politics here appears in a technical and depoliticized way, one in which a meaningful sense of contestation is foreclosed. Rebuilding and responding to climate change is posed as an act of security, and therefore not needing politics.

In New Jersey, headlines like "After Hurricane Sandy, Hoboken Joins United Nations' Making Cities Resilient Campaign" heralded a use of resilience that was largely about direct rebuilding to confront climate change,[21] and emphasizing infrastructure changes, such as installing additional water pumps to lessen the damage from future storms. The kind of resilience and the kind of socioecological transformation advocated by Transition Towns was absent here, giving way instead to a kind of Livestrong campaign mixed with post-9/11 security politics. In New York City, the discussion was somewhat different in content, though nonetheless containing the same kind of technical response. In a lengthy report entitled "A Stronger, More Resilient New York," issued after the storm, the mayor's office advocated a number of smaller-scale solutions, some of which linked resilience and ecology.[22] In addition to coastal fortifications and the use of natural areas to help control and direct storm surges, it endorsed the expansion of dune systems and wetlands—complete with biodiverse plant communities, in order to absorb rising waters—and the reestablishment of oyster beds in the harbor. The oyster beds help establish reefs, which in turn protect the city; as keystone species, they also anchor the development of a biodiverse and (ecologically) resilient ecosystem. Given that resilience here draws on its ecological meanings, we also might do well to think about the ways that resilience applies to ecosystems that are dysfunctional, and not just to the quality of their resilience.

While the mayor advocated some large-scale infrastructure, including the building of a brand-new neighborhood on landfill on the East River at a cost of $19.5 billion, the report steered clear of promoting the idea of building a massive wall around the city, via large-scale storm barriers and sea gates, citing exorbitant cost and time. At the same time, missing from the discussion were substantive discussion or recognition about the ways that Hurricane Sandy disproportionately affected poorer residents of New York and the kind of infrastructure within which they encountered the storm. Resilience, the front of the report says in bold letters, is synonymous with "tough." Resilience in post-Sandy New York City managed to mash plans for new material infrastructure with an ecological sense of adaptation to external perturbations and reference it all to a kind of postpolitical community driven by a quasi-permanent form of emergency management.

Finally, in ways that echo some of the fusion of cultural and biological diversity in World Heritage Sites, resilience has also been used to anchor new and sometimes uncomfortable hybrid formations of the human and the natural. For example, the Resilience Alliance, an international network of researchers aimed at generating and applying resilience theory, stretches the concept directly across social and ecological systems. On the one hand, biodiversity makes ecological systems resilient by preventing exogenous shocks from undermining the overall function of the system. It provides "functional redundancy," for example, providing multiple species that undertake the same kinds of ecological tasks. On the other hand, in a rather breathtaking parallel between species diversity and stakeholder diversity, the website states: "When the management of a resource is shared by a diverse group of stakeholders (e.g., local resource users, research scientists, community members with traditional knowledge, government representatives, etc.), decision-making is better informed and more options exist for testing policies."[23] For them, a social-ecological system consists of an ecosystem, simply with the added human capacity for learning, anticipation, and future planning. Diversity—from species to stakeholders—generates resilient socioecological systems.

In sum, biodiversity is a second-order principle that is generative of resilience, but is still intimately tied to securing—the boundaries of the city, the boundaries of the transition town, and the capacity for regeneration.

City Natures

Whereas previous discussions about nature in cities often emphasized the need for adding new nature as a way to improve the quality of human life—planting trees, building parks, and creating green spaces, all in the service of improving public health or as temporary escape from the pressures of work—a significant part of the urban biodiversity framing emphasizes the positive presence of already-existing biodiversity in cities, and urges us to see cities as beautiful and ecologically sound parts of nature. In an article on New York City as an ecological hot spot, journalist Robert Sullivan notes that a survey of bird species in Jamaica Bay Wildlife Refuge, which sits along the edge of John F. Kennedy International Airport in Queens, New York City, showed that it contained more bird species than Yellowstone and Yosemite combined. Here again, "counting species" becomes an important shorthand for marking biodiversity, and gesturing to the idea that, as Sullivan (2010, 2) puts it, "nature is . . . plentiful" and "New York is again a capital of nature." But it also masks the fundamentally *different* nature that is now there. While Sullivan notes that the megafauna of Manhattan have of course disappeared, he writes that "nature as a whole—the ecosystem that is the harbor—never went away." Using the metric of species, and the degrees of difference among them as a barometer of nature's well-being, this manages to gloss over entirely the massive geophysical transformation of Mannahatta into Manhattan and the destruction of the habitat for all of the major species that once lived there, such as bears, mountain lions, and minks.[24]

Perhaps this new ecosystem might simply be read as occupying a different equilibrium point, one that is not better or worse but simply lateral. Here, humans would be the keystone species who create fitness landscapes conducive to urban coyotes but not to wolves, create reserves for birds next to the landing strips for airplanes, and generate powerful mechanisms for determining the inclusion and exclusion of species in cities. But the evidence of human impact on natural processes suggests that we cannot see urban spaces in isolation in this way. As the limits to the "hotspots" approach to conservation has shown, we cannot treat nature—or cities—as isolated islands of biodiversity, and simply assume that they will continue to be diverse. Cities too are part of broader ecological systems that are (at least) regional, and increasingly are seen as continental in scale. For every effort to see the plant diversity in Central Park as evidence of rich biodiversity, the nesting of New York inside a massive swathe of urban and suburban development along the eastern seaboard and its pull of resources from across the planet suggests that biodiversity needs to have an appropriately large scale in order to be a meaningful gauge of ecological well-being. Birds in Jamaica Bay need to migrate, wolves that might hold red deer populations in check need a habitat, and areas that generate food and water for the city require wild nature to prosper. Urban biodiversity, if seen as decoupled from the socionatures around it, is a poor scale through which to see these problems. Created to avoid this very problem, biodiversity here functions to enable a process of shifting baselines.

For some commentators, the biodiversity in Jamaica Bay is powerful evidence of the need to see nature and culture as intertwined. Urban biodiversity is not all doom and gloom, on these accounts, and is more than a masquerade that facilitates ongoing ecological destruction. Rather, it represents a shift to trying to reconnect people to the biodiversity in front of them, and to create new categories for environmental politics, such as the urban wilds.[25] Unlike campaigns to save the Amazonian rainforest of the 1980s, this move tries to bring nonhuman life closer, forcing us to confront the nature in which we live and the array of human and nonhuman life that makes up urban landscapes. From this perspective, urban biodiversity can be a transformative category of practice that permits a politics across species lines. Steve Hinchliffe et al. argue that this "politicized ecology" is especially effective when it undercuts the general idea of species by promoting engagements with actual individual creatures and when it loosens the reliance on science as the sole mode of representing nature in liberal political systems.[26] Which species adapt to the urban landscape also shows the importance of material design and the unintentional and intentional ways it acts to determine fitness landscapes.[27] Rooftops never intended to select some species over others nevertheless do just that.

Rather than seeing nature only "out there" in wilderness areas, and humans in the city as apart from nature, Colin Jerolmack (2013, 236) likewise suggests that by better appreciating the "contaminated" biodiversity in the city, we can start to see the social and the natural as intertwined. Urban biodiversity, he argues in his study of the global pigeon, is a powerful way to place ourselves into the natural world again, while recognizing that nature is always socially constituted. At the same time, he notes that this suggests a paradox for conservation, in that the very reason we often conserve nature is because we think of it as transcendent or outside of us. To overcome this paradox, he urges us to rethink urbanism as a practice, to recognize that it is a fundamentally interspecies dance that makes up urban social order and urban spaces. While rethinking the city in these terms is a powerful way to break down the idea that cities are in some way outside of ecological relations, what it means for interspecies relations—or human interactions with nature—*outside* the city is somewhat more vexed. If urban biodiversity allows us to forget the extinction of major species and the transformation and conversion of habitats—processes that are, likewise, a matter of both social and natural factors—then urban biodiversity may allow for moments of connection with other species in the concrete jungle, but do little to create impetus for significant action to stop biodiversity loss elsewhere. The presence of the social in nature does not mean that vast wilderness areas should not exist, in other words, especially if they contribute to a richer flourishing of species and ecosystems. Instead, the same imaginary that sees cross-species urban entanglements, as Jerolmack puts it, as a positive socionature, can equally well admit new socially constituted wilderness areas, areas that are not preserved for being transcendent or outside, but as areas that are linked to urban areas, urban thinking, and multispecies flourishing.

In this strand of urban biodiversity, which validates cities as acceptable and even wonderful spaces of nature, the conceptual mobility of biodiversity as an ecological concept is important in facilitating its political slipperiness. Ecologically, biodiversity scales up and down, from global perspectives to local ones, finding species richness in a tree as well as a continent; this in turn enables the political (or antipolitical, to be more precise) claim that New York City is actually just fine as an ecological center. Biodiversity's mobility across taxonomic kingdoms—from animal to plant—also functions in a similar way, allowing the diversity of species in plant communities in a city to stand in as a marker of a well-achieved green society. In a sense, then, its mobility proves to be both a source of its strength to make us see the invisible (plant diversity) and a source of its weakness, in understaring the power of urbanization to eradicate ecosystems.

Biodiversity by Design

I have highlighted so far three strands of urban biodiversity, all three of which have sought to do more than describe species loss or point to how biodiversity works. The first, found largely within the global policy discussion, emphasizes urbanization (rather than urban-ness), and its connection with biodiversity lies in the impetus it creates for expanding green governance projects.

A second strand is built through a connection with resilience, where it has been both a means to buttress existing processes of securitization for states and cities, and part of a civil society effort to counteract the negative politics of environmentalism. A third strand has used urban biodiversity as a way to tell us that cities really are ecologically OK, encouraging urban dwellers to see the nature in front of them, and suggesting the beginnings of a new urbanism that thinks of its ecology locally. Biodiversity is not the sole point of reference in these three strands, but acquires distinct meanings as it connects with other discourses such as resilience or urbanization, and loses other meanings as it becomes re-formed into a generalized "diversity." While differing in some important ways, all three strands have involved a positive politics of biodiversity that go beyond conservation, and reach instead into remaking the ways that people think about the conduct of environmental politics, and about environment and politics themselves as terms in the Anthropocene.

These trends reach their most explicit zenith (or nadir, depending on your perspective) in "biodiversity by design"—that is, the construction of spaces in ways that are explicitly supposed to be conducive to species diversity, and in some cases, where biodiversity itself is brought in. Such explicit and intentional planning of biodiversity is somewhat more common in the United Kingdom and Europe, places where wild nature was overrun long ago and planned nature is not seen as the same kind of contradiction as it might be in the United States.[28] One major planning association publication in the UK that focuses on biodiversity and urban planning promises to show ways that "biodiversity can be created, protected, and enhanced" in the explicit service of "sustainable communities."[29] Self-consciously nesting itself into the UK Biodiversity Action Plan, which signatories agreed to create under the CBD, the document goes on to explore ways to design urban communities so as to maximize the benefits that biodiversity can deliver. A variety of master-planning ideas are suggested, ranging from street trees to communal doorstep spaces that help create "habitat mosaics" and "microclimate conditions" that will encourage nature to colonize areas appropriately.

Brought to the American context, biodiversity by design lends itself neatly to greenwashing, through direct commodification and commercial packaging. So-called conservation developments aim to connect biodiversity protection and sustainability with the classic American subdivision development (built from scratch, of course). The development of Harmony, Florida, for example, was established in 2002, with its founding documents containing explicit provisions for "harmony with nature" and "minimizing the circumstances that lead to conflict between humans and wildlife."[30] The development works to keep out invasive species that destroy Florida's biodiversity, educate homeowners about local species diversity and how it impacts their yard planting, and emphasizes a green lifestyle of organic foods and energy-efficient houses. Meanwhile, serious guides to "conserving biodiversity in subdivision development" offer design and management strategies to maintain biodiversity in areas zoned for development.[31]

While its connection to services and resilience suggests a self-negating quality, the focus on urban biodiversity ultimately can bring political questions more clearly to the fore—not about where we look for nature, now, but about the *quality* of our interactions with other species. What kind of engagements with coyotes—coyotes in the Bronx Zoo, or in the park? Diversity of species, but in what kind of ecosystem? Botanical gardens or parks, or the unused spaces between railroad ties? Do we want anything threatening at all? And how do such commitments interact with political institutions and governance? The simple presence or absence of species cannot answer these questions, nor can greater or lesser diversity of species.

Rewilding

Rewilding seems at first glance to oppose many of the ideas that urban biodiversity policy making and conservation embrace, and in some ways is its polar opposite. It eschews the small-scale intimacy of urban biodiversity in favor of a continental scale. It emphasizes a nature full of wild processes over a nature steered by technical management. It focuses on the areas least populated by humans, and aims to keep them that way.

In the most general terms, rewilding is the transformation or restoration of what has been domesticated, civilized, or tamed to its previous, wild state. Yet the variety of practices that are attached to it are surprisingly layered. In the North American context, rewilding references a conservation strategy that was summed up in its early days as "cores, corridors, and carnivores"—cores of protected wilderness areas, corridors for wildlife to move to and from those areas, and carnivores such as wolves and jaguars that are reintroduced into ecosystems.[32] In their early work on rewilding, Soule and Noss thought of these top species largely as predators, but rewilding has moved toward "keystone species," a broader category that refers to the species that appear to hold the key to the vitality of an ecosystem, whether carnivorous large species or herbivores like beavers or elephants.[33]

Whereas urban biodiversity is, almost by definition, an ecosystem dominated by one species (humans), the primary engine of change in rewilding is the reintroduction or protection of keystone species in large sprawling ecosystems that act as downward regulatory forces in the ecosystem, in what ecologists call trophic cascades.[34] The reintroduction of wolves to Yellowstone National Park in 1995, for example, triggered a wide series of changes in the Yellowstone ecosystem.[35] The elk population started to drop, due both to the direct effects of wolves hunting them as prey and to many of the indirect effects caused by the wolves' presence. But just as important, the behavior of elk also changed in response to wolves, as they avoided areas where they could be caught easily, such as riverbanks, and they stopped eating the vegetation in those areas. Left alone to regrow, the aspen, willow, and cottonwood trees that lined the valleys started to grow again. These trees, in turn, shaded the water, allowing fish and other species to increase in population, while species of birds who lived by the waterside also saw increasing numbers. Beaver and bison both benefited, while flooding patterns changed due to the roots of the trees holding the soil in. Finally, because wolves sometimes hunt coyotes or push them out of their territory, the prey of the coyotes (such as rabbits and mice) was now available for other species to hunt. In short, by focusing on the reintroduction of the wolf, with an adequate core wilderness area, major ecological changes occurred that on the whole strengthened biodiversity.

This is not to say that the presence of a keystone species is a guarantee for ecosystem equilibrium, or a "balance of nature," an ecological theory that was widely discredited by the end of the twentieth century. Like most complex systems, ecosystems are prone to emergent effects and unexpected points of instability, with substantial variation in the populations of various species over time, depending both on dynamics internal to the ecosystem and on external factors such as climate or the arrival of new species. But unlike the category of endangered species, which has guided environmental legal fights in the United States for many decades, keystone species goes beyond a politics based on saving one species, such as the famous spotted owl controversy in the Pacific Northwest, and provides a positive ecological argument about interspecies relationships and the conditions under which biodiversity can be generated.

Whatever its ecological merits, rewilding still requires a politics, however. In part, rewilding takes up some of the wilderness-based environmentalism of earlier decades, though it backs down from the grander plans to roll back civilization and establish wilderness across the United States. Some of those impulses remain strong, however. As Dave Foreman (2004), former Earth-First! activist and now head of the U.S.-based Rewilding Institute writes, "To halt mass extinction and to have an enduring resource of wilderness, we need to protect and restore sprawling wild landscapes with linked populations of keystone species, where natural ecological and evolutionary processes can roll on unhindered into wilderness-forever" (130). Whereas wilderness areas in the United States are currently a small fraction of the overall landscape, Foreman proposes a much broader wildlands network, based on four "megalinkages" that run the length and breadth of North America.

Whereas wilderness advocates in the 1980s and 1990s were accused, unfairly in some cases, of authoritarianism and ecofascism, rewilding advocates seem to have tacked toward a more politically interesting blend of bottom-up politics and ecological views at a grand scale.[36] Foreman's book on rewilding in North America walks through the fine-grained policy details involved in the creation and protection of wild areas, and emphasizes the need for bottom-up alliances across a range of political positions. George Monbiot, while discussing some vast changes to the British landscape, like reversing centuries of running sheep, makes it clear that rewilding cannot be an abstract concept applied around the world, but depends greatly on context and widespread popular support.

The most prominent plan for rewilding in the United States is the Yellowstone to Yukon (Y2Y) initiative, a corridor that runs from Wyoming to northern Canada. While a variety of keystone species reintroductions have been under way in the United States for many years, such as the gray wolf, the Y2Y initiative focuses on an already-present species (e.g., grizzly bears), and puts its emphasis on rewilding the geography of the corridor. Yet this rewilding initiative so far remains largely on paper. Like the other continent-wide proposals from rewilding proponents, they aim to think big, but encounter the fact that these big spaces are already deeply institutionally captured by local, state, and federal governments, and carved up by various landowners, whether ranchers, mining interests, or logging companies.

On its face, this version of rewilding is an entirely different strategy than the focus on urban biodiversity. Its scale is grand in design; its nature is "great, not good" (to reverse the Nature Conservancy's framing). Urban areas may play a role in rewilding plans, establishing areas that are waypoints on migratory routes, for example; but on the whole, rewilding's emphasis on corridors steers away from the heart of cities. Moreover, the ecological role of humans in the ecosystems of cities is as a dominant species, not a keystone species. Humans can, and have been, keystone species in other sorts of ecosystems—that is, they have crucial top-down effects on the ecosystem, but this requires a much smaller population of humans relative to the ecosystem.[37]

All of this, however, depends on being able to reference what the desired ecosystem looks like. How far back in time should one look for keystone species, for example? While the United States killed off its predators fairly recently

Figure 5. Map of four major North American wildlife corridors, the core areas targeted for rewilding by the Rewilding Institute. Four Continental Megalinkages. Wildlands Network Map by Todd Cummings/Kurt Menke.

and can look to them for a restoration baseline,[38] others have suggested looking further back in time. In a series of controversial scientific papers that stirred up public discussion in the United States, a group of conservation biologists advocated what they called "Pleistocene rewilding" in the United States.[39] Using the Pleistocene era as a baseline, the authors proposed restoring a variety of large vertebrates to the Great Plains, where populations are declining and land is becoming available. Where species were extinct, such as camelids, they proposed local "proxies" like the Bactrian camel. Where no local proxies were available as substitutes, they proposed bringing in species from another continent, such as African cheetahs, elephants, and lions.

The practice of rewilding has a number of important contextual factors that do not permit a uniform global strategy to be applied. In addition to the vast differences in ecological systems and trajectories across different contexts, rewilding also encounters political histories in different ways. The European rewilding effort is rooted in a significantly different ecopolitical history than the American one, for example.[40] Major predators have been absent for longer, to take one key difference, while the history of wilderness preservation has been minimal. When rewilding plays out, both the wilderness reserves and the keystone predators are very new introductions; the ecosystems are engineered on the assumption of *replaceability*. In the Oostvaardersplassen in the Netherlands, a privately held park, a rewilding effort has brought back species to substitute for the aurochs, a breed of cattle extinct since the 1600s—instead of aurochs, Heck cattle (famously a breed that the Nazis endeavored to reverse engineer), red deer from Scotland, and horses from Poland.[41] In short, rewilding ecology here was the very opposite of long-standing European efforts to focus on "native species," focusing solely on species from a much earlier time that function together in an ecosystem, but that can be imported from other geographical areas. In the face of falling and disappeared biodiversity, Oostvaardersplassen represents the chance to *make biodiversity anew*. Here, rewilding shares a politics in significant ways with urban biodiversity, in its top-down, design-heavy form of control.

Rewilding and urban biodiversity also tend to part ways on the issue of shifting baselines. Urban biodiversity embraces both the richness of nature in the center of human habitation and a future aimed at a pragmatic, functioning nature, able to provide for humans. Rewilding advocates, by contrast, suggest that ecosystems do have discernible stages of quality, and that those stages matter not just in an aesthetic sense, but in a pragmatic sense and sometimes a moral one. It is precisely because humans cannot easily and completely engineer complex ecosystems from the bottom-up that they have value.

But perhaps aiming at the *restoration* of an ecosystem, of whatever epoch, is the wrong way to think about rewilding. That is, perhaps the "wild" that is involved in rewilding is not about particular species, or a particular baseline arrangement of nature. Rather, it might be better thought of as endeavoring to restore a *process*, one where there is a chance for many species to inter-act—to create ecological systems that are more frequently self-regulating and complex.[42] Though there is no such teleology in ecology—ecosystems do not always become more complex over time and then stay at that peak level—there is a greater chance for such ecosystems when humans step back from their excessive influence on landscapes. Rewilding, in the sense of allowing more ecological processes to unfold in tandem with human actions with the aim of letting new ecosystems emerge in some places and permitting well-established ones to continue, is a kind of wilding that departs from the way that we have tended to think about wilderness. It is not about leaving nature alone, since wildness of this kind requires active political decision making and intervention on the part of humans. But neither is it about managing nature and the people who happen to be caught in it, which grants a kind of CEO-like position to humans. Instead, it looks more like a form of socio-nature, one explicitly aimed to create significant opportunities for wildness to emerge in order to generate more trophic diversity, and is therefore neither "managed" nor "wild."[43]

Urban biodiversity and rewilding are apparently different, and even oppo-site sides of the same coin. The former emphasizes the nature we have in cit-ies, not the nature that once was, and urges us to focus on changing the way that city centers act as a magnet for material resources. The latter emphasizes continent-wide conservation corridors and the reintroduction of important species, or substitutes for them, to generate working ecosystems. Yet there are also heterodox strands to both sets of practices. Some urban biodiversity work focuses on the amazing capacity of nature to outrun designs, to con-stantly innovate and evolve in situations where it seems impossible for non-human presence to thrive. Rewilding advocates, meanwhile, offer a variety of strategies, some of which are more interested in wilderness-by-design than others. Some rewilding is wrapped up with troubling historical concepts of wilderness, especially in its connection to forms of nationalism, whiteness, and masculinity, as well as its pristine variant in which humans are (ostensi-bly) absent. On the whole, however, even the most ardent hands-off propo-nents of rewilding are involved in depth with a variety of planning initiatives, and awareness of the cultural and political history of wilderness has also changed over the past decades.

In comparing these two practices, the relevant opposition is ultimately not between planning on one hand and free nature on the other, as if the mere suggestion of contact between the two necessarily means contamination. While American sensibilities about wilderness may once have involved the fantasy that it was a nature pure and untouched by human hands, the reality of the Wilderness Act of 1964 was that wilderness required active political and social design. In the decades since William Cronon's much-discussed piece on wilderness as a social construction, it has become standard critical practice to examine wilderness practices as politically charged and infused with social values. Cronon's (1995) argument has been somewhat overapplied, overemphasizing the social construction of wilderness at the expense of its materiality.[44] Cronon himself gestures to this at the end of the chapter, writing about his ambivalence toward critiquing wilderness and making clear that "the autonomy of nature seems to [be] an indispensable corrective to human arrogance" and that wilderness, for all its troubles, has also fostered "responsible behavior" by articulating "deep moral values" about the nonhuman world (87). While the overall argument is aimed at showing how the idea of wilderness has been socially constructed in different ways over time, he does not want to jettison wilderness making as a practice; rather, he suggests that the task is to find a way to find wildness *both* in the wilderness *and* in the places where we live (89–90).

Bringing this point to bear on both urban biodiversity and rewilding proposals, the issues are therefore not limited to how these visions of nature— biodiversity by design—construct the natural world. Instead, they include the ways that human–nonhuman systems can constitute themselves given significant uncertainties over possible futures. Here, rewilding advocates call on the knowledge of ecology and conservation biology—some draw on a map of nature that seems to have worked in the past and then reverse-engineer it; others emphasize a more experimental approach. Urban biodiversity takes a more experimental position with nature, looking for new points of stability. Both require experimentation in ecological worlds, where nonhuman species, their affiliations, their proclivities, and their slight transformations are also part of what count. Social constructions do not take place in material vacuums, in other words, but in embedded contexts, and the social planning of nature entails a kind of conversation with the space, the materials, and the species involved, determining its contours, limits, and possibilities, alongside the creation and deployment of political ideas about that space.[45]

The success of ideas requires both the transformation of human political subjectivity (and the institutions within which they are nested) and a material accommodation with the fluctuations of the nonhuman world. As urban bio-diversity advocates note, a significant aspect of emphasizing nature in the city is that it can transform urban attitudes toward nature. What John Muir wrote of wilderness areas—that they "provide a refuge for weary urban souls"—might well apply to the microrefuge of an individual species, or of an urban forestland. But as a political term, rewilding might also be interpreted in the way I have been reading biodiversity: as a sign that organizes and directs relations that are both ecological and political, and attaching to other political concepts along the way. If biodiversity's attachment to 1990s multicultural-ism traded on liberal notions of difference, its full partnership with postmod-ern capitalism in the 2000s culminated with ecosystem services and dollar valuations of nature; and its connection to the security state beginning in the 2000s played out through ecological resilience, what is rewilding as a mode of thinking about biodiversity and generating new political ecologies starting to attach to?

Undoubtedly, many of those previous points of attachment will continue within rewilding projects. Yet rewilding is also generating new points of attach-ment. Its relationship to biodiversity tends to emphasize trophic diversity rather than species diversity, moving in part away from some of the problems that plague the latter. Trophic diversity is based on the food chain or food web, within which there are a number of trophic levels, or positions. Emphasizing diversity of trophic levels puts a premium on expanding the number of levels that are present in the food chain, which in turns generates new opportunities for inter-species interactions and greater opportunities for systems to self-constitute.[46] Its emphasis on diverse systems producing emergent outcomes that are largely mutually beneficial and the enhancement of individual opportunities as the goal of system-steering certainly have some affinity with principles of market organization, and are likely to continue to draw on the already-existing dis-cursive alliances between economy and ecology (such as ecosystem services and economic valuations of nature). Trophic diversity nonetheless promotes a kind of intervention that falls between a completely hands-off approach and a direct form of outcome management.

A tension that remains involves who, precisely, will be allowed to engage in rewilding activities. To the extent that it retains a firm technical manage-rialism in deciding the proper progress of species reintroductions, rewilding will remain an activity of the state, with the input of approved conservation organizations and mediated by science. Citizens may engage in rewilding activ-ities in places like Harmony, Florida, but in their backyards and after appro-priate education. There are a few groups, mostly on the margins, undertaking rewilding in other ways. Guerrilla gardening often involves planting vegetable gardens on unused parcels of land, but others use the practice to plant native species in public spaces, thus contributing to a smaller scale, bottom-up version of rewilding. But just as frequently, people dump unwanted pets into wild areas, leading to problems like the Burmese pythons overrunning the Florida Everglades.

Toward Wilding

How, then, might we start to square rewilding and urban biodiversity in order to better understand the context of biodiversity by design? I have emphasized already some of their common points of overlap and divergence, but I want to conclude by considering what kind of politics could bind them together.

Much depends on the problems one sees with the political. On the one hand, neither rewilding nor urban biodiversity seems to lead to serious organized, collective action that creates concrete social movements and positive platforms. To the extent that the problem lies in the depoliticizing trends of contemporary biopolitics and in the loss of true political contestation and organized politics, neither development is likely to challenge such moves. When the state does intervene for biodiversity by design, it is on the basis of a technical, scientific managerialism, in the name of saving life itself.

Other parts of rewilding and urban biodiversity that emphasize a transformation of individual political subjects are equally problematic from this perspective. The brief encounters that individuals have with biodiversity in the city, or the encounters that individuals have with wilderness and wildness that rewilding projects base some of their political clout on are likewise a small-scale politics that do not tackle depoliticization particularly well. Other versions of rewilding such as anarcho-primitivism that aim to rewild not just nature but people—what Bookchin (1995) dismissively called "lifestyle anarchism"—likewise seem to forgo directed collective action in favor of forms of self-fashioning.[47]

One of the most intricate defenses of this kind of self-fashioning comes from Jane Bennett's (1994) book on Henry David Thoreau, in which she argues that self-fashioning was not a retreat from politics for Thoreau, but a considered way to limit the normalizing effects of political life.[48] She suggests that Thoreau thinks of the wild as "the pesky remainder produced in the wake of human attempts to organize or combat or know or love nature" (53). As such, nature (or the universe) is not unified or harmonious, but is rather a "heteroverse," which suggests how "heterogeneous elements intersect or influence one another" and where the perfection of nature "lies not in completeness but in the richness of its heterogeneity" (53). Connecting to this heterogeneity forms the basis of a better democratic politics. Thoreau was deeply skeptical of the state, of course, which "never made men a whit more just; and, by means of their respect for it, even the well-disposed are daily made the agents of injustice" (86).

The top-down politics of biodiversity by design would pose similar worries for Thoreau. But as Bennett points out, he was equally skeptical of organized collective action *against* the state (such as social movements, opposition parties, or group activism) because it was a "crucible of normalization" and creates a mood that is antithetical to right thinking—"explicitly public and deliberately inflammatory in character" (86). Wildness, then, requires various "techniques of the self," involving practices by which the individual makes herself through thoughtful encounters with nature producing something extra in the individual. In short, while occasional participation in politics is necessary and important, to think about rewilding means to be only occasionally engaged with politics, and to focus instead on the more Herculean task of fighting the normalizing effects of social life. Self-fashioning, then, can be embedded in political participation, and takes place in parallel with politics, not in opposition to it or abdication from it.

In the end, rewilding can be not only a technique for generating ecological reserves but also a parallel and necessary activity of encouraging individuals to remake themselves through encounters with the nonhuman nature that exceeds human design. From a cosmopolitical perspective on politics, one emphasizing the importance of making politically potent assemblages of humans and nonhumans as a counterweight to depoliticization, both urban biodiversity and rewilding have significant elements of such a parallel politics of ecology and self. This politics is perhaps starting to emphasize a different opposition—not a spatial one between wilderness and urban, or between nature and culture, but rather between wildness and technical. What this political practice might require, then, is a wilding in the present, across natural, personal, and political lines, rather than a rewilding by looking backward and away from politics.

Conclusion   Agency Revisited and the
Future of Biodiversity

THIS BOOK HAS TRACED THE POLITICS of global biodiversity from its inception in the 1980s to the end of the 2000s. Some aspects of biodiversity—including the centrality of species, the generative power of abstract differences, and conceptual scalability and contextual mobility—stayed relatively constant over that period, providing continuity to the concept and to the practices associated with it. So too did much of the narrative and reality of species loss and the general decline of biodiversity at global scales. While these aspects localized in particular ways, they nonetheless provided a somewhat stable reference point for conservation policy and environmental politics. Part of what I argued, however, is that excessive focus on this stability hides the plurality of ways that biodiversity has worked in practice. Treating biodiversity only as an ecological referent hides the diversity of the politics that have worked through it and misses the ways that biodiversity, in turn, has affected some of the political discourses with which it has had significant contact. Taken as a jointly political-ecological sign, this book has shown some of the variation in global biodiversity formations, ranging from its affiliation with the politics of multiculturalism, to biopolitical projects of governing life, to the politics of security and resilience.

The rise of biodiversity as an object of global environmental governance has meant attachment to things well beyond conservation—as enshrined in the CBD, biodiversity more clearly became a natural and economic resource, attached to national sovereignty. Its attachment to cultural diversity was part of its discursive strength, positioning it against the flattening power of globalization and framing it as a kind of identity politics. That link also resulted in a new formation: the bioculturally diverse World Heritage Site, where the difficult politics of hybridizing natural and cultural, global and local, and Western and indigenous played out in uneven ways. Later, its move to the urban context, and its partially twinned practice of managed rewilding, completed a turn in biodiversity politics that increasingly has accepted the so-called "end of nature" argument, leaving wilderness and wildness politics behind and resigning environmental politics to the management of the leftovers of the Anthropocene.

What are the implications of the past few decades of the politics of global biodiversity for the important questions of this book? This concluding chapter revisits both of the touchstones set out in the introduction, the first regarding a set of theoretical questions surrounding political agency, and the second about where environmental politics and biodiversity might go in the future.

Agency: Freedom, Effects, Resistance

The changing configurations of stability and change over three decades of biodiversity politics could be read through the lenses of structure and agency, where the stable components of biodiversity discourse were forms of social structure within which, and against which, social individuals exercised varying degrees of agency. More broadly, in political science, the politics of global biodiversity can be understood as taking place within the structural constraints of the interstate system or the global political economy, and it is within these structural contexts that the agency of states, individuals, scientists, and non-state actors can be pinpointed. The same can be said for the lack of agency in significantly addressing biodiversity loss at the international level, due partly to the constraints of the state system and the way in which that structure shapes the interests of states and limits their capacity to reach effective environmental agreements. Agent-structure thinking of this kind in political science and international relations has tended to understand agency as the degree of autonomy or *freedom* from deterministic structure, opposing them in roughly zero-sum terms.[1] The free decision-making capacity of an individual or group is set against political or social constraints or structure. The goals of theorizing agency in tandem with structure are to figure out the constraints under which agents act or to highlight the ways in which microlevel actions produce structural constraints that then rebound back onto agents.

In more recent revisions, the relation of agency and structure are cast slightly differently as mutually constituting, not diametrically opposed and in different locations. Central to Anthony Giddens's notion of agency, to take one prominent influence on international relations, is the duality of structure. Structure is not something external to agents, either in the sense of an outside constraint or in the sense that it is a product of previously existing agents. Instead, the structural properties of society are "both medium and outcome" of that which they organize, and as such, "the rules and resources drawn upon in the production and reproduction of social action [agency] are at the same time the means of system reproduction."[2] Structure, moved inside the heads and experiences of human agents, is "not to be equated with constraint, but is both constraining and enabling," and it is in this sense that, to paraphrase Alexander Wendt, structure is effectively a cultural formation that is what agents make of it.[3]

This reformulation of structure is important in connecting agent-level processes to the structures that constrain them. But if agency is not to be completely dissolved into structure, there must be an agentic (enabled) dimension of agency that remains a version of autonomy against power. Walking something of a tightrope, agency for Giddens, on the one hand, is bound up with the reproduction of its structured conditions; on the other hand, "agency concerns events of which an individual is the perpetrator, in the sense that individuals could, at any phase in a given sequence of conduct, have acted differently."[4] Agency continues to exist in the ongoing exercise of individual choice against socially determining structures. One might understand the choices of conservation biologists to undertake a mission-oriented form of science as an exercise of individual agency on these terms, then. The actions of individual states in negotiating the CBD can be seen as states working within, and constituted by, the distribution of power and interests in the international system. Yet the agentic dimension of agency here is still not far from the sovereign liberal agent acting against structure, in which it is difficult to reconcile the highly social nature of the individual with the assertion of sovereign autonomy and interests. While some forms of sovereign agency may be politically desirable in liberal political traditions, its application has often been uneven, importing assumptions about race, gender, and class to decide who counts as a sovereign agent and who doesn't. Equally, it does not seem to be an adequate ontology of political life, which appears much more deeply social than even nuanced versions of sovereign agency allow.

Instead, in this book I have approached agency as a *distributed* phenomenon, highlighting the ways that things, ideas, people, and species have had agency through their relations with other entities. This sense of agency is different from the one found in agent-structure thinking in international relations. Rather than emphasizing freedom or autonomy, agency here means the *ability to have effects through relations* and the ability to gather in, or enroll, other agents in networks that help produce those effects. Much of the agency found in the context of biodiversity is of this relational sort. The way that biodiversity, as a productive sign, has changed and created effects over time makes it agentic, particularly if we follow how it materializes across different locations, whether texts (ranging from the CBD to scientific articles to conservation treatises), physical sites (such as the Brazilian Amazon, the Australian desert, and New York City), or technological places (like the online Catalogue of Life). Uluru Rock, in this sense of agency, might also be understood as having agency in its encounter with biodiversity politics, world heritage, and the emergence of biodiverse life forms at its base.

There is a another mode of agency that has emerged over the course of the book, one centered on *resistance*. While easier to see in nonhumans than freedom, it is also more difficult to think about than the creation of effects. Resistance characterized some of the escapes of nonhuman life in the biodiversity census and the concept of species itself. It also arose in the limit cases of Uluru Rock and Meteora, as resistance in a material sense, which as Andrew Pickering (1992) has suggested, constitute an important and perhaps agentic part of scientific knowledge projects. Ideas themselves also seemed to display qualities of obdurateness over time, showing a resistance to change even in spite of evidence to the contrary.

To what extent is resistance to constraint or to hegemonic power a plausible way of approaching agency, whether human or nonhuman? This is an important political question because forms of political resistance are often understood as the exercise of agency, or at least as forms of creating the conditions of noninterference through which agency may be exercised.[5] If extended to biodiversity, forms of natural action can be understood as resistance to human action. Do these constitute political agency, and if so, in what sense?

On its own terms, agency as resistance is problematic in at least two ways. First, acts of resistance may be too deeply implicated with power to be properly understood as agentic. Resistance may be defined in opposition to the power it is resisting, where the terms of resistance reinscribe that which is being struggled against. Moreover, as Sabba Mahmood persuasively argues, resistance may also inscribe other forms of unfreedom, and as such, not represent agency-as-freedom at all.[6] Resistance to a form of cultural practice can manifest in ways that actually reduce agency. Mahmood points out the example of the young Bedouin women wearing lingerie as resistance to dominant social mores and parental authority structures, but also reinscribing new and different kinds of power relations (e.g., capitalist consumerism or urban bourgeois aesthetics). In short, although resistance may indicate agency, it need not do so.

The stipulation of interests for nonhumans is arguably even more difficult to establish than it is for most humans in most contexts. Since resistance requires a clear baseline of interests against which agentic capacity can be judged, it makes it difficult to interpret whether nonhuman resistance is agentic. Agency as resistance is also problematic because it can be a way of positing that there is a sovereign subject who should assert their desires, interests, and needs.[7] Yet it denies the social processes by which subjects are formed and the constitution of their interests by others. Agency as resistance largely assumes the inherence of interests and sovereign subjects in the first place, and this is again as difficult to establish, if not more so, for nonhuman life forms than for humans. Resistance, as a form of material resistance to human inquiries, ultimately looks much more like a kind of agency driven by an ability to have effects.

Using a somewhat different lexicon that fits more closely with the biotic conception of agency outlined at the beginning of the book, Judith Butler (1997) has argued that modern subject formation is itself a process that is deeply entwined with power. She suggests that humans are formed as subjects through a paradoxical social process of subjection where the subject is itself dependent for its existence on the very power that forms it in the first place (1, 11, 20). That is, the very condition of being (or becoming) a subject is the assumption of power; even more, this enactment of being a subject entails the production of a "passionate attachment" to subjection that is part of the condition of subjectivity (6, 9). As such, agency cannot be grounded in a resisting subject, or in fact a subject at all, at least not if one is concerned with having a kind of agency that is independent of power. Agency, in Butler's formulation, instead comes through the necessary iteration of the practices of subjection. Because these practices can never be exactly repeated, social meanings can change in their iteration. There is thus what Butler calls a "temporally based vulnerability" in the conditions of reproducing the self (12).[8] In these iterations, rather than agency-as-freedom, agency seems to effect newness in the world in ways that are unexpected or not determined by power. Such a formulation can lend itself to thinking about nonhuman agency as well, assuming that nonhumans can take part, in some way, in a world of social meanings where iteration can be agentic.

But there is an important paradox in Butler's formulation, which is that even though it is an interior subject that is enacting the practices and acting in the world, such a subject may never be able to directly experience or inhabit the agentic dimension of those practices. Butler thinks that power itself is what "fabricates the distinction between interior and exterior life (19). But if agency necessarily lies where power is not, then an interior experience of agency may not be able to take place at all, since to experience agency interiorly would be to enact an already-demarcated set of conditions of agency. In this sense, if agency actually happens for Butler, it seems to happen altogether somewhere beyond the interior experience of those who enact it, or on a plane of experience in which an interior/exterior distinction has no hold. Public weeping, pretenses of modesty, or veiling can be read as these kind of enacted practices.[9] It is in the repeated acts that the very desires of the interior self are created. Agency here is read not as something exercised from within, but as the embodied exterior acts *themselves*, which enable the freedom of the interior agent.

Such a plane of experience might be a useful place to consider the operation of agency for nonhuman life, though subject formation and subjectivity remain contested ideas when it comes to nonhumans. If the agentic dimension of agency is neither a capacity (as it is for the sovereign autonomous subject) nor experienced by the subject as such, it follows that agency could be enacted by nonhumans, living or otherwise, in a plane of social meaning or, to extend Butler, in a biosemiotic sphere in which living things engage with and are constituted by signs. Agency, on this account, does requires the presence of interiority (or embodied mind), but the interior "moment" in the circle of agency is significantly downplayed. It is exterior performances and social relationality that are the stuff of agency. It is the enactment and reenactment of practices over time that create and change social meanings, with agency taking place in each iteration. Being a human biodiversity subject in the ways considered in this book, for example, often involves this kind of agency—the exterior modality of agency involves practices like public defenses of reasons to value biodiversity, the regular invocation of crisis and loss, mourning for the loss of species and the destruction of nature, and the defense of difference as a generative force.[10] The major acts of environmental governance related to biodiversity—whether the once-per-decade international Earth Summits in Rio and Johannesburg, the declarations of the Decade of Biodiversity, or the greening of the language surrounding World Bank projects—also display a collective performance and collective agency with similar dynamics. Although they have been a relative failure in stopping biodiversity loss, they have not been failures at extending governance—indeed, the performance itself is precisely the point, and is the point at which agentic effects of these summits can be found.[11]

Each of these moments also involves a passionate attachment to the conditions of subjection, in Butler's terms: the terms of biodiversity loss as a management tool for conservation policy, the resignation to species loss, and the kinds of solutions that take global capitalism for granted, as something that biodiversity must enmesh itself in. Yet the fact that agency can be found through the iteration of practices (Butler's temporally based vulnerability) does not mean that all agentic aspects are somehow politically or ecologically desirable, or that all iterations are equally agentic in their microtransformations. There can be a fetishization of agency, partly involving the study of agency in contexts that appear politically favorable, much as norms in the study of international politics have tended to study the emergence of liberal norms.[12] Agency, by its nature, is more politically malleable than that. The emergence and existence of global biodiversity evinces a number of such agentic moments, and not all of them are for the good. A general appreciation of nonhuman agency, though necessary in opening the doors to the complexity of ecological politics, does not appear sufficient.

This iterative kind of agency is thicker in many ways than the agency of creating effects, and it also limits the sort of "things" that can be agentic to those able to have an interiority and those capable of engaging with semiotic processes in a significant way. While it remains an open question as to where such boundaries might be drawn, if at all, the focus on exteriorly performed and relational agency by living creatures, especially humans, opens new perspectives on nonhuman agency. Rather than seeing the escapes of nonhuman life as exits from human narratives, they appear as glimpses of alternate forms of culture or society. Rather than seeing the performances of nonhuman life in biodiversity knowledge projects like species gathering merely as behaviors, they can appear as moments of agency in which the species may not fully appreciate their own transformative effects. Such accounts of agency might change, too, what we think of by ecological politics, which would appear less as a politics of the human environment, and more as a politics of intra- and interspecies encounters.

Looking to the Future of Environmental Politics and Biodiversity

This book started by noting that even though biodiversity as a mode of green governance has seen significant expansion over the past three decades, global biodiversity loss is a forgotten crisis, especially compared to climate change. Climate change and biodiversity loss are tightly coupled in ecological terms. The things that drive biodiversity loss, such as loss of wildlife habitat through development and deforestation, negatively impact the possibility of adaptation to climate change. Meanwhile, climate change erodes the potential for species and ecosystems to survive by shifting their habitat zones at a rate that not all species will be able to adapt to. But climate change and biodiversity have become increasingly coupled in political terms too, sharing common policy languages, an emphasis on markets and market solutions, a long-term horizon, and a discourse of crisis coupled with a technical approach to problem solving. To overstate it slightly, climate change is, as a mode of thinking and acting on environmental politics, largely an economic issue with economic solutions, with only a hint of a political edge.

Parts of biodiversity have succumbed to this kind of thinking, as traced in this book, attaching themselves to the idea that giving biodiversity dollar valuations can fundamentally transform and stop species loss. The shift to talking about biodiversity in terms of "ecosystem services" was not only a nod to market economics but also partly a capitulation to the issue success of climate change, making biodiversity a calculable problem, with economic costs that demand mitigation and adaptation. "The environment *is* the economy," writes Caroline Fraser (2009, 8) in a recent book on rewilding, gesturing to the way that ecosystems generate millions in "undercounted" economic services. As this book has traced, that idea has evolved from a more deeply opposed understanding of economy and environment within conservation biology, one where the intrinsic value of other species, and of nature itself, stood firmly against seeing it solely for its instrumental value in economic terms. While intrinsic value arguments for biodiversity did not preclude economic use, they did aim to anchor that use in an overall framework of value that limited and constrained human action for moral reasons.

Current solutions tend to involve various rearrangements of "economy" and "ecology." That these terms have common linguistic roots in the Greek word *oikos* (household) is an oft-noted reason why they are coupled, as environmental magazines named *Oikos* suggest.[13] Both economy and ecology, as they exist today (as capitalism and conservation management, respectively) are essentially *technical* discourses and practices, harnessed to enormous knowledge projects. They share a perspective of management, classification, organization, and optimization, harnessed to the desires, energies, and processes of life. While it is possible that they may find common ground within which to operate, such common ground is likely to be a place where both nature and politics are relatively poor. If it is not simply a technical matter of squaring ecology and economics to work well together, and if the language and practice of ethics (whether ethical consumption or a shift in moral value) is insufficient to counter the tight coupling of ecology and markets, in what ways might a revamped, *political* biodiversity provide a different trajectory for global environmental politics?

Though global climate is a joint product of living and nonliving elements, the main nonhuman actants in climate change are abiotic—carbon, coal, tailpipes, smokestacks, electric power, and oil. Biodiversity, by contrast, forces us more explicitly into the murky, biological world of living creatures. Entering the domain of the living raises more complicated questions but also offers different kinds of opportunities for what Val Plumwood (2002) called an interspecies ethics. Relations between living species, Plumwood suggests, potentially raises issues of reciprocity, communication, community, justice, and signification. Encounters with other life—even mediated deeply by technology and media—push us toward more difficult moral questions about how we related to other life and to death, and by extension, or our own lives and mortality.[14] As such, biodiversity offers a location for environmental politics that is more than the aesthetic politics of conserving for recreation, and more than a technical and economic politics of addressing climate change; it is potentially a politics of life itself, political all the way through.

To build on the previous chapter, an expanded idea of rewilding is a potential touchstone for this kind of politics. Biodiversity, itself conceptually rewilded, might be more than ecological planning at large scales with modest aims (though it must also be that)—it might also be a remaking of the self by encounters with the heterogeneity of nature. The remaking of the self, meanwhile, cannot exist only as a counterpoint to wilderness and wildness in ecological terms. It must also involve the political creation of the conditions through which the heterogeneity of nature can come to exist, both across time (emphasizing the slow process of evolution) and space (allowing areas for wild activity and biodiversity). Importantly, the politics of this heterogeneity cannot emphasize just the material existence of species, in zoos or seed banks, for example, but rather could emphasize a particular material-semiotic quality of *wildness*. Such wildness would be a quality to pursue as an individual, as a political aim within existing political communities, and on the part of other species—especially keystone species, which generate trophic diversity.

We cannot answer with any finality whether other species "want" to be domesticated rather than left to the wild, or prefer the conditions of species autonomy in the woods to a spot in front of the fire or in a zoo. It is not entirely clear whether we can answer that question for humans, either, who are adaptable and malleable across a wide range of cultural and political forms. But given the cultural malleability of many other species, who differ widely as living beings depending on the conditions in which they are born, grow up, experience life, and die, it seems clear that a politics of biodiversity focused on wilding, rather than on technical management, ought to direct us to a different kind of biodiversity that emphasizes politics across species lines.

We might think about this rewilding as three legged: personal, ecological, and political. The first leg is a Thoreauvian rewilding of the self, indispensable at least for urban populations with sufficient means but also valuable for others who access it as a means for human flourishing. This implies not just engagement with "wilds" per se, but rather with a rich heterogeneity, as a form of buttressing and remaking the self. The second is a large-scale ecological rewilding—backing keystone species where they have existed in the recent past and creating corridors aimed at generating trophic diversity. Such projects would not only be ecological in a generalized sense but aimed at specific keystone species, with an openness to the kinds of species that might become involved. Under conditions of climate change in particular, such flexibility will be particularly necessary as the ranges of species habitats will be changing significantly. Insisting on the wild character of the post–climate change era in ecological settings, rather than its managed one, forms an important plank of a new politics of biodiversity.

Ecologically, a further possibility would be to move away from "species" as a dominant concept in biodiversity discourses and toward markers that reflect or translate more clearly the material-semiotic relations between humans and other living species. Biodiversity, as chapter 1 noted, has been founded on species; and scientifically as well as politically, species remains the major unit of currency in biodiversity. But species, like biodiversity as a whole, has been deeply commodified and neoliberalized, arguably eviscerating biodiversity of its critical potential as a concept.[15] Its emphasis on form rather than context ends up contributing to some of the problematic political visions of green governance as well. While the rights of species have been extensively debated in moral philosophy and put into place (via the Endangered Species Act in the United States, for example), a promising turn would be toward other levels in the Linnaean taxonomic system, or to ecological concepts like trophic levels (as discussed in chapter 4). Although there are very good reasons to be skeptical about the long-term ability of this taxonomic system to break free of its epistemological embeddedness in colonial histories of expansion and extraction, it is also important to work within existing frames of knowledge and to redirect them if possible. In particular, an ecological politics of biodiversity based on *communities*—which still draws on the notion of "species"—might be a promising turn. Cutting against both the highly individualized animal rights arguments and the hyper-decontextualizing power of species as such, communities of species as the constituents of biodiversity and its politics emphasize place, context, and relations between species communities. Communities are not part of the Linnaean taxonomic scheme, emerging instead from ecological analysis. While suffering from some similar conceptual difficulties when it comes to specification, communities nonetheless are a functioning ecological unit, and hold the advantage of being localized and identified as actual, materialized living beings, relating to one another.

The third leg of rewilding is the occasional, but regular and passionate, engagement in politics aimed at extending the personal and the ecological into new political structures and categories of practice. Rather than inventing new politics from whole cloth, however, this is more likely to mean taking up and reworking explicitly political categories, such as rights, sovereignty, justice, equality, and security, and thinking them through interspecies lenses. Such a rethinking might take place not in a naive extensionist way, but in a way that furthers both a rethinking of its human variation and an openness to how those categories can exist as a way to better our engagement with non-human life, and its engagement with us.

Emerging social movements and legal changes are beginning to bring some of these political practices into place, designating the status of nature, animals, and ecosystems in ways that are flexible, generative, and political. New forms of constitutional rights for nature have been put into place that connect the counterhegemonic aspirations of parts of the Latin American Left with explicit protection of ecosystems. Yet these rights have also remained deeply open to instrumental, national manipulation for national resource extraction. Elsewhere, rights for ecosystems exist in New Zealand, an explicitly legal fiction that aims to give greater voice to indigenous claims as well as environmental protection.

None of this is to suggest that an interspecies politics can fully replace or supplant the work of critiquing and transforming political systems and political economy. And there are significant and valid concerns about the way that these political categories can be used to speak for nonspeaking nature. As with any term that references nonhuman nature, it can be used as a shortcut to circumvent politics. Yet these developments offer a promising direction for biodiversity and environmental politics, a way to move into the present moment where a Romantic conception of nature from centuries past is gone, but the nature—the socionature, or nature-culture—that is here now becomes an issue that we address as a more central part of political life, rather than a material constraint on our economic lives or a technical problem to be solved without politics at all.

Appendix Mixed-Criteria World Heritage Sites
By Type of Interaction between Nature and Culture

MODE OF NATURE—CULTURE INTERACTION	SITE NAME	COUNTRY	YEAR INSCRIBED	INTERACTION BETWEEN NATURE AND CULTURE
None	Ibiza	Spain	1999	N/A—biodiversity and Renaissance architecture are next to one another
	Rio Abiseo NP	Peru	1990 (1992)	N/A—existing endemic biodiversity preservation and archaeological remains of pre-Incan society are not directly related
	Mt. Wuyi	China	1999	N/A—natural features (Nine Rivers, endemic biodiversity, Mt Wuyi) not related directly to sites related to birthplace of neo-Confucianism
Past or declining national way of life	Tassili n'Ajjer	Algeria	1982	Cave paintings are of local flora, fauna; cave location and setting is important to cultural heritage
	Willandra Lakes	Australia	1981	Site of a "dead" cultural landscape involving co-evolutionary processes (archaeological artifacts used to process nature); cultural heritage is of ancient humans (not clearly connected to living Aboriginal culture)
	Pyrenees (Mt. Perdu)	France/Spain	1997 (1999)	Preserving a "pastoral way of life" in decline, relationship between farmers, animals, landscape
	Tikal National Park	Guatemala	1979	Ruins of urban Mayan life are important for the transition from hunting/gathering to farming and relationship with nature in that transition; e.g., ruins include evidence of fruits and vegetables domesticated from the surrounding forest; natural conservation includes preservation of 300 species of trees "useful to humans"
	Macchu Picchu	Peru	1983	Contour of mountain landscape is directly central to architectural form; land and fortress are an integrated complex

Appendix—*Continued*

MODE OF NATURE–CULTURE INTERACTION	SITE NAME	COUNTRY	YEAR INSCRIBED	INTERACTION BETWEEN NATURE AND CULTURE
	uKhahlamba–Drakensberg Park	South Africa	2000	Main cultural heritage (cave paintings) is of natural heritage (flora, fauna); caves and rock shelters are also an important part of the dramatic rock formations of the natural setting; preservation of a past cultural landscape (inhabited by the San people)
	Göreme National Park	Turkey	1985	Byzantine art in "rock-hewn sanctuaries" inspired by Göreme Valley setting
	Hierapolis-Pamukkale	Turkey	1988	Heritage of Roman imperial spas linked directly to the naturally beautiful setting in which they were built
Sacred/Religious	Mt. Emei	China	1996	Mountain and surrounding area of natural beauty into which human elements have been directly integrated and inspired; giant Buddha statue carved into side of mountain reflects attempt to integrate the religious/cultural/natural
	Mt. Huangshan	China	1990	Cultural heritage (art, architecture) is related directly to natural heritage
	Mt. Taishan	China	1987	Art and architecture at the site undertaken with ideal of "perfect harmony with the landscape"
	Meteora	Greece	1988	Cultural value of monasteries and the hermetic ideal are structured around and permitted by the sandstone spikes on which they are built

Appendix—*Continued*

N/C CODE	SITE NAME	LOCATION	YEAR INSCRIBED	INTERACTION BETWEEN N/C
Postcolonial/ Postimperial	Ohrid Region	Macedonia	1979	Lake, city, and monastery are historically intertwined in the production of natural and cultural heritage (religious iconography, fishing way of life, protected lake)
	Cliff of Bandiagara	Mali	1989	Site protects natural cliffs, architecture built into them, and ongoing cultural practices of Dogon people (for ethnological and tourist purposes)*
	Kakadu National Park	Australia	1981 (1987, 1992)	Protected mixed heritage involves ongoing confusion of Aboriginal population with nature; cultural heritage being protected is of colonized people
	Tasmanian Wilderness	Australia	1982 (1989)	Cultural heritage is archaeological; natural scenic beauty and biodiversity protected; enabled by removal of Aboriginal population in 1830s†
	Uluru-Kata Tjuta National Park	Australia	1987 (1994)	Central feature (Uluru-Ayers Rock) initially appropriated by Australian government, subsequently returned to Aboriginal hands, and promptly converted into a government-managed park protecting Aboriginal sacred site
	Tongariro National Park	New Zealand	1990 (1993)	Maori cultural landscape; first cultural landscape inscribed as a World Heritage Site
	Laponian Area	Sweden	1996	Lapps herding native reindeer form a nature-culture complex
	St. Kilda	United Kingdom	1986 (2004, 2005)	Subsistence culture and archaeological remains on the island related directly to its natural setting, available natural resources

Sources: Data from UNESCO 2007 and WCMC 2006.

* The Dogon are a minority group (701,460 out of total population of 12,291,529) in a country of 50 percent Mande people. They remain largely animist in a mostly Sunni Islamic (nominally) country (though traditional practices remain strong). I coded this as postcolonial/postimperial rather than sacred/religious, since there is no clear history of imperial violence and because the main incentive is tourism rather than imperial guilt.

† The long time span between Aboriginal removal and Heritage Site status makes this a borderline postcolonial site; could also have been coded under past national way of life, suggesting the incorporation of natural beauty (with the indigenous population expunged) into dominant national narratives (e.g., Yellowstone or Yosemite in the United States).

Notes

Introduction

1. On the debate about a new World Environmental Organization, see Biermann 2002 and Najam 2003.

2. "Nature™Inc" comes from work in critical political ecology. See Arsel and Buscher 2012 for a collection of recent work under the heading of "Nature™Inc," which builds on the work of, among others, Harvey (1996) and Peet and Watts (1996). On antipolitics, see Ferguson 1990. Also, a very good more recent work in the environmental context is Buscher 2013.

3. See www.TEEBweb.org.

4. Foucault (1978, 1997, 2007) discusses biopower as a contrast to sovereign power. Biopolitics has been developed by a number of other theorists, including Hardt and Negri (2000) and Esposito (2008); see chapter 3 of this work for a discussion.

5. In particular, see Dillon and Reid 2009 on the links between complex emergency, liberal political thought, and security; and in the environmental context, see Buell 2003 and Mulligan 2010.

6. Jane Bennett's work on agency and assemblage has been particularly central to political science. See Bennett 2005b on assemblage and Bennett 2005a on a way to think about the political as a moment of disruption involving human and nonhuman things. On nonhuman agency and a modern-day vitalism, see Bennett 2010. Assemblage-based approaches are gaining increased traction in international relations as well; see Cudworth and Hobden 2011 and Barry 2013.

7. See the Millennium Ecosystem Assessment 2005a, 4–5. For a detailed look at biodiversity, see the Biodiversity Synthesis (Millennium Ecosystem Assessment 2005b). Using the most conservative estimates, which are based only on confirmed species extinctions (i.e., they ignore species likely to be extinct but not confirmed by extended scientific surveying), the rate of species extinction in the twentieth century was between fifty and five hundred times greater than the background rate of extinction naturally occurring through evolution. If we add in species that are possibly extinct, that rate climbs to one thousand times the background rate. Species are disappearing faster than evolution can keep up, by substantial orders of magnitude.

8. See Wilson 1992, 31.

9. A growing analysis from environmental quarters is that we are also witnessing the end of "nature" as a guiding idea (see McKibben 1989), and for some, this is not an entirely bad outcome (see Morton 2007).

10. See the CBD text at http://www.cbd.int/convention/text/. On the CBD, see McConnell 1996; LePrestre 2003; and Chasek, Downie, and Brown 2010, 226–35.

11. See DeSombre 2007a, 187–88.

12. Biodiversity loss is an unusual global environmental issue because it is in some ways not an issue of the global commons (see DeSombre 2007b, 179–82). Unlike climate change, for example, in which individual states are degrading a good that is not territorially located, biodiversity is generally confined to specific territories with sovereign governments, and concentrated more in some places than others. This means that, in theory, there is already political authority in place to deal with its loss, and if enough states valued it equally and were in a political and economic position to act on it, biodiversity loss could be addressed through sovereign state actions, via the greening of the sovereignty, as Eckersley (2004) argues. More pragmatically, given differing levels of interest in conserving it, and differing political and economic resources, it might be addressed by common agreement, or by bilateral or multilateral cooperation.

13. On the intersections of global biodiversity with national and subnational contexts, see Lowe 2006 regarding Indonesia and Lewis 2003 regarding India.

14. For representative liberal-rationalist work in international environmental politics, see Haas, Keohane, and Levy 1993 and R. Mitchell 2010. For a survey of the vast number of international environmental treaties that are the object of this literature's inquiry, see R. Mitchell 2003. For critiques that argue that both realist and liberal-rational approaches to environmental issues contribute to ongoing environmental degradation by misframing the problem, see Laferriere and Stoett 2006; Paterson 2000; and Mulligan 2010. Another strand of liberal-rationalist work sees biodiversity as an issue of global governance. It combines a similar positivist approach to the study of political life with a broader concern about how actors are bound by norms, how rules and roles are generated, and how state and non-state actors can form governance complexes. See Young 1997 and Esty and Ivanova 2002. And for a persuasive critique of global environmental governance, see Najam, Chrisopoulu, and Moomaw 2004.

15. The growing literature on the "new materialism" in politics includes Bennett 2010; Coole and Frost 2010; and Braun and Whatmore 2010.

16. For an early discursive take on environmentalism, see Hajer 1995, which seeks to recognize the "time and space specific nature of environmental discourse" (17). Other scholarship taking a discursive approach to environmental issues includes Litfin 1994; Dryzek 2005; and Epstein 2008. A subliterature on environmentality pursues the way that environmental discourses have intersected with governmentality, though again, generally emphasizing human agency or the agency of human discourses (see Agrawal 2005; Goldman 2001; Kuehls 1996; and Luke 1995). On discourse and

biodiversity, see Arturo Escobar's (1998) article, as well as Escobar 1995 and 1996. Environmental scholars, perhaps more so than in other disciplines, are split deeply around discursive approaches, with vehement debate over whether discursive analysis (or social construction more broadly) implies a rejection of nature as a dynamic materiality with its own, independent existence. See Soper 1994 and Kidner 2000.

17. Charlotte Epstein's (2008) excellent book on whaling discourses provides an example—while in no way denying the reality or materiality of whales, the book focuses entirely on how whales are made meaningful through human discourses (5). All of the "material practices" in the book revolve around the human aspect of whaling; thus, without denying the materiality of whales, Epstein manages to make that materiality irrelevant to the question of meaning—since a "social actor is also a speaking actor" (13), and only human speech counts as discourse. Jacques Derrida's (2008) work on response and reaction and the question of the animal persuasively suggests that such assumptions are unsustainable (see also Youatt 2012). But the book does not ask whether whales, too, have some kind of discourse that formed part of the context for the shift in whaling practices, or how it might matter for contemporary debates over whaling if they did. As new work on interspecies relations is increasingly showing (see Haraway 2008; Livingston and Puar 2011; and Kirksey and Helmreich 2010), we can in fact study and think about social relations across species lines in semiotic terms, of which human discourse is one part.

18. Anthropologists have fared somewhat better on this count—on biodiversity, see Raffles 2002 and Lowe 2006. This work carefully traces the different interconnections between global and local, insisting on the way that global discourses like biodiversity are particularized, and sometimes appropriated, in national and subnational contexts. My focus here is on the local production of the idea of global biodiversity from largely Western centers of power, and thus complements, rather than challenges, those other accounts. See also Whatmore 2002; Hinchcliffe and Whatmore 2006; and Bingham 2006 for work that integrates actor-network theory (ANT) with political-ecological analysis, and Castree 2002 on the ways to bridge Marxist and ANT-inspired approaches.

19. Latour (1987, 1993) develops ANT in his early work (along with Law [1991]; Law and Hassard [1999]; Callon [1986]; and others); but Latour (1996) then disavows ANT, writing that his work is neither about actors nor networks, nor is it a theory. However, his ongoing commitment (see Latour 1999, 2004) to seeing nonhumans as agentic and participating in networks with humans is less easy to disavow, and some of his more recent work takes the mantle of ANT back. See Latour 2005.

20. As cited in Kirsch and Mitchell 2004, 689.

21. See also Casper 1994. For other sustained criticisms of Latour, see Fuller 1994 and Elam 1999. A more recent treatment of Latour can be found in Harman 2009.

22. See Latour 1999, chapter 2.

23. As Giorgio Agamben (1998, 2004) argues, this exclusion is not complete, but is a constitutive exclusion that constitutes sovereign power. In a much-discussed passage

in the *Politics*, Aristotle (1996, 13) wrote: "Man is by nature a political animal. . . . Nature, as we often say, makes nothing in vain, and man is the only animal with the gift of speech. And whereas mere voice is but an indication of pleasure and pain, and is thereby found in other animals . . . the power of speech is intended to set forth the expedient and inexpedient, and therefore likewise the just and the unjust." In this same passage, Aristotle also says that "man is *more* of a political animal than bees or any other gregarious animal" (emphasis added), which suggests that human politics is not radically exceptional and species specific, but only relatively so. As such, while reasoned speech constitutes the main criterion of the (human) political in the Western philosophical tradition, it is not necessary for political life as such, even on Aristotle's terms.

24. See Derrida 2008, 2009.

25. Emphasis in original. A range of nonlinguistic or quasi-linguistic concepts offers other ways of approaching this continuum—affect (see Deleuze and Guattari 1987, xvi, 256–65); synergy (see Mathews 2003); biosemiosis (see Uexkull 1982 and Deely 1990); and actancy (see Latour 1999).

26. See P. Singer 1990 and Eckersley 1999.

27. See Deely 1990, 2001a, b.

28. The slight surprise of action for Latour (1999, 281) is at first relative to a human agent: "I never act; I am always slightly surprised by what I do," by which he means to refer to the nonsovereignty of human agency, and the way our own actions are always "overtaken" by events. But he also writes that "that which acts through me is also surprised by what I do, by the chance to mutate, to change, and to bifurcate," suggesting that the surprise of action is simply relative to an event involving actants, whether or not they are human. See also Bennett 2010, 103.

29. More accurately, for Haraway, the purity of "human," "natural," and "technological" as categories is deeply compromised, and in their stead, we ought to pay more attention to hybrid figures like cyborgs and companion species, and to actually hybridized things like OncoMouse. See Haraway 1991 and 1997.

30. See Hayles 1999 on the generative metaphysics of information, and for a history of cybernetics. The distinction between the concepts of information and meaning is critical both because of the way it seems to constitute some technical objects as participating in circuits of meaning making and because information is increasingly encroaching on human meaning and biotic semiosis itself.

1. The Awful Symmetry of Biodiversity Hotspots

1. This story is from Takacs 1996, 153–54.

2. Ibid., 11–21.

3. The full text of the CBD is available at http://www.cbd.int/convention/text/.

4. See McGraw 2002.

5. See http://www.unep-wcmc.org/what-is-biodiversity_50.html. See Groombridge and Jenkins 2002 for the full discussion.

6. The proceedings were turned into Wilson 1988.

7. See Takacs 1996, 37.

8. Ibid.

9. On transition towns, see Hopkins 2008 and Scott-Cato and Hillier 2010.

10. See DeLong 1996.

11. On the theoretical integrability of levels, see J. D. Singer (1969), who suggests that as social kinds, levels are not integrable; by contrast, Kenneth Waltz's (2001) classic three-part levels of analysis takes the levels to be explanatory lenses, rather than actually existing things, and therefore sees less trouble in forging links between them. See also Wendt 1992; 1999, 145–47, on the ways that levels are mutually constituting. The levels of analysis issue is largely a problem of the conceptualization of world processes (not a problem with the world itself), which finds ways to integrate itself through means that may or may not work within an imagery of levels. While it is possible to think about natural levels of analysis as working in ways different from social ones, with the latter existing only in intersubjective space and the former as a material fact, I do not see them as fundamentally different kinds of problems.

12. While there are arguably an infinite number of ways that biological differences could be organized, Gaston and Spicer (2004, 6) note that species is the most commonly used element for studying it. Species diversity is also the organizing concept for Norman Myers's analysis of hotspots, which I discuss in the next section. Similarly, for E. O. Wilson, species is the "fundamental unit" of biodiversity. Wilson (1992) also suggests that there is a communicative imperative to using species. Without using the idea of species to describe biodiversity and ecosystems, "biologists would find it difficult to compare results from one study to the next" (38).

13. Scott Atran (1990, chapter 2) argues in his comparative study of "folkbiology"— namely, how "ordinary" (i.e., nonspecialist) people in different cultures organize local flora and fauna—that modern species taxonomies standardize already-existing ways of classifying living things. Though cultures do not do so in exactly the same way, Atran suggests that there are some hierarchical ordering patterns in common, including the Russian doll pattern of nesting differences within one another. E. O. Wilson (1992, 42–43) similarly suggests that although taxonomy is not a direct mirror of natural kinds, the range of classification is not infinite either. He cites an example comparing colonial European ornithological classifications of bird species in New Guinea with the indigenous Arfak system of naming birds, where there was correspondence on 136 out of 137 species. Such evidence, however anecdotal, suggests that species may have a certain level of self-organization that can be recognized among different cultures. Thus, the often stark distinctions drawn between different ways of knowing, and the juxtaposition of local knowledge to scientific knowledge is perhaps overstated. Indeed, the fact that biodiversity, as a form of political economy, has been relatively successful in appropriating local knowledge about plants and animals is evidence of the connectedness between modes of knowing nature. Nonetheless, the fact that the species concept is *internally* contested should give us pause for reflection.

14. For a thorough analysis and historical tracing of the idea of species in the Western scientific tradition, including its contestation in the centuries since Linnaeus, see Wilkins 2009. Species was also deeply wrapped up with colonial, racial, gender, and national histories, and there is much more to say about this in the biodiversity context than I do here. As Harriet Ritvo (1997) notes, there is no strictly necessary connection between classification and ranking (or hierarchy), but historically this connection has nonetheless been commonplace. In the Victorian context, the link was between biological classification and lingering ideas about the Great Chain of Being, on the one hand, and the emerging rhetoric of progress and evolution, on the other (122). Moreover, classification was linked to significant anxieties about who was doing the classifying, linking to issues of class in particular. Biodiversity classification practices show some of the same tendencies and anxieties, as well as connecting to new internationalized forms of hierarchy, such as global sustainability indexes, green certification regimes, and global development regimes.

15. The closer one looks at the apparent disunity of science, the more, as Peter Galison (1999, 138) puts it, "it seem[s] as if any two cultures (groups with very different systems of symbols, and procedures for their manipulation) would seem utterly condemned to passing one another without any possibility of significant interaction." But, drawing from anthropology and trade, he suggests that "two groups can agree on rules of exchange, even if they ascribe utterly different significance to the objects being exchanged; they may even disagree on the meaning of the exchange process itself. Nonetheless, the trading partners can hammer out *local* coordination despite vast *global* differences." Against the sharper breaks of Foucaultian epistemes and Kuhnian paradigms, Galison (1996, 14) suggests that in the boundaries between paradigms and epistemes, and even between subdisciplines, "trading zones" are worked out in which practices are coordinated. Yet "the possibility of working out such partial, local, and specific linkages is what [he suspects] underlies the experience of continuity that these various groups feel as they work out trading zones between them" (15). Similar dynamics may partially account for the ongoing unity of the species idea—and even more so in nonscientific arenas, where much of the conceptual disagreement is either unknown or ignored.

16. See Ritvo 1997.

17. See Mayr 2001, 284.

18. See Wilson 1992, 38.

19. See Mayr 2001, 166–67.

20. See Wilson 1992, 45–50.

21. See Wilkins 2009, 225.

22. The idea of the co-configuration of abstract and particular is drawn from White 2001.

23. See Wheeler and Meier 2000 for a sample of the contemporary debate over the species problem.

24. Wilson (1992), Mayr (2001), and Wilkins (2009) advocate the former; Ereshefsky (2001) advocates the latter.

25. See Wilson 1992, 144.

26. See Myers et al. 2000, 853, and Gaston and Spicer 2004, 66.

27. See DeSombre 2007b, 181.

28. See Worster 1977, who details the emergence of ecological thinking from the mid-nineteenth century forward, particularly his focus on Gifford Pinchot and Aldo Leopold, who embody some of the key tensions in the "conservation vs. preservation" debate that still structures ecological management. Managing nature (and therefore also managing people) at global levels came out of the limits to growth literature of the 1970s, rooted especially in population management thinking (see Meadows et al. 1972), and from the Stockholm Conference of 1972, the first global environmental summit that paved the way for the agreements reached at Rio twenty years later.

29. See Myers 1988, 1990.

30. See Conservation International 2005.

31. See Myers 1988 and Wilson 1992. Although there are ways of defining hotspots that do not rely on endemic species—e.g., using "rare" species as a measure rather than "endemic" (see Prendergast, Quinn, and Lawton 1993 and Possingham and Wilson 2005)—Myers's use of endemic species is the most widespread approach.

32. See Conservation International 2005.

33. In 2000, CI's analysis listed twenty-five hotspots. In 2005, CI revised its analysis of hotspots, adding six new hotspots and subdividing two others, for a total of thirty-four.

34. See Mittermeier, Myers, and Mittermeier 1999 and Conservation International 2005. On the science of hotspots, using a broader definition than CI, see Willis, Gillson, and Knapp 2007.

35. By "conceptual object," I mean here something like Latour's (1993, 51–55) quasi-object: a quasi-object is neither an object nor a subject, neither a thing nor an idea, but a relation that has both material and semiotic properties. Michel Serres (2007) uses the example of the ball and players in a soccer game—the ball is not just acted on by players, though its animacy relies on human activity; it also acts on the players, modifying their activities, thinking, and skills. It is difficult to understand the playing of soccer without a greater elaboration of how the ball relates to the game, and to the players.

36. See Cincotta, Wisnewski, and Engelman 2000, 990.

37. See ibid., 244, on "hemorrhage" and Kareiva and Marvier 2003 on "triage."

38. This rhetoric leads to questionable consequences, as environmental skeptics such as Ferry (1995) suggest. See Buell 2003 for an excellent look at the history of the "crisis mentality" in American environmentalism.

39. See Mayr 2001, 202.

40. See http://www.conservation.org/where/priority_areas/hotspots/Pages/hotspots _in_context.aspx.

41. See Mittermeier and Myers 1998.

42. See Wilson 1992, 197. There is slightly different data in DeSombre 2007b, 181.

43. The clearest analysis of these overlaps is in the political ecology literature, particularly Escobar 1995 and 1999. See also Adams 1990; Harvey 1996; and Peet and Watts 1996 and, more recently, Peet, Robbins, and Watts 2011. Political geographers have also been receptive to the implications of Latour's work, and actor-network theory more generally. For ecological politics, see Whatmore 2002 and Robbins 2007.

44. See Possingham and Wilson 2005, 920.

45. Jepson and Canney (2001) make this criticism in the biodiversity context.

46. Although I have mostly drawn on the science studies literature here that is part of the actor-network theory lineage, I was initially inspired to look further into biodiversity sciences as socially produced from a different strand of scholarship that emphasized the social construction of scientific truth. In science studies, this debate is famously captured in the "epistemological chicken" exchange between Collins and Yearly, and Callon and Latour, in Pickering 1992. A range of scholarship takes up this approach—see Knorr-Cetina 1981, 1999; Poovey 1998; Rabinow 1989; and Jasanoff 2006.

47. Much like political ideas such as democracy, class, or détente come into being at particular times and subsequently fade away, Latour suggests that yeast literally has historicity—that it did not exist until it was constituted in the relation with Pasteur and the broader social assemblage of institutions, norms, and media. In essence, he wishes to do away with an independent reality, but without insisting on a subjective relativism, and his solution is to grant the same kind of material-semiotic sociality to all things equally, including historicity. Here, I part ways with Latour. Although I agree that mind-independent reality is an idea, not a thing, it is an idea that I do not much worry about as being false. Rather, because material-semiotic *relations* precede things, mind-independent reality should be seen as a useful but nonetheless secondary effect of a mind-experienced reality. The very possibility of positing a mind-independent reality, in other words, requires a mind-experienced reality first. The best discussion of this I have found is John Deely's (1990) discussion of semiotics. Indeed, as many kinds of historical examples suggest, mind-independent reality (as it has been understood) has, time after time, shown itself to be "wrong" (under its own criteria of truth/falsehood)— all the wrong science, the thousands of years of geocentric universes, the Salem witches who were not witches, the impermeability or hard materiality of walls, atoms as basic units of the universe, and so on. A mind-independent reality, as a primary ontology, makes little sense—a mind would be necessary to conceive of that idea, which would make it not mind-independent at all. The only possible existence of a mind-independent reality comes from the existence of a mind-in-the-world in the first place. A mind-independent reality can still exist as a semiotic entity, then, and in fact a very useful one (even if we get its contours wrong all the time), but only as a secondary phenomenon.

48. See Takacs 1996, 6, 35.

49. See, for example, the pieces by Soule, Ehrenfeld, and Janzen in *Conservation Biology*, vol. 1.

50. See Takacs 1996, 35.

51. "Ecosystem services" was first used in the late 1970s by ecologists, but did not become fully articulated as an ecological and a conservation concept until the mid-1990s. See Mooney and Ehrlich 1997.

52. See McCann 2000 and Tilman 2000.

53. See Gaston and Spicer 2004, 99.

54. See, for example, Devall and Sessions 1985; Fox 1990; and Mathews 1991.

55. See Katz 1985.

56. The cosmopolitan/communitarian debate played out in political theory, but also had an interesting variation in international relations as the liberalism/realism debate; see Buzan, Held, and McGrew 1998 for an overview, and Linklater 1998 and Archibugi, Held, and Kohler 1998. On humanitarian intervention, see Wheeler and Morris 1996 and Onuf 2004, and on humanitarianism in international relations, see Fixdal and Smith 1998; Campbell 1998; Orford 1999; Belloni 2007; and Barnett and Weiss 2008.

57. See Wilson 1992, 198.

58. Erwin explicitly rejects the idea of intrinsic value. See Takacs 1996, 249–50.

59. Livingston and Puar 2011 and Haraway 2008 both raise this issue as well. See Ereshefsky 2001 on alternative taxonomies in biology and the prodigious literature on folk taxonomies/classifications that Atran pulls together in anthropology. A particularly interesting history of how the endangered species concept has been used in political life, as a proxy for the politics of place in the western United States, is Alagona 2013.

2. Biopower, the Global Biodiversity Census, and the Escapes of Nonhuman Life

1. See Raven and Wilson 1992; Wilson 1992; Kelly 2000; Lawler 2001; and Wilson 2003.

2. See Heywood and Watson 1995.

3. See Gaston and Spicer 2004, 43.

4. See Hayden 1998, 39.

5. See Takacs 1996, 85. See also Stork 1997 and Harmon 2002, chapter 2, on the debates over methods for gauging biodiversity.

6. Political controversy has dogged efforts to change the United States census from an attempt to achieve a direct headcount to using statistical methods to achieve greater accuracy. The Supreme Court ruled in 1999 that statistical sampling could not be used to determine congressional apportionment; however, it allowed the use of statistical sampling for other uses, such as distribution of funds for federal programs. Partisan debates over the effects of statistical adjustments have also hindered the full implementation of sampling procedures to overcome chronic undercounting. See Peterson 1999.

7. See Lovejoy 1994; May, Lawton, and Stork 1995; Wheeler 1995; Dobson 1996; Decker and O'Dor 2002, 33–40; and Harmon 2002.

8. See Escobar 1998 and 1999; Luke 1995; and Goldman 2001.

9. See Maffi 2001.

10. See Foucault 1978 and Anderson 1983.

11. See Latour 1999.

12. Duvall and Barnett (2005) offer a useful framing of four kinds of power, which I use to organize the discussion here. The first kind of power, compulsory power (i.e., direct control or coercion), is largely not applicable to the kinds of power at use in the biodiversity census. The second form of power, institutional power, and the third form, structural power, inform the discussion in this section. While more diffuse than compulsory power, these two forms of power are nonetheless identifiable in their effects and structures. By contrast, the fourth form of power, productive power, which Duvall and Barnett call "the socially diffuse production of subjectivity in systems of meaning and signification" (4), is more difficult to pin down. I therefore use Foucault's work on biopower as a way of understanding how productive power relates to the biodiversity census.

13. The idea of seductive power having particular dynamics of its own comes from Allen 2003. Unlike forms of power like domination, coercion, and manipulation, seduction "leaves open the possibility that a subject can opt out" (30). In this respect, seduction resembles authority, which is also based on the recognition of power as legitimate by a subject, and thus holds the potential for refusal. The nature of seductive power, paradoxically, lies partly in that right of refusal—what allows someone to be seduced by a panoptic discourse is the sense that there is nothing dominating or coercive about its appeal.

14. From www.allspecies.org. See www.sp2000.org for the current publicly available data in the Catalogue of Life.

15. See Stein 2002.

16. See www.gbif.org and www.itis.gov.

17. From http://www.gbif.org/GBIF_org/bg1#whyneed.

18. On panopticism, see Foucault 1995, 195–228, and for applications in international relations, see Der Derian 1990; Lucas 1992; Gill 1995; and Debrix 1999.

19. From www.allspecies.org.

20. The distinction between modern and postmodern capitalism comes from O'Connor 1994.

21. See Bamford 2002.

22. On the role of scientists in steering global environmental governance, see Haas 1990 and 1992.

23. See Latour 1993. As an earlier reviewer pointed out, the force of human/nonhuman hybridity is not in introducing the nonhuman into the human; it is pointing out that it is already there and always has been. The matter is one of undoing discursive denials.

24. The question is Donna Haraway's (1997, 113).

25. I use Rabinow and Rose's (2006) scaffolding in exploring the biodiversity census in relation to Foucault's early work on biopower, but the literature on biopolitics and biopower is now quite vast and interdisciplinary, with its own internal debates. See, for example, Agamben 1998; Braun 2007; Foucault 2007; Esposito 2008; and

Dillon and Reid 2009. Although most biopolitical analyses do not consider nonhuman subjectivities, see the wonderful work by Lewis Holloway (2007, Holloway and Morris 2007), where he uses the biopower frame to consider bovine subjectivities in the context of farming techniques; see also Shukin 2009 and Wolfe 2010.

26. See Escobar 1996.

27. See Foucault 1978, 141.

28. See Rabinow and Rose 2003, 2.

29. On the testimony of nonhumans, see Latour 1993.

30. See Allen 2004. See also Allen 2003, chapter 4, where Allen questions whether it is possible to see "almost anything and everything . . . as a technique or relation of power" (68). For Allen, even if power is immanent rather than a capacity or an external force, it cannot be everywhere. Rather, he suggests that we need topologies or cartographies of power that show "specific diagrams" of power in particular institutions or sites (68). Pushed beyond these sites, however, descriptions of immanent power start to become metaphorical, and in Allen's view, they begin to lose sight of the ways that spatiality intervenes in and mediates the practices of power.

31. See Foucault 1978, 95: "Where there is power, there is resistance, and yet, or rather consequently, this resistance is never in a position of exteriority in relation to power. Should it be said that one is always 'inside' power, there is no 'escaping' it, there is no absolute outside where it is concerned, because one is subject to the law in any case? . . . This would be to misunderstand the strictly relational character of power relationships. Their existence depends on a multiplicity of points of resistance. . . . These points of resistance are present everywhere in the power network. Hence, there is no single locus of great Refusal, no soul of revolt, source of all rebellions, or pure law of the revolutionary. Instead there is a plurality of resistances, each of them a special case."

32. Yet see Shaw 2000 and Wendt 2003.

33. See Goldman 2001.

34. See Archibugi, Held, and Kohler 1998 and Linklater 1998.

35. See Wolf 1999. And see Moravscik 2002 for a contrary perspective on the democratic deficit.

36. See Goldman 2001, 502.

37. See, for example, Young 1997.

38. See Zureik 2001.

39. See Hardt and Negri 2000.

40. Ibid., 29–30.

41. See O'Connor 1994.

42. Wilson (1992, 142) uses the term in reference to the sheer numbers of bacterial species; however, his metaphor also gestures to the work that bacteria do in ecological terms, in breaking down vast quantities of organic matter. Perhaps the term overstates the Marxist analogy—bacteria, after all, do not have class consciousness—but it nonetheless seems to me to be a way to acknowledge their ecological importance relative to human scale.

43. In the material-semiotic perspective advanced by Donna Haraway (1991, 1997) and Bruno Latour (1993), meaning is made not only through language but also through bodies and biology—"meaning" literally circulates through materiality as well as language, moving from one realm into the other and back again. Material things are semiotic, both in the sense that they carry signs that human minds interpret and in the sense that they transform those signs through the very act of being. Similarly, for postmodern theorists of gender like Judith Butler (1993), who read bodies as texts, it is not just that bodies can be read "as" texts in a metaphorical sense; rather, it is that texts and bodies share in the process of making meaning. Neither society nor nature determines gender; it is made through linked circuits of meaning that move through both realms in performed discourse. Discourse, in this postmodern sense, is not just "talk," but is a series of practices that involve both speech/language and materiality, linking them into a structured regime of meanings. My concern here is with the category of "human" and, particularly, with the way that its meaning is made in discursive practices that include biological and bodily similarities as well as linguistic constructions like cosmopolitanism and human rights.

44. See Devall and Sessions 1985 and Fox 1990.

45. Ecocentric thinking, as Robyn Eckersley (1992, 28) points out, takes "our [human] proper place in the rest of nature as logically prior to the question of what are the most appropriate social and political arrangements for human communities." For some deep ecologists, this perspective has meant considering the human species as a whole in relation to the global ecosystem, as in EarthFirst!'s infamous identification of human beings as a "cancer" in the global ecosystem (see Zimmerman 1991) or in taking the Gaia hypothesis to its logical extreme. The "wider self" that Arne Naess (1985) proposes likewise finds its ultimate expression in the global ecosystem. Nonetheless, many ecocentric thinkers, like Eckersley, are careful to safeguard some human interests and politics outside the perceived demands of the global ecosystem (see Dryzek 2000, chapter 6).

46. See, for example, Flannery 2001.

47. On the Chipko movement, see Escobar 1995; though see Mawdsley 1998 for a critique that the Chipko movement has been overromanticized as a neopopulist movement

48. See Pollan's (2006) popular account.

49. Among many arguments for moral obligations on these grounds, see Singer 1990 and Rolston 1988.

3. World Heritage Sites, Rocks, and Biocultural Diversity

1. See Elizabeth Shakman Hurd 2008 on the intersections of secularism and international relations.

2. "Natureculture," unwieldy though it is, is a term used by Donna Haraway and Bruno Latour to point to the deep inseparability of nature and culture. They use the term mostly in analyses of modern Western society and politics, where those two terms

have had sustained powers of separation. I use it here to label the complex of agents around Aboriginal societies who, it is too often said, do not have concepts of nature and culture as such (as if they exist outside of modernity, still). As the chapter shows, these societies are paradoxically positioned as being part of a natureculture in UNESCO heritage practices, in juxtaposition to the nature and culture of nonindigenous societies. The productive power of this paradoxical logic is what I wish to emphasize here.

3. In *Sand County Almanac* (1949, 129), Leopold writes that "only the mountain has lived long enough to listen objectively to the howl of a wolf. . . . Perhaps this is behind Thoreau's dictum: In wildness is the salvation of the world. Perhaps this is the hidden meaning in the howl of the wolf, long known among mountains, but seldom perceived among men." Leopold's idea is that you can only apprehend the living relations in ecology by starting with the mountain's perspective—but here, Leopold does not mean the mountain as the rocks and stone, but rather the mountain as the living biota of the mountain as a whole, playing out on the abiotic context of the mountain. By contrast, I am more interested here in thinking like, about, and with the abiotic elements of a mountain, especially since Uluru and Meteora do not have substantial biota. "Useful anthropomoprhism" is Bennett's (2010) phrase.

4. See McPhee 1998 and Bush 2000.

5. Stallybrass (1993) offers an interesting inquiry into the dynamic relationship between historical memory and material things by considering the way that things (such as clothes) bear the material and semiotic traces of the past, suggesting a distributed understanding of historical memory. See also Sturken 1997.

6. See Frisch 1998. See also Davison 1991 and Hewison 1989. Hewison agrees with Lowenthal that heritage should be kept distinct from history, but sees the two as increasingly blended in practice.

7. See Star and Griesemer 1989, 393.

8. See the Convention at www.unesco.org.

9. See Wager 1995 and Heyd 2005.

10. On wilderness being just as cultural as it is natural, see the famous essay by Cronon (1995).

11. Olwig (1989) points out that the first Anglo-American visitors to view Yellowstone's nature had to be protected by army troops against Native Americans who considered the area part of their territory.

12. See Latour 1993, esp. 29–32.

13. This debate is framed in Uzzell 1989.

14. See UNESCO 1994.

15. Ibid.

16. Ibid. This work is ongoing.

17. Data drawn from UNESCO website.

18. Phillips (1995) makes the point about noncultural nature being an imperial conceit that masked the presence of non-European cultures.

19. See von Droste, Plachter, and Rossler 1995 on cultural landscapes.

20. These three definitions were developed at a meeting of experts at La Petit Pierre in September 1992, and adopted by the Seventeenth Session of the World Heritage Committee in Santa Fe in 1992. For a detailed account of UNESCO's process, see Rossler 1995.

21. See Phillips 1995, 382.

22. See UNESCO 2005, iii, 10.

23. Wolfe 1991 assesses the impact of anthropology's dualistic interventions.

24. See UNESCO 2005, paragraph 46.

25. As of September 2011, out of 936 World Heritage Sites, 28 properties had been selected for both cultural and natural value. Source: UNESCO website.

26. According to the WCMC (the World Conservation Monitoring Centre, a British NGO monitoring World Heritage Sites): "It was subsequently realised that the area was also internationally important for its geology, fauna and flora. Some of the important elements of the park include the geological formations which are of outstanding scenic interest (precambrian crystalline formation and eroded sandstones). The Tassili is important for wildlife and includes 28 national plant rarities and one internationally threatened plant species and over five endangered mammal species. . . . The entire region is important for resting migratory Palaearctic birds. *Cupressus dupreziana* is one of 12 critically endangered plants selected by IUCN's Species Survival Commission to highlight the serious threats to species around the world" (WCMC 2006).

27. See UNESCO 2004, IV.I.2, MLA 2.

28. See Nicol 1963, 1. Roughly translated from the Greek, Meteora means "suspended in air."

29. Ibid. Chapter 2 of this work contains a useful discussion of the tradition of Byzantine monasticism and how it differed from the Western Christian monastic tradition.

30. As quoted in Nicol 1963, 4.

31. Ibid., 3.

32. See the ICOMOS recommendation of July 1988 and the IUCN evaluation of Meteora of May 1988, available at http://whc.unesco.org/en/documents/.

33. See UNESCO's Twelfth Session of the World Heritage Committee, Brasilia, Brazil, December 5–9, 1988, available at whc.unesco.org/archive/repcom88.htm.

34. Dipesh Chakrabarty (2000) points out how secular Western history has difficulty grasping the apparent agency of divine figures in driving peasant rebellions in India.

35. See https://portals.iucn.org/library/efiles/html/BP4%20-%20Indigenous_and _Traditional_Peoples_and_Protected_%20Areas/casestudy11.html.

36. See http://whc.unesco.org/en/list/147.

37. See UNESCO 1998.

38. See IUCN 2004, summary of the nomination submitted by the government of Australia.

39. See World Heritage Committee Meeting, July 12, 1999, minutes, at http://whc .unesco.org/en/soc/2330.

40. Ibid.

41. See Layton 1986; Layton and Titchen 1995; and WCMC 2006.

42. The technical but also graphic term "excised" appears both in Layton and Titchen 1995 and on the UNESCO World Heritage site description at http://whc.unesco.org/en/list/447.

43. See Layton and Titchen 1995, 176–77. See also Barwick 1990; Chatwin 1987; Price-Williams and Gaines 1994; and Wolfe 1991.

44. On the geology of Uluru Rock, see Sweet and Crick 1992.

45. Recent work in continental philosophy, gathered under the heading of "speculative realism," has pushed the boundaries of what we think objects, including rocks, do and are. Graham Harman (2011) has suggested that rocks access one another as what he calls "sensuous objects," yet have an interiority that cannot be accessed by other objects (whether other rocks or humans). See also Harman, Srnicek, and Bryant 2011 and Bogost 2012. If Harman is right, then rocks are agents in the strong sense, rather than just the virtual sense that I have suggested here, because of their capacity for interiority. But it is difficult to see how one might give more substance to the "withdrawn" quality of Uluru Rock (or any objects), given the premise that this interior is a withdrawn one, while the point of encounter is with the sensuous aspect of the object. Unlike living creatures, whose interior experiences we also cannot access but whose exterior performances occur in recognizably semiotic terms, rocks do not have an interior experience we can easily recognize. This may, though, be a failure of imagination to understand the very long temporalities within which rocks move and experience, such as the tilting of Uluru Rock.

46. See Oviedo, Maffi, and Larsen 2000.

47. See UNESCO 2004.

48. Maffi 2001 is one cornerstone of the BCD literature; Posey (1999) was the first to argue for the links between bio and cultural diversity, as a response to the Global Biodiversity Assessment that I looked at in the biodiversity hotspots chapter. Harmon (2002) considers the philosophical arguments for biocultural diversity, drawing on William James's theory that human consciousness is defined most importantly by the effort to make sense of difference. See also Posey 1999; Oviedo, Maffi, and Larsen 2000; and Joe et al. 2002.

49. See Harmon and Loh 2004 and Moore et al. 2002.

50. See Nabhan and St. Antoine 1993.

51. See Cocks 2006 for a critical appraisal of the limited application of BCD to indigenous peoples.

52. See also Rossler 1995 on the way that the managerial vision of UNEP finds its way into indigenous heritage politics.

53. The literature on sustainability, and particularly sustainable development, is enormous. Some of the strongest and most persuasive critiques have come from political ecologists. W. M. Adams (1990, 2) argues that the discourse of sustainable development has a "beguiling simplicity" and a "terrible versatility" that gives an appearance

of reform but does not, and cannot, radically alter the substantive causes of environmental degradation. Arturo Escobar (1996) pushes this point even further. Sustainable development's basic problem, he argues, is how we can continue to have global capitalism without destroying the environment. Thus, far from changing the direction of development, "the Brundtland Report inaugurated a period of unprecedented gluttony in the history of vision and knowledge with the concomitant rise of a global eco-cracy" (50). By incorporating individuals and local populations into a flexible labor pool (based in part on heritage tourism) and by bringing them further into the orbit of state power in order to serve purportedly global needs, UNESCO's heritage program might thus be read as the mutually reinforcing structures of capitalism and eco-governmentality, held together via the glue of "environmental" sustainability discourse. See Adams 1990; Peet and Watts 1996; Shiva 1999; Bryant and Bailey 1997; Escobar 1995; and Stott and Sullivan 2000.

54. See Laland and Galef 2009 for a collection of the contemporary debate on nonhuman animals and culture.

55. "Sharing a World of Difference" is the title of a volume published by UNESCO on BCD. See Skutnabb-Kangas, Maffi, and Harmon 2003.

56. I adapt these from Hayles 1999. See also the analyses of complexity theory in the social sciences, which sometimes endeavors to explain the world in these terms (for example, Cederman 1997 and Jervis 1998), and to understand the world through them (for example, Dillon and Reid 2001; Connolly 2011; and Cudworth and Hobden 2011).

57. See Hayles 1999, 285.

58. See Serageldin, Shluger, and Martin-Brown 2001.

4. Urban Biodiversity in New York City and the New Rewilding

1. See Kareiva 2011, 35, and Kareiva et al. 2007.

2. The literature on the ways that neoliberalism and nature have been brought together is vast and varied. Peet, Robbins, and Watts 2011 brings together a number of recent contributions from global political ecology.

3. On Victorian zoos in London, see Ritvo 1987, 205–42. On the history and evolution of zoos in America, see Hanson 2004.

4. This rethinking was led by William Whyte Jr., Lewis Mumford, and Joanne Jacobs, among others. For the early turn toward integrating urban planning and ecology, see McHarg 1995.

5. See Platt, Rowntree, and Muick 1994, 9.

6. In a number of fields, including geography and political economy, metabolism has been the central metaphor through which to think about these flows—not just of materials but also energy and information. See Gandy 2004. An excellent history of how metabolism mutually constitutes the urban and rural in American history is Cronon 1992, which traces the development of Chicago from the outside in.

7. See Platt, Rowntree, and Muick 1994, 11.

8. See Oliviera et al. 2010, 9–10.

9. From UNEP on urban biodiversity: http://www.unep.org/urban_environment/issues/biodiversity.asp.

10. See Blaustein 2013.

11. See http://www.iclei.org/our-activities/our-agendas/biodiverse-city.html.

12. The UN Millennium Ecosystem Assessment dedicated only one chapter to "Urban Systems," emphasizing the ecosystem services aspect of urban ecology in particular.

13. See Secretariat of the Convention on Biological Diversity 2012. While these conferences are often dismissed as empty talk, they actually perform important aspects of global governance, though for reasons other than those explicitly stated. The same is true for the power of their policy reports. On the theatrical politics of these global environmental summits, see Death 2011, who argues that their performative power in enacting governance far exceeds their stated aim to achieve agreements.

14. See Guha 2000.

15. See Secretariat of the Convention on Biological Diversity 2012, 7.

16. On green governmentality, see Luke 1995 and 1999; Goldman 2001; Agrawal 2005; and Rutherford 2007. On governmentality in international relations, and especially climate change, see Methman 2013.

17. See Swyngedouw and Heynen 2004 and Heynen, Kaika, and Swyngedouw 2006.

18. Holling (1973) first proposes this. On the links between biodiversity and resilience, see Walker et al. 2004 and Elmqvist et al. 2003.

19. See Hopkins 2008, 55. For general information about transition towns, see the U.S. website for the transition town movement: http://transitionus.org/home.

20. See Scott-Cato and Hillier 2010, 875.

21. See http://www.nj.com/hudson/index.ssf/2013/04/in_aftermath_of_hurricane_sand.html.

22. The report is available at http://www.nyc.gov/html/sirr/html/report/report.shtml.

23. See http://www.resalliance.org/index.php/resilience. On the possibilities of stretching resilience across social and ecological systems, see Adger 2000, which compares the conceptual differences in resilience in ecosystems with resilience communities, and questions whether the former aids the latter.

24. See Sanderson 2009.

25. See Hinchcliffe et al. 2005.

26. Ibid.

27. For competing visions of the relationship between design and politics, see Margolin 2002 and Fry 2011. Fry argues that liberal democracy is in essence unable to deliver the goods necessary for ecological sustainability, and that the design of materials and spaces can step into the breach as a new form of politics. This resonates with Latour's politics of material experimentation conceptually, but suffers from some of the same difficulties with institutionalization.

28. This is true in ecological thought as well. See Whiteside 2003 for an engagement with the alternatives that French ecological thought offers to environmental thinking.

29. See Town and Country Planning Association 2004, 4.

30. Harmony, Florida, bylaws are available at http://www.harmonyfl.com/Central -Florida-Community/resident-guidelines.

31. See Hostetler 2012.

32. See Soule and Noss 1998, 22.

33. See Fraser 2009, 9–10.

34. On keystone species and trophic cascades, see Eisenberg 2010.

35. This account of the Yellowstone rewilding is drawn from Monbiot 2013, 84–86.

36. Ferry (1995) was one prominent critic. See (Wolfe 1997) for a multipronged rebuttal.

37. Ecologists use biomass, rather than population, as a gauge to make this distinction. But functionally speaking, a lower population of humans also results in a lower biomass. See Davic 2003.

38. For a regional perspective on rewilding in the northeastern United States, see Klyza 2001.

39. See Donlan et al. 2006. These scientific proposals cross over in interesting ways to rewilding movements in the United States aimed at the rewilding of human beings through various forms of anarcho-primitivism. Paul Shephard (1998), in one important anarcho-primitivist text, argues that the genetic makeup of humans was developed in the Pleistocene, and locates the roots of the global environmental crisis in our cultural and ecological departure from that era. Here, the emphasized turn is backward in time, organizing our current practices around our genetic roots.

40. For rewilding projects in continental Europe, see www.rewildingeurope.com.

41. See Kolbert 2012 and Lorimer and Driessen 2013.

42. This argument is similar to the line taken by Monbiot (2013), who argues that the "process is the outcome" for rewilding (83), and rejects Pleistocene rewilding as missing the target of rewilding, which is to allow "self-willed" processes to take place with a minimum of human interference.

43. Likewise, the reintroduced species that would come to inhabit these areas are somewhat unique. As Sarah Rinfret (2009) notes, wild reintroductions are creating a new class of animal that is managed—they are neither domesticated nor truly wild, but rather, a constructed and disciplined animal, increasingly subject to forms of both physical surveillance and forms of discipline (such as the use of shock collars on wolves when they approach a ranch).

44. For a collection of some of the debates, see Callicott and Nelson 1998 and Chaloupka 2000. Academically speaking, conservation biology and critical environmental history are arguably not mutually exclusive, each emphasizing different objects of knowledge and with differing academic standards of knowledge. Much of the resulting

debate was instead about the kind of politics that each perspective implies. For those concerned with the social contingency of wilderness, it suggests a great focus on changing what wilderness means and a greater turn to finding wilderness in places like cities, a turn that critics took to be political fodder for economic exploitation. Similarly, the emphasis on the extrasocial reality of wilderness by conservation biologists suggests a continued effort to preserve wilderness areas, with political values acting merely as a distraction from the real task. But this shows the tone-deaf quality of taking a purely ecological perspective to politics, and is justifiably the very point of Cronon's critique.

45. Two of the best examples of this are Mitchell 2002, chapter 1, and Scott 1998.

46. See Eisenberg 2010 and Monbiot 2013, 84.

47. On self-fashioning, see Greenblatt 1980. On anarcho-primitivism, see also John Zerzan and Derrick Jensen.

48. There is also a second Thoreau, who spends many of his later years as a scientist (see Worster 1977, 59–111)—so much so that he ends up feeling alienated from the very nature that he celebrates at Walden: "I have become sadly scientific. . . . My views have become narrowed to the microscope. I see details, not wholes nor the shadow of a whole. Once I was part and parcel of nature; now I am observant." Nonetheless, he spends the second act of his life doing something entirely different: he turns to becoming a scientist-politician of sorts. He works on questions of forest succession in particular, looking at how forests change and recover after logging. In New England at that time, woods were being cut down rapidly for use as timber as well as for railroads and housing. Over time, these trees could replenish themselves, which people were aware of. But the species that would grow back was often a different one than was cut—pine instead of oak, for example. This, in turn, caused people to burn the young pine trees out, and then plant crops on it like rye, and then move on.

In this context, Thoreau questions how tree species succeed one another. By paying close attention he finds that what determines the species of tree depends on the way squirrels bury the seeds of the trees and the way that pine seeds carry in the wind and lodge at the base of oaks. It is simply a matter of chance. He starts to think about succession of species—patterns that occur after a clearcut, or after a fire, which leads from a weedy open area to a mature forest. The question was how biodiversity builds over time, to put it in contemporary language. He publishes a paper in a scientific journal on this issue, and delivers lectures getting these ecological interdependencies into people's heads, and trying to get them to manage the woodlands better. He works harder at botany and identification of species, and he notices that even though he was in the middle of nature at Walden, he hadn't noticed *the deep diversity of life* that was there. It wasn't until after he became more scientific, in other words, that he was able to notice natural variety in depth. He reads Linnaeus—whose system of taxonomy is still influential. He read Darwin and Charles Lyell. This second Thoreau, at least in broad strokes, is a good stand-in for many aspects of how current American environmentalism and conservation policy approach biodiversity. In this second Thoreau, rewilding and urban biodiversity projects seem very much at home.

Conclusion

1. For a discussion of the agent-structure problem in international relations and ways of thinking about agency outside this dualistic conception, see Wendt 1992 and 1999, 26–27; Doty 1997; and Debrix 2003. More recently in international relations, much of this debate about agency and structure turns on the disagreements between rational choice ontologies and constructivist theory (see Sil 2000). See, more generally, Jackson 2011.

2. See Giddens 1984, 19, 25.

3. Ibid. and Wendt 1992.

4. Giddens 1984, 9.

5. Fanon (1967) understands resistance to colonial power as a form of agency. Shiva (1993) similarly thinks of resistance to monoculture and global seed companies as resistance that express local forms of agency. See Petit 2003 on the idea of option-freedom as a weaker form of free choice.

6. Agency as resistance can be characterized as "the capacity to realize one's own interests against the weight of custom, tradition, transcendental will, or other obstacles" (Mahmood 2004, 10).

7. See Assad 2003, 71.

8. See also Mahmood's (2004, 25) discussion of Butler.

9. Mahmood's (2004) study of Islamic religious practices is useful in thinking through a concrete way in which the relationship between interiority, exteriority, and agency works. Her aim is in part to show that there is an alternative to an analysis of religious practice that relies on a liberal vision of agency as autonomy. This alternative, she suggests, turns on a different experience of freedom that needs to be understood on its own grounds. The liberal version of agency involves an interior experience of freedom as autonomous will; agency thus emanates outward in an attempt to establish uniqueness or specificity. By contrast, an exterior modality of agency, which Mahmood suggests better characterizes the pioutous practices of Islamic women, means that freedom is experienced as coming from the enactment of a series of practices themselves.

10. The biodiversity subject is much like Paul Robbins's (2007) lawn subject, or turf-grass subject. As Epstein (2008) notes, there is also an important distinction between subjectivity and subject position—a subject position can be inhabited by an individual or a group but does not require subjectivity or consciousness.

11. See Death 2011.

12. The same can be said of the study of norms in international relations, which have had a tendency to highlight liberal, progressive norms in world politics. See Epstein 2012.

13. See Worster 1977.

14. See Haraway 2008.

15. See Buscher 2014. Precisely because of its abstracted quality that privileges form, species can be turned into "species banking": see http://www.speciesbanking .com/. Buscher rightly points to the possibility of reemphasizing the long-term time horizons and emergent qualities needed to generate biodiversity as a way to reanimate the critical political potential of the term.

Bibliography

Adams, W. M. 1990. *Green Development: Environment and Sustainability in the Third World*. New York: Routledge.

Adger, Neil. 2000. "Social and Ecological Resilience: Are They Related?" *Progress in Human Geography* 24, no. 3: 347–64.

Agamben, Giorgio. 1998. *Homo Sacer: Sovereign Power and Bare Life*. Stanford, Calif.: Stanford University Press.

———. 2004. *The Open: Man and Animal*. Stanford, Calif.: Stanford University Press.

Agrawal, Arun. 2005. "Environmentality: Community, Intimate Government, and the Making of Environmental Subjects in Kumaon, India." *Current Anthropology* 46, no. 2: 161–90.

Alagona, Peter. 2013. *After the Grizzly: Endangered Species and the Politics of Place in California*. Berkeley: University of California Press.

Allen, John. 2003. *Lost Geographies of Power*. Oxford: Blackwell.

———. 2004. "The Whereabouts of Power: Politics, Government, and Space." *Geografiska Annaler: Series B, Human Geography* 86B, no. 1: 19–32.

Anderson, Benedict. 1983. *Imagined Communities*. London: Verso.

Archibugi, Danielle, David Held, and Martin Kohler, eds. 1998. *Re-imagining Political Community*. Stanford, Calif.: Stanford University Press.

Arendt, Hannah. 1958. *The Human Condition*. Chicago: University of Chicago Press.

Aristotle. 1996. *The Politics and the Constitution of Athens*. New York: Cambridge University Press.

Arsel, Murat, and Bram Buscher. 2012. "Nature™Inc.: Changes and Continuities in Neoliberal Conservation and Market-Based Environmental Policy." *Development and Change* 43, no. 1: 53–78.

Asad, Talal. 2003. *Formations of the Secular: Christianity, Islam, Modernity*. Stanford, Calif.: Stanford University Press.

Atran, Scott. 1990. *Cognitive Foundations of Natural History: Towards an Anthropology of Science*. Cambridge: Cambridge University Press.

Bamford, Sandra. 2002. "On Being 'Natural' in the Rainforest Marketplace: Science, Capitalism, and the Commodification of Biodiversity." *Social Analysis* 46, no. 1: 35–50.

Barnett, Michael, and Thomas G. Weiss, eds. 2008. *Humanitarianism in Question: Politics, Power, Ethics*. Ithaca, N.Y.: Cornell University Press.

Barry, Andrew. 2013. "The Translation Zone: Between Actor-Network Theory and International Relations." *Millennium* 41, no. 3: 413–29.

Barwick, Linda. 1990. "Central Australian Women's Ritual Music: Knowing through Analysis versus Knowing through Performance." *Yearbook for Traditional Music* 22:60–79.

Belloni, Roberto. 2007. "The Trouble with Humanitarianism." *Review of International Studies* 33:451–74.

Bennett, Jane. 1994. "Why Thoreau Hates Politics." In *Thoreau's Nature: Ethics, Politics, and the Wild*, 1–13. Lanham, Md.: Rowman and Littlefield.

———. 2001. *The Enchantment of Modern Life: Attachments, Crossings, and Ethics*. Princeton: Princeton University Press.

———. 2005a. "In Parliament with Things." In *Radical Democracy: Politics between Abundance and Lack*, ed. Lars Toender and Lasse Thomassen, 133–48. Manchester: Manchester University Press.

———. 2005b. "The Agency of Assemblages and the North American Blackout." *Public Culture* 17, no. 3: 445–65.

———. 2010. *Vibrant Matter: A Political Ecology of Things*. Durham, N.C.: Duke University Press.

Biermann, Frank. 2002. "Green Global Governance: The Case for a World Environment Organisation." *New Economy* 9, no. 2: 82–86.

Bingham, Nick. 2006. "Bees, Butterflies, and Bacteria: Biotechnology and the Politics of Nonhuman Friendship." *Environment and Planning A* 38, no. 3: 483–98.

Blaustein, Richard. 2013. "Urban Biodiversity Gains New Converts." *Bioscience* 63:72–77.

Bogost, Ian. 2012. *Alien Phenomenology; Or, What It's Like to Be a Thing*. Minneapolis: University of Minnesota.

Bookchin, Murray. 1995. *Social Anarchism or Lifestyle Anarchism*. Stirling: AK Books.

Braun, Bruce. 2007. "Biopolitics and the Molecularization of Life." *Cultural Geographies* 14:6–28.

Braun, Bruce, and Sarah Whatmore, eds. 2010. *Political Matter: Technoscience, Democracy, and Public Life*. Minneapolis: University of Minnesota Press.

Broad, William. 1979. "Paul Feyerabend: Science and the Anarchist." *Science* 206, no. 4418: 534–37.

Brown, Chris. 1997. "Universal Human Rights: A Critique." *International Journal of Human Rights* 1, no. 2: 41–65.

Bryant, Raymond L., and Sinead Bailey. 1997. *Third World Political Ecology*. New York: Routledge.

Buell, Frederick. 2003. *From Apocalypse to Way of Life: Environmental Crisis in the American Century*. New York: Routledge.

Buggey, Susan. 1995. "Cultural Landscapes in Canada." In *Cultural Landscapes of*

Universal Value, ed. B. von Droste, H. Plachter, and M. Rossler, 252–71. New York: Gustav Fischer.

Buscher, Bram. 2013. *Transforming the Frontier: Peace Parks and the Politics of Neoliberal Conservation in Southern Africa*. Durham, N.C.: Duke University Press.

———. 2014. "Biodiversity." In *Critical Environmental Politics*, ed. Carl Death, 13–21. New York: Routledge.

Bush, Sargent. 2000. "America's Origin Myth: Remembering Plymouth Rock." *American Literary History* 12, no. 4: 745–56.

Butler, Judith. 1997. *The Psychic Life of Power*. Stanford, Calif.: Stanford University Press.

Buzan, Barry, David Held, and Anthony McGrew. 1998. "Realism vs Cosmopolitanism: A Debate." *Review of International Studies* 24, no. 3: 387–98.

Callicott, J. Baird, and Michael P. Nelson, eds. 1998. *The Great New Wilderness Debate*. Athens: University of Georgia Press.

Callon, Michel. 1986. "Some Elements of a Sociology of Translation: Domestication of the Scallops and the Fishermen of St. Brieuc Bay." In *Power, Action, Belief: A New Sociology of Knowledge*, ed. John Law, 196–223. London: Routledge.

Campbell, David. 1998. "Why Fight: Humanitarianism, Principles, and Post-Structuralism." *Millennium* 27, no. 3: 497–521.

Casper, Monica. 1994. "Reframing and Grounding Nonhuman Agency." *American Behavioral Scientist* 37, no. 6: 839–56.

Castree, Noel. 2002. "False Antitheses? Marxism, Nature, and Actor-Networks." *Antipode* 34, no. 1: 111–46.

Cederman, Lars-Erik. 1997. *Emergent Actors in World Politics: How States and Nations Develop and Dissolve*. Princeton: Princeton University Press.

Chakrabarty, Dipesh. 2000. *Provincializing Europe: Postcolonial Thought and Historical Difference*. Princeton: Princeton University Press.

Chaloupka, William. 2000. "Jagged Terrain: Cronon, Soule, and the Struggle over Nature and Deconstruction in Environmental Theory." *Strategies: Journal of Theory, Culture & Politics* 16, no. 2: 23–38.

Chasek, Pamela S., David L. Downie, and Janet Welsh Brown, eds. 2010. *Global Environmental Politics*. Boulder, Colo.: Westview Press.

Chatwin, Bruce. 1987. *The Songlines*. New York: Penguin Books.

Cincotta, R. P., J. Wisnewski, and R. Engelman. 2000. "Human Population in the Biodiversity Hotspots." *Nature* 404:990–92.

Cleere, Henry. 1993. *Framework for a Global Study*. Paris: ICOMOS.

Cocks, Michelle. 2006. "Biocultural Diversity: Moving Beyond the Realm of 'Indigenous' and 'Local' People." *Human Ecology* 34, no. 2: 185–200.

Connolly, William. 2011. *A World of Becoming*. Durham, N.C.: Duke University Press.

Conservation International. 2005. "Biodiversity Hotspots." http://biodiversityhotspots.org/xp/Hotspots/hotspotsScience.

Coole, Diana, and Samantha Frost, eds. 2010. *New Materialisms; Ontology, Agency, Politics*. Durham, N.C.: Duke University Press.

Cronon, William. 1992. *Nature's Metropolis: Chicago and the Great West.* New York: W. W. Norton.

———. 1995a. "The Trouble with Wilderness; or, Getting Back to the Wrong Nature." In *Uncommon Ground: Toward Reinventing Nature,* 69–90. New York: W. W. Norton.

———, ed. 1995b. *Uncommon Ground: Toward Reinventing Nature.* New York: W. W. Norton.

Cudworth, Erika, and Stephen Hobden. 2011. *Posthuman International Relations: Complexity, Ecologism, and Global Politics.* New York: Zed Books.

Davic, Robert D. 2003. "Linking Keystone Species and Functional Groups: A New Operational Definition of the Keystone Species Concept." *Conservation Ecology* 7, no. 1: r11.

Davison, Graeme. 1991. "The Meanings of 'Heritage.'" In *A Heritage Handbook,* ed. G. Davison and C. McConville, 1–13. North Sydney: Allen and Unwin.

Death, Carl. 2011. "Summit Theatre: Exemplary Governmentality and Environmental Diplomacy." *Environmental Politics* 20, no. 1: 1–19.

Debrix, Francois. 1999. "Space Quest: Surveillance, Governance, and the Panoptic Eye of the United Nations." *Alternatives* 24:269–94.

———, ed. 2003. *Language, Agency, and Politics in a Constructed World.* New York: M. E. Sharpe.

Decker, Cynthia J., and Ron O'Dor. 2002. "A Census of Marine Life: Unknowable or Just Unknown?" *Oceanologica Acta* 25, no. 5: 179–86.

Deely, John. 1990. *Basics of Semiotics.* Bloomington: Indiana University Press.

———. 2001a. "A Sign Is What? A Dialogue between a Semiotician and a Would-Be Realist." *Sign Systems Studies* 29, no. 2: 705–43.

———. 2001b. "Umwelt." *Semiotica* 134, no. 1: 125–35.

Deleuze, Gilles, and Félix Guattari. 1987. *A Thousand Plateaus: Capitalism and Schizophrenia.* Translated by Brian Massumi. Minneapolis: University of Minnesota Press.

DeLong, Don C., Jr. 1996. "Defining Biodiversity." *Wildlife Society Bulletin* 24:738–49.

Der Derian, James. 1990. "The Space of International Relations: Simulation, Surveillance, and Speed." *International Studies Quarterly* 34, no. 3: 295–310.

Derrida, Jacques. 2008. *The Animal That Therefore I Am.* Translated by David Wills. Edited by Marie Louise Mallett. New York: Fordham University Press.

———. 2009. *The Beast and the Sovereign.* Translated by Geoffery Bennington. Chicago: University of Chicago Press.

DeSombre, Elizabeth. 2007a. "Science, Uncertainty, and Risk." In *The Global Environment and World Politics,* 39–47, 50–53. New York: Continuum.

———. 2007b. *The Global Environment and World Politics.* 2nd ed. New York: Continuum.

Devall, Bill, and George Sessions. 1985. *Deep Ecology: Living as If Nature Mattered.* Salt Lake City: Peregrine Smith Books.

Dillon, Michael, and Julian Reid. 2001. "Global Liberal Governance: Biopolitics, Security, and War." *Millennium* 30, no. 1: 41–66.

———. 2009. *The Liberal Way of War: The Martial Face of Global Biopolitics.* New York: Routledge.

Dobson, Andrew P. 1996. *Conservation and Biodiversity*. New York: Scientific American Library.

Dobson, Andrew P., and Robert M. May. 1986. "Disease and Conservation." In *Conservation Biology: The Science of Scarcity and Diversity*, ed. Michel Soule, 345–65. Sunderland, Mass.: Sinauer.

Donlan, C. J., J. Berger, C. Bock, J. Bock, and D. Burney. 2006. "Pleistocene Rewilding: An Optimistic Agenda for Twenty-First Century Conservation." *American Naturalist* 168, no. 5: 660–81.

Doty, Roxanne L. 1997. "Aporia: A Critical Exploration of the Agent-Structure Problematique in International Relations Theory." *European Journal of International Relations* 3, no 3: 365–92.

Dryzek, John. 2000. *Deliberative Democracy and Beyond: Liberals, Critics, and Contestations*. Oxford: Oxford University Press.

———. 2005. *The Politics of the Earth: Environmental Discourses*. 2nd ed. New York: Oxford University Press.

Duvall, Raymond, and Michael N. Barnett. 2005. "Power and Global Governance." In *Power and Global Governance*, ed. Raymond Duvall and Michael N. Barnett, 1–32. New York: Cambridge University Press.

Eckersley, Robyn. 1992. *Environmentalism and Political Theory: Toward an Ecocentric Approach*. Albany: State University of New York Press.

———. 1999. "The Discourse Ethic and the Problem of Representing Nature." *Environmental Politics* 8, no. 2: 24–49.

———. 2004. *The Green State: Rethinking Democracy and Sovereignty*. Cambridge: MIT Press.

Eisenberg, Cristina. 2010. *The Wolf's Tooth: Keystone Predators, Trophic Cascades, and Biodiversity*. Washington, D.C.: Island Press.

Elam, Mark. 1999. "Living Dangerously with Bruno Latour in a Hybrid World." *Theory, Culture, and Society* 16, no. 4: 1–24.

Elmqvist, Thomas , Carl Folke, Magnus Nyström, Garry Peterson, Jan Bengtsson, Brian Walker, and Jon Norberg. 2003. "Response Diversity, Ecosystem Change, and Resilience." *Frontiers in Ecology and Environment* 1, no. 9: 488–94.

Epstein, Charlotte. 2008. *The Power of Words in International Relations: Birth of a Whaling Discourse*. Cambridge: MIT Press.

———. 2012. "Stop Telling Us How to Behave: Socialization or Infantilization?" *International Studies Perspectives* 13, no. 2: 135–45.

Ereshefsky, Marc. 2001. *Poverty of Linnaean Hierarchy: A Philosophical Study of Biological Taxonomy*. Portchester, N.Y.: Cambridge University Press.

Erwin, Terry. 1983. "Beetles and Other Insects of Tropical Forest Canopies at Manaus, Brazil, Sampled by Insecticidal Fogging." In *Tropical Rain Forest: Ecology and Management*, ed. S. L. Sutton, T. C. Whitmore, and A. C. Chadwick, 59–75. London: Blackwell.

Escobar, Arturo. 1995. *Encountering Development: The Making and Unmaking of the Third World*. Princeton: Princeton University Press.

———. 1996. "Constructing Nature." In *Liberation Ecologies: Environment, Development, and Social Movements*, ed. Richard Peet and Michael Watts, 46–68. New York: Routledge.

———. 1998. "Whose Knowledge, Whose Nature? Biodiversity, Conservation, and Political Ecology of Social Movements." *Journal of Political Ecology* 5:53–82.

———. 1999. "After Nature: Steps to an Antiessentialist Political Ecology." *Current Anthropology* 40, 1:1–30.

Esposito, Roberto. 2008. *Bios: Biopolitics and Philosophy*. Minneapolis: University of Minnesota Press.

Esty, Daniel, and Maria Ivanova. 2002. "Revitalizing Global Environmental Governance: A Function-Driven Approach." In *Global Environmental Governance: Options and Opportunities*, ed. Daniel Esty and Maria Ivanova, 181–204. New Haven: Yale School of Forestry & Environmental Studies.

Fanon, Frantz. 1967. *Black Skin, White Masks*. New York: Grove Press.

Ferguson, James. 1990. *The Anti-Politics Machine: 'Development,' Depoliticization, and Bureaucratic Power in Lesotho*. Minneapolis: University of Minnesota Press.

Ferry, Luc. 1995. *The New Ecological Order*. Translated by Carol Volk. Chicago: University of Chicago Press.

Fixdal, Mona, and Dan Smith. 1998. "Humanitarian Intervention and Just War." *Mershon International Studies Review* 42:283–312.

Flannery, Tim. 2001. *The Eternal Frontier: An Ecological History of North America and Its Peoples*. New York: Grove Press.

Foreman, Dave. 2004. Rewilding North America: A Vision for Conservation in North America. Washington, D.C.: Island Press.

Foucault, Michel. 1978. *The History of Sexuality: Volume 1*. New York: Vintage Books.

———. 1995. *Discipline & Punish: The Birth of the Prison*. New York: Vintage Books.

———. 1997. *Society Must Be Defended: Lectures at the Collège de France, 1975–1976*. New York: St. Martin's Press.

———. 2007. *Security, Territory, Population: Lectures at the Collège de France*. New York: Palgrave Macmillan.

Fox, Warwick. 1990. *Towards a Transpersonal Ecology: Developing New Foundations for Environmentalism*. Boston: Shambhala.

Fraser, Caroline. 2009. *Rewilding the World: Dispatches from the Conservation Revolution*. New York: Picador.

Frisch, M. 1998. "Possessed by the Past: The Heritage Crusade and the Spoils of History." *American Historical Review* 103, no. 5: 1567–68.

Fry, Tony. 2011. *Design as Politics*. New York: Berg.

Fuller, Steve. 1994. "Making Agency Count." *American Behavioral Scientist* 37, no. 6: 741–53.

Galison, Peter. 1996. "Introduction: The Context of Disunity." In *The Disunity of Science: Boundaries, Contexts, and Power*, edited by Peter Galison and David Stump, 1–36. Stanford, Calif.: Stanford University Press.

———. 1999. "Trading Zone: Coordinating Action and Belief." In *Science Studies Reader*, edited by M. Biagoli, 137–60. New York: Routledge.

Gandy, Matthew. 2002. *Concrete and Clay: Reworking Nature in New York City*. Cambridge: MIT Press.

———. 2004. "Rethinking Urban Metabolism: Water, Space, and the Modern City." *City* 8, no. 3: 363–79.

Gaston, Kevin J., and John I. Spicer. 2004. *Biodiversity: An Introduction*. Malden, Mass.: Blackwell.

Giddens, Anthony. 1984. *The Constitution of Society*. Berkeley: University of California Press.

Gill, Stephen. 1995. "The Global Panopticon? The Neoliberal State, Economic Life, and Democratic Surveillance." *Alternatives* 20, no. 1: 1–49.

Goldman, Michael. 2001. "Constructing an Environmental State: Eco-governmentality and Other Transnational Practices of a 'Green' World Bank." *Social Problems* 48, no. 4: 499–523.

Greenblatt, Stephen. 1980. *Renaissance Self-Fashioning: From More to Shakespeare*. Chicago: Univeristy of Chicago.

Groombridge, Brian, and Martin Jenkins. 2002. *World Atlas of Biodiversity: Earth's Living Resources in the 21st Century*. Berkeley: University of California Press.

Guha, Ramachandra. 2000. *Environmentalism: A Global History*. New York: Longman.

Haas, Peter. 1990. "Obtaining International Environmental Protection through Epistemic Consensus." *Millennium* 90:347–64.

———. 1992. "Introduction: Epistemic Communities and International Policy Coordination." *International Organization* 46, no. 1:1–35.

Haas, Peter M., Robert O. Keohane, and Marc A. Levy, eds. 1993. *Institutions for the Earth: Sources of Effective International Environmental Protection*. Cambridge: MIT Press.

Hajer, Maarten A. 1995. *The Politics of Environmental Discourse: Ecological Modernization and the Policy Process*. Oxford: Clarendon Press.

Hanson, Elizabeth. 2004. *Animal Attractions: Nature on Display in American Zoos*. Princeton: Princeton University Press.

Haraway, Donna. 1991. *Simians, Cyborgs, and Women*. New York: Routledge Press.

———. 1997. *Modest_Witness@Second_Millennium.FemaleMan(c)_Meets_Oncomouse (tm): Feminism and Technoscience*. New York: Routledge.

———. 2008. *When Species Meet*. Minneapolis: University of Minnesota Press.

Hardt, Michael, and Antonio Negri. 2000. *Empire*. Cambridge: Harvard University Press.

Harman, Graham. 2009. *Prince of Networks*. Melbourne: re.press.

———. 2011. *The Quadruple Object*. New Alresford, UK: John Hunt.

Harman, Graham, Nick Srnicek, and Levi Bryant, eds. 2011. *The Speculative Turn: Continental Materialism and Realism*. Melbourne: re.press.

Harmon, David. 2002. *In Light of Our Differences: How Diversity in Nature and Culture Makes Us Human*. Washington, D.C.: Smithsonian Institution Press.

Harmon, David, and Jonathon Loh. 2004. "A Global Index of Biocultural Diversity." *Paper presented at the International Congress on Ethnobiology*, University of Kent, UK.

Harvey, David. 1996. *Justice, Nature, and the Geography of Difference*. Cambridge, Mass.: Blackwell.

Hayden, Corinne P. 1998. "A Biodiversity Sampler for the Millennium." In *Reproducing Reproduction: Kinship, Power, and Technological Innovation*, ed. S. Franklin and H. Ragone, 173–206. Philadelphia: University of Pennsylvania Press.

Hayles, N. Katherine. 1999. *How We Became Posthuman: Virtual Bodies in Cybernetics, Literature, and Informatics*. Chicago: University of Chicago Press.

Hewison, Robert. 1989. "Heritage: An Interpretation." In *Heritage Interpretation: The Natural and Built Environment*, ed. D. Uzzell, 15–23. New York: Belhaven Press.

Heyd, Thomas. 2005. "Nature, Culture, and Natural Heritage: Toward a Culture of Nature." *Environmental Ethics* 27, no. 4: 339–54.

Heynen, Nikolas, Maria Kaika, and Erik Swyngedouw, eds. 2006. *In the Nature of Cities: Urban Political Ecology and the Politics of Urban Metabolism*. New York: Routledge.

Heywood, V. H., and R. T. Watson. 1995. *Global Biodiversity Assessment*. Cambridge: Cambridge University Press.

Hinchcliffe, Steve, Matthew B. Kearnes, Monica Degen, and Sarah Whatmore. 2005. "Urban Wild Things: A Cosmopolitical Experiment." *Environment and Planning D* 23, no. 5: 643–58.

Hinchcliffe, Steve, and Sarah Whatmore. 2006. "Living Cities: Towards a Politics of Conviviality." *Science as Culture* 15, no. 2: 123–38.

Holling, C. S. 1973. "Resilience and Stability of Ecological Systems." *Annual Review of Ecology and Systematics* 4:1–23.

Holloway, Lewis. 2007. "Subjecting Cows to Robots: Farming Technologies and the Making of Animal Subjects." *Environment and Planning D* 25, no. 6: 1041–60.

Holloway, Lewis, and Carol Morris. 2007. "Exploring Biopower in the Regulation of Farm Animal Bodies: Genetic Policy Interventions in UK Livestock." *Genomics, Society and Policy* 3, no. 2: 82–98.

Hopkins, Rob. 2008. *The Transition Handbook: From Oil Dependency to Local Resilience*. Totnes Devon, UK: Green Books.

Hostetler, Mark. 2012. *The Green Leap: A Primer for Conserving Biodiversity in Subdivision Development*. Berkeley: University of California Press.

Hurd, Elizabeth Shakman. 2008. *The Politics of Secularism in International Relations*. Princeton: Princeton University Press.

ICOMOS 1988. Recommendation for Inscription. http://whc.unesco.org/archive/advisory_body_evaluation/455.pdf.

IUCN. 2004. "The World Heritage List: Future Priorities for a Credible and Complete List of Natural and Mixed Sites." Twenty-Eighth Session of the World Heritage Committee, Suzhou, China.

Jackson, Patrick T. 2011. *The Conduct of Inquiry in International Relations: Philosophy of Science and Its Implications for the Study of World Politics*. New York: Routledge.

Jasanoff, Sheila. 2006. "Biotechnology and Empire: The Global Power of Seeds and Science." *History of Science and Society* 21:273–92.

Jepson, Paul, and Susan Canney. 2001. "Biodiversity Hotspots: Hot for What?" *Global Ecology and Biology* 10:225–27.

Jerolmack, Colin. 2013. *The Global Pigeon*. Chicago: University of Chicago Press.

Jervis, Robert. 1998. *System Effects: Complexity in Political and Social Life*. Princeton: Princeton University Press.

Joe, Tony, Luisa Maffi, Gary Paul Nabhan, and Patrick Pynes. 2002. *Safeguarding the Uniqueness of the Colorado Plateau: An Ecoregional Assessment of Biocultural Diversity*. Flagstaff, Ariz.: Center for Sustainable Environments.

Kareiva, Peter. 2011. "The Future of Conservation: Balancing the Needs of People and Nature." *Nature Conservancy* 61, no. 1: 38–39.

Kareiva, Peter, and Michelle Marvier. 2003. "Conserving Biodiversity Coldspots." *American Scientist* 91:344–51.

Kareiva, Peter, Sean Watts, Robert McDonald, and Tim Boucher. 2007. "Domesticated Nature: Shaping Landscapes and Ecosystems for Human Welfare." *Science* 316, no. 5833: 1866–69.

Katz, Eric. 1985. "Organism, Community, and the 'Substitution Problem.'" *Environmental Ethics* 7, no. 3: 241–55.

Kelly, Kevin. 2000. "All Species Inventory: A Call for the Discovery of All Life-Forms on Earth." *Whole Earth* (Fall): 4–9.

Kidner, David W. 2000. "Fabricating Nature: A Critique of the Social Construction of Nature." *Environmental Ethics* 22, no. 4: 339–58.

Kirksey, S. Eben, and Stefan Helmreich. 2010. "The Emergence of Multispecies Ethnography." *Cultural Anthropology* 25, no. 4: 545–76.

Kirsch, Scott, and Don Mitchell. 2004. "The Nature of Things: Dead Labor, Nonhuman Actors, and the Persistence of Marxism." *Antipode* 36, no. 4: 687–705.

Klyza, Christopher, ed. 2001. *Wilderness Comes Home: Rewilding the Northeast*. Hanover, Vt.: Middlebury College Press.

Knorr-Cetina, Karin. 1981. *The Manufacture of Knowledge*. New York: Pergamon Press.

———. 1999. *Epistemic Cultures: How the Sciences Make Knowledge*. Cambridge: Harvard University Press.

Kolbert, Elizabeth. 2012. "Recall of the Wild." *New Yorker* 88, no. 41: 50–60.

Kuehls, Thom. 1996. *Beyond Sovereign Territory*. Minneapolis: University of Minnesota Press.

Laferriere, Eric, and Peter J. Stoett, eds. 2006. *International Ecopolitical Theory: Critical Approaches*. Vancouver: University of British Columbia Press.

Laland, Kevin N., and Bennett G. Galef, eds. 2009. *The Question of Animal Culture*. Cambridge: Harvard University Press.

Latour, Bruno. 1987. *Science in Action*. Cambridge: Harvard University Press.

———. 1993. *We Have Never Been Modern*. Cambridge: Harvard University Press.

———. 1996. "On Actor-Network Theory: A Few Clarifications." *Soziale Welt* 47:369–81.

———. 1999. *Pandora's Hope: Essays on the Reality of Science Studies*. Cambridge: Harvard University Press.

———. 2004. *Politics of Nature: How to Bring the Sciences into Democracy*. Cambridge: Harvard University Press.

———. 2005. *Reassembling the Social: An Introduction to Actor-Network Theory*. Oxford: Oxford University Press.

Law, John, ed. 1991. *A Sociology of Monsters: Essays on Power, Technology, and Domination*. London: Routledge.

Law, John, and John Hassard, eds. 1999. *Actor Network Theory and After*. Oxford: Blackwell.

Lawler, Andrew. 2001. "Up for the Count?" *Science* 294, no. 5543: 769–70.

Layton, Robert. 1986. *Uluru: An Aboriginal History of Ayers Rock*. Canberra: Aboriginal Studies Press.

Layton, Robert, and Sarah Titchen. 1995. "Uluru: An Outstanding Australian Aboriginal Cultural Landscape." In *Cultural Landscapes of Universal Value*, ed. B. von Droste, H. Plachter and M. Rossler, 174–81. New York: Gustav Fischer.

Lee, Nick, and Steve Brown. 1994. "Otherness and the Actor Network." *American Behavioral Scientist* 37, no. 6: 772–89.

Leopold, Aldo. 1949. "Thinking Like a Mountain." In *A Sand County Almanac*, 129–33. New York: Oxford.

LePrestre, Phillipe, ed. 2003. *Governing Global Biodiversity: The Evolution and Implementation of the Convention on Biological Diversity*. Aldershot: Ashgate.

Lewis, Michael. 2003. *Inventing Global Ecology: Tracking the Biodiversity Ideal in India, 1947–1997*. Athens: Ohio University Press.

Linklater, Andrew. 1998. *The Transformation of Political Community*. Columbia: University of South Carolina Press.

Litfin, Karen. 1994. *Ozone Discourses*. New York: Columbia University Press.

Livingston, Julie, and Jasbir Puar. 2011. "Interspecies." *Social Text* 29, no. 1: 1–14.

Lorimer, Jamie, and Clements Driessen. 2013. "Wild Experiments at the Oostvaardersplassen: Rethinking Environmentalism for the Anthropocene." *Transactions of the Institute of British Geographers* 39, no. 2: 169–81.

Lovejoy, Thomas E. 1994. "The Quantification of Biodiversity: An Esoteric Quest or a Vital Component of Sustainable Development?" *Philosophical Transactions of the Royal Society of London B* 345:81–87.

Lowe, Celia. 2006. *Wild Profusion: Biodiversity Conservation in an Indonesian Archipelago*. Princeton: Princeton University Press.

Lowenthal, David. 1995. "Fabricating Heritage." *History and Memory* 10, no. 1: 5–24.

———. 1998. *Possessed by the Past: The Heritage Crusade and the Spoils of History*. Cambridge: Cambridge University Press.

Lucas, Colin. 1992. "Power and the Panopticon." In *Critical Essays on Michel Foucault*, ed. Peter Burke, 135–38. Brookfield, Vt.: Ashgate.

Luke, Timothy. 1995. "On Environmentality: Geo-Power and Eco-Knowledge in the Discourses of Contemporary Environmentalism." *Cultural Critique* 31:57–81.

———. 1999. "Environmentality as Green Governmentality." In *Discourses of the Environment*, ed. E. Darier, 121–51. Malden, Mass.: Blackwell.

Maffi, Luisa, ed. 2001. *On Biocultural Diversity: Linking Language, Knowledge, and the Environment*. Washington, D.C.: Smithsonian Institute.

———. 2005. "Linguistic, Cultural, and Biological Diversity." *Annual Review of Anthropology* 29:599–617.

Mahmood, Sabba. 2004. *Politics of Piety: The Islamic Revival and the Subject of Feminism*. Princeton: Princeton University Press.

Margolin, Victor. 2002. *The Politics of the Artificial*. Chicago: University of Chicago Press.

Mathews, Freya. 1991. *The Ecological Self*. London: Routledge.

———. 2003. *For Love of Matter: A Contemporary Panpsychism*. Albany: State University of New York Press.

Mawdsley, Emma. 1998. "After Chipko: From Environment to Region in Uttaranchal." *Journal of Peasant Studies* 25, no. 4: 36–54.

May, R. M., J. H. Lawton, and N. E. Stork. 1995. "Assessing Extinction Rates." In *Extinction Rates*, ed. J. H. Lawton and R. M. May, 1–24. Oxford: Oxford University Press.

Mayr, Ernst. 2001. *What Evolution Is*. New York: Basic Books.

McCann, Kevin Shear. 2000. "The Diversity-Stability Debate." *Nature* 405:228–33.

McConnell, Fiona. 1996. *The Biodiversity Convention: A Negotiating History*. London: Kluwer Law International.

McGraw, Desiree M. 2002. "The Story of the Biodiversity Convention: From Negotiation to Implementation." In *Governing Global Biodiversity: The Evolution and Implementation of the Convention on Biological Diversity*, ed. Phillipe LePrestre, 7–38. Aldershot: Ashgate.

McHarg, Ian. 1995. *Design with Nature*. New York: John Wiley and Sons.

McKibben, Bill. 1989. *The End of Nature*. New York: Random House.

McPhee, John. 1998. *Irons in the Fire*. New York: Farrar, Straus & Giroux.

Meadows, Donella H., Dennis L. Meadows, Jorgen Randers, and Williams W. Behrens III. 1972. *The Limits to Growth: A Report for the Club of Rome's Project on the Predicament of Mankind*. New York: Universe Books.

Methman, Chris. 2013. "The Sky Is the Limit: Global Warming as Global Governmentality." *European Journal of International Relations* 19, no. 1: 69–91.

Millennium Ecosystem Assessment. 2005a. *Ecosystems and Human Well-Being: Synthesis Report*. Washington, D.C.: Island Press.

———. 2005b. *Ecosystems and Human-Well Being: Biodiversity Synthesis*. Washington, D.C.: World Resources Institute.

Mitchell, Ronald B. 2003. "International Environmental Agreements: A Survey of Their Features, Formation, and Effects." *Annual Review of Environmental Resources* 28:429–61.

———. 2010. *International Politics and the Environment*. Los Angeles: Sage.

Mitchell, Timothy. 2002. *Rule of Experts: Egypt, Techno-Politics, Modernity*. Berkeley: University of California Press.

Mittermeier, Russell A., and Norman Myers. 1998. "Biodiversity Hotspots and Major Tropical Wilderness Areas: Approaches to Setting Conservation Priorities." *Conservation Biology* 12, no 3: 516–20.

Mittermeier, Russell A., Norman Myers, and Cristina Mittermeier. 1999. *Hotspots: Earth's Biologically Richest and Most Endangered Terrestrial Ecoregions*. Mexico City: CEMEX.

Monbiot, George. 2013. *Feral: Searching for Enchantment of the Frontiers of Rewilding*. New York: Penguin Books.

Mooney, Harold, and Paul Ehrlich. 1997. "Ecosystem Services: A Fragmentary History." In *Nature's Services: Societal Dependence on Natural Ecosystems*, ed. Gretchen Daily, 11–22. Washington, D.C.: Island Press.

Moore, J. L., L. Manne, T. Brooks, N. D. Burgess, R. Davies, C. Rahbek, P. Williams, and A. Balmford. 2002. "The Distribution of Cultural and Biological Diversity in Africa." *Proceedings of the Royal Society of London B* 269:1645–53.

Moravscik, Andrew. 2002. "Reassessing Legitimacy in the EU." *Journal of Common Market Studies* 40, no. 4: 603–25.

Morton, Timothy. 2007. *Ecology without Nature*. Cambridge: Harvard University Press.

Mühlhäusler, Peter. 1996. *Linguistic Ecology: Language Change and Linguistic Imperialism in the Pacific Rim*. London: Routledge.

Mulligan, Shane. 2010. "Reassessing the Crisis: Ecology and Liberal International Relations." *Alternatives: Global, Local, Political* 35:137–62.

Myers, Norman. 1988. "Threatened Biotas: 'Hot Spots' in Tropical Forests." *Environmentalist* 8, no. 3: 187–208.

———. 1990. "The Biodiversity Challenge: Expanded Hot-Spots Analysis." *Environmentalist* 10, no. 4: 243–56.

Myers, Norman, Russell Mittermeier, Cristina Mittermeier, Gustavo A. B. de Fonseca, and Jennifer Kent. 2000. "Biodiversity Hotspots for Conservation Priorities." *Nature* 403:853–58.

Nabhan, Gary Paul, and Sara St. Antoine. 1993. "The Loss of Floral and Faunal Story: The Extinction of Experience." In *The Biophilia Hypothesis*, ed. Stephen R. Kellert and Edward O. Wilson, 229–50. Washington, D.C.: Island Press.

Naess, Arne. 1985. "Identification as a Source of Deep Ecological Attitudes." In *Deep Ecology*, ed. Michael Tobias. Santa Monica: IMT Productions.

Najam, Adil. 2003. "The Case against a New International Environmental Organization." *Global Governance* 9:367–84.

Najam, Adil, Ioli Chrisopoulu, and William R. Moomaw. 2004. "The Emergent 'System' of Global Environmental Governance." *Global Environmental Politics* 4, no. 4: 23–35.

Nicol, Donald M. 1963. *Meteora: The Rock Monasteries of Thessaly*. London: Chapman and Hall.

Nordhaus, Ted, and Michael Shellenberger. 2004. "The Death of Environmentalism." www.thebreakthrough.org/images/Death_of_Environmentalism.pdf

————. 2007. *Breakthrough: From the Death of Environmentalism to the Politics of Possibility.* Boston: Houghton Mifflin.

O'Connor, Martin. 1994. "On the Misadventures of Capitalist Nature." In *Is Capitalism Sustainable: Political Economy and the Politics of Ecology,* ed. Martin O'Connor, 125–51. New York: Guilford Press.

Office of Technology Assessment. 1988. *Technologies to Maintain Biodiversity.* Washington, D.C.: Office of Technology Assessment.

Oliviera, Jose Antonio Puppim de, Osman Balaban, Christopher Doll, Raquel Moreno-Penaranda, Alexandros Gasparatos, Delijana Iossifova, and Aki Suwa. 2010. *Cities, Biodiversity and Governance: Perspectives and Challenges of the Implementation of the Convention on Biological Diversity at the City Level.* Singapore: United Nations University Institute for Advanced Study.

Olson, David., and Eric Dinerstein. 1998. "The Global 200: A Representation Approach to Conserving Earth's Most Biologically Valuable Ecoregions." *Conservation Biology* 12, no. 3: 502–15.

Olwig, Kenneth R. 1989. "Nature Interpretation." In *Heritage Interpretation: The Natural and Built Environment,* ed. David Uzzell, 132–41. New York: Belhaven.

Onuf, Nick. 2004. "Humanitarian Intervention: The Early Years." *Florida Journal of International Law* 16, no. 4: 753–87.

Orford, Anne. 1999. "Muscular Humanitarianism: Reading the Narratives of the New Interventionism." *European Journal of International Law* 10, no. 4: 679–711.

Oviedo, Gonzalo, Luisa Maffi, and Peter B. Larsen. 2000. *Indigenous and Traditional Peoples of the World and Ecoregion Conservation: An Integrated Approach to Conserving the World's Biological and Cultural Diversity.* Gland: World Wildlife Fund for Nature.

Paterson, Matthew. 2000. *Understanding Global Environmental Politics: Domination, Accumulation, Resistance.* Houndmills: Macmillan Press.

Peet, Richard, Paul Robbins, and Michael Watts. 2011. *Global Political Ecology.* New York: Routledge.

Peet, Richard, and Michael Watts, eds. 1996. *Liberation Ecologies: Environment, Development, Social Movements.* New York: Routledge.

Peterson, Ivars. 1999. "Census Sampling Confusion." *Science News Online* 155, no. 10: 1–7.

Petit, Philip. 2003. "Agency-Freedom and Option-Freedom." *Journal of Theoretical Politics* 15, no. 4: 387–403.

Phillips, Adrian. 1995. "Cultural Landscapes: An IUCN Perspective." In *Cultural Landscapes of Universal Value,* ed. B. von Droste, H. Plachter, and M. Rossler, 380–92. New York: Gustav Fischer.

Pickering, Andrew, ed. 1992. *Science as Practice and Culture.* Chicago: University of Chicago Press.

Platt, Rutherford H., Rowan A. Rowntree, and Pamela C. Muick, eds. 1994. *The Ecological City.* Amherst: University of Massachusetts Press.

Plumwood, Val. 2002. "Towards a Dialogical Interspecies Ethics." In *Environmental Culture: The Ecological Crisis of Reason*, 167–95. New York: Routledge.

Pollan, Michael. 2006. *The Omnivore's Dilemma*. New York: Penguin Press.

Poovey, Mary. 1998. *A History of the Modern Fact: Problems of Knowledge in the Sciences of Wealth and Society*. Chicago: University of Chicago Press.

Posey, Darrell A., ed. 1999. *Cultural and Spiritual Values of Biodiversity*. London: Intermediate Technology (in association with UNEP).

Possingham, Hugh P., and Kerrie A. Wilson. 2005. "Biodiversity: Turning Up the Heat on Hotspots." *Nature* 436, no. 18: 919–20.

Prendergast, J. R., R. M. Quinn, and B. C. Lawton. 1993. "Rare Species, The Coincidence of Diversity Hotspots, and Conservation Strategies." *Nature* 365, no. 6444: 335–37.

Price-Williams, Douglass, and Rosslyn Gaines. 1994. "The Dreamtime and Dreams of Northern Australian Aboriginal Artists." *Ethos* 22, no. 3: 373–88.

Rabinow, Paul. 1989. *French Modern: Norms and Forms of the Social Environment*. Cambridge: MIT Press.

Rabinow, Paul, and Nikolas Rose. 2003. "Thoughts on the Concept of Biopower Today." http://www.lse.ac.uk/sociology/pdf/rabinowandrose-biopowertoday03.pdf.

———. 2006. "Biopower Today." *BioSocieties* 1:195–217.

Raffles, Hugh. 2002. *In Amazonia: A Natural History*. Princeton: Princeton University Press.

Raven, Peter H., and Edward O. Wilson. 1992. "A Fifty-Year Plan for Biodiversity Surveys." *Science* 258, no. 5085: 1099–100.

Rinfret, Sara. 2009. "Controlling Animals: Power, Foucault, and Species Management." *Society and Natural Resources* 22: 571–78.

Ritvo, Harriet. 1987. *The Animal Estate: The English and Other Creatures in the Victorian Age*. Cambridge: Harvard University Press.

———. 1997. *The Platypus and the Mermaid (and Other Figments of the Classifying Imagination)*. Cambridge: Harvard University Press.

Robbins, Paul. 2007. *Lawn People: How Grasses, Weeds, and Chemicals Make Us Who We Are*. Philadelphia: Temple University Press.

Rolston, Holmes. 1988. *Environmental Ethics: Duties to and Values in the Natural World*. Philadelphia: Temple University Press.

Rossler, Mechtild. 1995. "UNESCO and Cultural Landscape Protection." In *Cultural Landscapes of Universal Value*, ed. B. von Droste, H. Plachter, and M. Rossler. New York: Gustav Fischer.

Rutherford, Stephanie. 2007. "Green Governmentality: Insights and Opportuntiies in the Study of Nature's Rule." *Progress in Human Geography* 31, no. 3: 291–307.

Sanderson, Eric. 2009. *Manahatta: A Natural History of New York City*. New York: Harry N. Abrams.

Scott, James. 1998. *Seeing Like a State: How Certain Schemes to Improve the Human Condition Have Failed*. New Haven: Yale University Press.

Scott-Cato, Molly, and Jean Hillier. 2010. "How Could We Study Climate-Related Social Innovation? Applying Deleuzean Philosophy to Transition Towns." *Environmental Politics* 19, no. 6: 869–87.

Secretariat of the Convention on Biological Diversity. 2012. *Cities and Biodiversity Outlook*. Montreal: Secretariat of the Convention on Biological Diversity.

Serageldin, Ismail, Ephim Shluger, and Joan Martin-Brown, eds. 2001. *Historic Cities and Sacred Sites: Cultural Roots for Urban Futures*. Washington, D.C.: World Bank.

Serres, Michel. 2007. *The Parasite*. Minneapolis: University of Minnesota Press.

Shaw, Martin. 2000. *Theory of the Global State*. Cambridge: Cambridge University Press.

Shephard, Paul. 1998. *Coming Home to the Pleistocene*. Washington, D.C.: Island Press.

Shiva, Vandana. 1993. *Monocultures of the Mind*. New York: Zed Books.

———. 1999. "Ecological Balance in an Era of Globalization." In *Global Ethics and Environment*, ed. Nicholas Low, 47–69. London: Routledge Press.

Shukin, Nicole. 2009. *Animal Capital: Life in Biopolitical Times*. Minneapolis: University of Minnesota Press.

Sil, Rudra. 2000. "The Foundations of Eclecticism: The Epistemological Status of Agency, Culture, and Structure in Social Theory." *Journal of Theoretical Politics* 12, no. 3: 353–87.

Singer, J. David. 1969. "The Level-of-Analysis Problem in International Relations." In *International Politics and Foreign Policy*, ed. James Rosenau, 20–29. New York: Free Press.

Singer, Peter. 1990. *Animal Liberation*. New York: Avon Books.

Skutnabb-Kangas, Tove, Luisa Maffi, and David Harmon. 2003. *Sharing a World of Difference: The Earth's Linguistic, Cultural, and Biological Diversity*. Paris: UNESCO Publishing.

Soper, Kate. 1994. *What Is Nature?* Oxford: Blackwell.

Soule, Michael. 1985. "What Is Conservation Biology?" *BioScience* 35:727–34.

Soule, Michael, and Reed Noss. 1998. "Rewilding and Biodiversity: Complementary Goals for Continental Conservation." *Wild Earth* 8, no. 3: 18–28.

Stallybrass, Peter. 1993. "Worn Worlds: Clothes, Mourning, and the Life of Things." *Yale Review* 81, no. 2: 35–50.

Star, Susan Leigh, and James R. Griesemer. 1989. "Institutional Ecology, Translations, and Boundary Objects: Amateurs and Professionals in Berkeley's Museum of Vertebrate Zoology, 1907–29." *Social Studies of Science* 19:387–420.

Stein, Lincoln. 2002. "Creating a Bioinformatics Nation." *Nature* 417, no. 6889: 119–20.

Stille, Alexander. 2002. *The Future of the Past*. New York: Farrar, Straus & Giroux.

Stork, Nigel E. 1997. "Measuring Global Biodiversity and Its Decline." In *Biodiversity II: Understanding and Protecting Our Biological Resources*, ed. M. L. Reaka-Judla, D. E. Wilson, and E. O. Wilson, 41–68. Washington, D.C.: Joseph Henry Press.

Stott, Phillip, and Sian Sullivan, eds. 2000. *Political Ecology: Science, Myth, and Power*. New York: Oxford University Press.

Sturken, Marita. 1997. "Absent Images of Memory: Remembering and Reenacting the Japanese Internment." *Positions* 5, no. 3: 687–707.

Sullivan, Robert. 2010. "The Concrete Jungle: How Did New York City Become a Diverse Ecological Hot Spot?" *New York Magazine,* September 12, 2010.

Sweet, I. P., and I. H. Crick. 1992. *The Geological History of Uluru (Ayers Rock) and Kata Tjuta (the Olgas).* Canberra: Bureau of Mineral Resources, Geology and Geophysics.

Swyngedouw, Erik, and Nikolas Heynen. 2004. "Urban Political Ecology, Justice and the Politics of Scale." *Antipode* 35, no. 5: 898–918.

Takacs, David. 1996. *The Idea of Biodiversity: Philosophies of Paradise.* Baltimore: Johns Hopkins University Press.

Tilman, David. 2000. "Causes, Consequences, and Ethics of Biodiversity." *Nature* 405, no. 6783: 208–11.

Town and Country Planning Association. 2004. *Biodiversity by Design: A Guide to Sustainable Communities.* Manchester: TCPA.

Uexkull, Jakob von. 1982. "The Theory of Meaning." *Semiotica* 42, no. 1: 25–82.

UNESCO. 1994. "Expert Meeting on the 'Global Strategy' and Thematic Studies for a Representative World Heritage List." Eighteenth Session of the World Heritage Committee, Paris, France, June 20–22. http://whc.unesco.org/archive/global94.htm.

———. 1998. "World Heritage Committee Report of 22nd Session." Twenty-Second Session of the World Heritage Committee, Kyoto, Japan, November 27–28. http://whc.unesco.org/en/sessions/22COM/documents/.

———. 2004. "UNESCO Culture Sector—Programme 2004–5." http://portal.unesco.org/culture/en/ev.php-URL_ID=11500&URL_DO=DO_TOPIC&URL_SECTION=201.html.

———. 2005. "Operational Guidelines for the Implementation of the World Heritage Convention." http://whc.unesco.org/en/guidelines.

———. 2007. "Cultural Landscape." http://whc.unesco.org/en/culturallandscape/.

Uzzell, D., ed. 1989. *Heritage Interpretation: Volume 2.* London: Belhaven Press.

von Droste, B., H. Plachter, and M. Rossler, eds. 1995. *Cultural Landscapes of Universal Value.* New York: Gustav Fischer.

Wager, Jonathan. 1995. "Environmental Planning for a World Heritage Site: Case Study of Angkor, Cambodia." *Journal of Environmental Planning and Management* 38, no. 3: 419–34.

Walker, B., C. S. Holling, S. R. Carpenter, and A. Kinzig. 2004. "Resilience, Adaptability and Transformability in Social–Ecological Systems." *Ecology and Society* 9, no. 2: 5.

Waltz, Kenneth. 2001. *Man, the State, and War: A Theoretical Analysis.* New York: Columbia University Press.

WCMC. 2006. "Parc national de Tassili N'Ajjer." http://www.biologie.uni-hamburg.de/b-online/afrika/wcmc/tassili.htm.

Wendt, Alexander. 1992. "Anarchy Is What States Make of It." *International Organization* 46, no. 2: 391–425.

———. 1999. *Social Theory of International Politics*. Cambridge: Cambridge University Press.

———. 2003. "Why a World State Is Inevitable." *European Journal of International Relations* 9, no. 4: 491–542.

Whatmore, Sarah. 2002. *Hybrid Geographies: Natures, Cultures, Spaces*. Thousand Oaks, Calif.: Sage.

Wheeler, Nicholas, and Justin Morris. 1996. "Humanitarian Intervention and State Practice at the End of the Cold War." In *International Society after the Cold War*, ed. R. Fawn and J. Larkin, 135–71. New York: St. Martin's Press.

Wheeler, Quentin D. 1995. "Systematics and Biodiversity: Policies at Higher Levels." *BioScience* 45:21–28.

Wheeler, Quentin D., and Rudolf Meier, eds. 2000. *Species Concepts and Phylogenetic Theory*. New York: Columbia University Press.

White, Stephen. 2001. "Three Conceptions of the Political: The Real World of Late Modern Democracy." In *Democracy and Vision: Sheldon Wolin and the Vicissitudes of the Political*, ed. A. Botwinick and William Connolly, 173–92. Princeton: Princeton University Press.

Whiteside, Kerry. 2003. *Divided Natures*. Cambridge: MIT Press.

Wilkins, John. 2009. *Species: A History of the Idea*. Berkeley: University of California Press.

Willis, Katherine, Lindsey Gillson, and Sandra Knapp. 2007. "Biodiversity Hotspots through Time: An Introduction." *Philosophical Transactions of the Royal Society of London B* 362:169–74.

Wilson, E. O. 1984. *Biophilia: The Human Bond with Other Species*. Cambridge: Harvard University Press.

———, ed. 1988. *Biodiversity*. Washington, D.C.: National Academy Press.

———. 1992. *The Diversity of Life*. Cambridge: Harvard University Press.

———. 2003. "The Encyclopedia of Life." *Trends in Ecology and Evolution* 18, no. 2: 77–80.

Wolf, Klaus Dieter. 1999. "The New Raison d'État as a Problem for Democracy." *European Journal of International Relations* 5, no. 3: 333–63.

Wolfe, Cary. 1997. "Old Orders for New: Ecology, Animal Rights, and the Poverty of Humanism." *Electronic Book Review* 4:1–38.

———. 2003. *Animal Rites: American Culture, the Discourse of Species, and Posthumanist Theory*. Chicago: University of Chicago Press.

———. 2010. "Before the Law: Animals in a Biopolitical Context." *Law, Culture, and the Humanities* 6, no. 1: 8–23.

Wolfe, Patrick. 1991. "On Being Woken Up: The Dreamtime in Anthropology and in Australian Settler Culture." *Comparative Studies in Society and History* 33, no. 2: 197–224.

Worster, Donald. 1977. *Nature's Economy: A History of Ecological Ideas*. New York: Cambridge University Press.

Youatt, Rafi. 2012. "Power, Pain, and the Interspecies Politics of Foie Gras." *Political Research Quarterly* 65, no. 2: 346–58.

Young, Oran, ed. 1997. *Global Governance: Drawing Insights from the Environmental Experience.* Cambridge: MIT Press.

Zimmerman, Michael. 1991. "Deep Ecology, Ecoactivism, and Human Evolution." *ReVision* 13, no. 3: 122–28.

Zureik, Elia. 2001. "Constructing Palestine through Surveillance Practices." *British Journal of Middle Eastern Studies* 28, no. 2: 205–27.

Index

Page numbers in italics indicate photographs, tables, and other illustrations.

112–13, 134, 159n12; scalability
of, 10, 29; science of, 10, 16, 20,
37–43, 64; sustainability of, 44, 51,
102; taxonomy of, 27–28, 29–30,
115, 147n13, 148n14; transformations of, 4, 9, 21, 114, 133; trophic,
23, 122. *See also* census, global
biodiversity; hotspots, biodiversity;
politics, biodiversity; species,
biodiversity of
biodiversity, loss of: global, 26, 47, 101,
133; impacts of, 2, 35, 36; international treatment of, 12–13, 128;
politics of, 4, 5, 7–9, 37, 144n12;
stopping, 106, 115, 132. *See also*
species, loss of
biodiversity, urban, 102–26; baselines
for, 121–22; by design, 115–17;
global, 103–9; nature in, 113–15;
politics of, 103, 121, 125–26;
resilience and, 110–13, 116, 117;
rewilding and, 22–23, 117–26,
127–28, 135, 161–62n48
Biodiversity Action Plan (UK, CBD), 116
biological species concept (BSC), 30–31,
47, 61
biologists and biology, conservation, 27,
123, 134, 160–61n44; biodiversity
hotspots identified by, 25, 43–44;
cultural, 50; development of, 16,
37–43; global biodiversity census
conducted by, 21, 47, 57; motivations of, 13, 129; panoptic future of,
51–52, 52–53. *See also* conservation
biomass, 49, 160n37
biophilia hypothesis, 16, 40
biopolitics, 3, 125, 143n4. *See also*
politics, biodiversity
biopower, 53–64; authorities and, 48,
56–58, 152n13; biosocial collectivities and, 48, 58–64; ecological, 53,
54, 56, 58, 61, 64; Foucault's

concept of, 3, 47–48, 53–58, 60–61,
143n4, 152–53n25; humans'
participation in, 3, 48, 54–55, 58,
61; nonhumans' participation in,
22, 48, 53–56, 58, 61, 64,
152–53n25; sovereign power
contrasted with, 53–54, 55, 143n4.
See also power
bioprospecting, 41
biotic agency, 17–19, 21, 131, 155n3;
abiotic agency's interactions with,
20, 90; nonhuman, 17, 48, 55, 61
Bookchin, Murray, 125
Bradford, William, 68
Brazil, rainforests in, 3–4, 25. *See also*
Rio Earth Summit (Brazil, 1992)
Brown, Chris, 16, 42
Brundtland Report, 157–58n53
BSC. *See* biological species concept
(BSC)
Buggey, Susan, 75
Buscher, Bram, 163n15
Butler, Judith, 131, 132–33, 154n43

Callon, Michel, 150n46
capitalism, 48, 134; global, 2, 157–
58n53; postmodern, 52, 61, 124.
See also economy
Catalogue of Life (global biodiversity
census), 51
cave paintings, 78, 85
CBD. *See* Convention on Biological
Diversity (CBD)
census, global biodiversity, 47–64;
authority of, 56–58; biopower and,
53–64, 152–53n25; biosocial
collectivities and, 58–64; conservation biologists conducting, 21, 47,
57; discursive power of, 50, 52;
hybridizing force of, 52–53; power
used in, 22, 152n12; proposal for,
47, 48–50, 51, 52; scientific work

Rafi Youatt is assistant professor of politics at the New School for Social Research and Eugene Lang College.